What leaders in our field are saying

David lives, eats, and breathes narrative; it's what he does and who he is. It is like he can see into people's souls through their narratives and help them see all of who they are. When we taught together, it was evident how profound and powerful narratives are in revealing and healing our deepest shadows. Narrative Coaching illustrates this important work in a way that we can use in our work and lives. Brilliant!

Donna Karlin
The Shadow Coach, Canada

David is a global thought-leader in Narrative Coaching, and this book will stimulate, educate, and provide valuable insights and tools for all coaches. An essential read.

Anthony M. Grant, PhD
Director of the Coaching Psychology Unit, University of Sydney, Australia

David is one of my favorite coaching thought leaders, shining bright as a coaching scholar. His star also radiates warmth and compassion, poured into narrative coaching, a coaching domain David founded. This book integrates the best of David's thinking over the past 15 years. It is a rich and evocative resource for everyone interested in coaching.

Margaret Moore,
Founder and CEO of Wellcoaches

This book is a powerful source of inspiration and resources for coaches who have outgrown the simplistic and mechanical models taught in many coaching programs and who are ready to take their skills to a new level.

Prof. Konstantin Korotov, PhD,
Director of the Center for Leadership Development Research, ESMT-Berlin

David Drake charts the waters for any coach or trainer willing to help a fellow soul change the stories that bind him or her. Wonderful examples and a healthy respect for the diverse and unpredictable variability of two humans talking (or sitting in silence) makes this book entertaining as well as useful.

Annette Simmons
Group Process Consulting, US

David has taken his doctoral research and created a globally recognized body of work. It has been a joy to watch narrative coaching evolve and David along with it. His systemic approach to developing people is on the leading edge of coaching. I highly recommend this book for both its scholarship and its profound insights on practice.

Judy Stevens-Long, PhD
PhD Faculty, Fielding Graduate University,
School of Human & Organizational Development, US

David Drake understands — truly and deeply understands — how *the stories we tell about ourselves* are the genesis of our identities, and from that deep awareness he has pioneered the field of narrative coaching. What an astonishing achievement, and what a potent contribution to the field of human development! If your vocation calls you now into this journey of learning, then this book is your map… and Dr. David Drake is your wise and compassionate guide.

David Hutchens
Author and organizational story consultant

There are very few coaching approaches that are fully theory-based and also serve as a sensitive guide to practice. Narrative coaching as developed by David Drake represents an outstanding example of such an approach. It includes a skillful synthesis of the best ideas in the field of human change, made richer by his years of thoughtful refinement and integration into coaching practice. This book truly extends the knowledge of the coaching field and beyond.

Tatiana Bachkirova, PhD
Co-director of the International Centre for
Coaching and Mentoring Studies, UK

Most coaches deal with the surface of life, focusing on arranging behaviors and tasks. David has a way of quickly getting to the deeper personal narrative that shapes how we perceive daily life. Once I understood the story I was living in, I had the power to change it. Behavioral changes that had been a challenge seem much less daunting now that they are tied to a deeper intention.

Brian Lanahan
Brand strategist, US

David's book is the most thorough and robust guide to Narrative coaching available. The tools and models are presented in easy to understand, simple and clear language. This book will be useful to both beginning practitioners as well as the most experienced coaches and leadership development specialists. But beware . . . there is a depth here that offers a limitedness guide for our learning. The simplicity belies the sophistication of this model that will stand the test of time.

Loretta Brown
Director, New Zealand Coaching and Mentoring Centre

David Drake brings a rare combination of rigour and humanity to this long-awaited book. Rooted in both academic research and ground-breaking practice, he has written the seminal work on Narrative Coaching. I'm delighted to see this new and expanded second edition. A well-thumbed copy should be on the desk of every professional coach and anyone interested in exploring and changing the story of their lives.

Geoff Mead, PhD
Director, Narrative Leadership Associates and
Associate Fellow, Saïd Business School, University of Oxford

David gives us the inside story on Narrative Coaching and how it brings not only our stories to life but our practice as well. He shares his decades of research and coaching experience and kindly includes the reader in his own journey to better coaching. This is an inspiring and remarkably generous book. I'll be returning to it again and again. Relax, trust, and listen. Everything we need is in the stories.

Moya Sayer-Jones
Founder and story activist, Only Human, Australia

Wow—it is so good to read something about coaching with this degree of freshness and energy! It offers a genuine and helpful alternative by highlighting narrative as a key way to understand and appreciate one's patterns and life events. Whatever you are doing right now, just stop and read this book; you won't be disappointed!

Professor Bob Garvey
Faculty Head of Research, York St. John Business School, UK

This is a book for anyone who is seriously concerned with the business of personal and professional transformation. It is written with great authority—an authority grounded in many years of diligent scholarship and reflective practice.

Most importantly it tells the "story" of narrative coaching in an engaging way, and it is very accessible and practically useful. I can see our students benefiting enormously from it.

Gordon Spence, PhD
Director, Master of Business Coaching, Sydney
Business School/University of Wollongong, Australia

This book is a superb guide to narrative coaching and an important and innovative resource. It is a must-have for any coach wishing to develop new perspectives on their skills in helping clients reflect on their experience and test new stories for themselves. Narrative Coaching offers plenty of practical advice, underpinned by David's unique and ground-breaking theory about how people develop through coaching.

Sunny Stout-Rostron, DProf
University of Stellenbosch, School of Business, South Africa

David has created a multifaceted book that offers a scholarly text on narrative coaching. . . . It is a lovely book, written as though we are walking with him on a long pilgrimage. The book encourages "listening" to familiar tales differently and being open and attentive to the moment when people seek new stories. This book will become a highly valued reference for people interested in narrative work.

Ann Whyte
Former Managing Director, Whyte & Co, Australia

Listen to the story behind the story . . . that is what I take away from David's work. As coaches, we often get hung up on getting on with business and changing behavior. David is always reminding us to help each other learn how our stories affect us and can be realized to set free our potential.

Lew Stern, PhD
Senior Advisor to the Institute of Coaching,
Co-founder and Director, The Executive Coaching Forum

This is a deeply thoughtful yet highly practical account of narrative coaching. David Drake has made a significant contribution to the field of coaching, not just to narrative approaches. I highly recommend this book.

Professor David Lane
Professional Development Foundation and Middlesex University, UK

This book by David Drake represents a great contribution to the field. Narrative Coaching represents a powerful framework for helping clients find meaning and develop new perspectives effectively and efficiently. It integrates seamlessly with existing theoretical foundations while adding a deeper sense of humanity into the coaching conversation!

Wade Azmy
CEO, Pharos Institute (Asia Pacific)

David Drake's work with Narrative Coaching gives you a new mindset, useful frameworks and specific questions to ask yourself or your coachees in critical moments. Based on sound theory and practice, it is food for the brain and the soul. Absorb what is in this book and you will be a better leader and coach.

Carol Kauffman PhD
Founder, Institute of Coaching

David works as a scientist practitioner, and this is one of the greatest strengths of his work. His ability to navigate academic rigour and to work effectively with robust organisational cultures has produced a high impact coaching methodology that delivers change in thinking, feeling and decision making for those who experience it.

Terri Mandler
Former Group Head, Leadership & Learning
QBE Insurance Group. Pty. Ltd.

With a passion for narratives and stories that began early in life, David Drake offers an approach to coaching that integrates different theoretical positions—from psychodynamic to social constructionist—into a coherent and striking bouquet. Reflective practitioners will value this book as an inspiring and insightful source for their professional development.

Reinhart Stelter, PhD
Coaching Psychology Unit, University of Copenhagen, Denmark

narrative
COACHING

the definitive guide to bringing new stories to life

DAVID B. DRAKE, PhD

CNC Press, Petaluma, California

Second Edition

NARRATIVE COACHING
The Definitive Guide to Bringing New Stories to Life
David B. Drake, PhD

CNC Press
Petaluma, CA, USA
www.momentinstitute.org/cncpress
For information on author appearances and quantity orders
contact: admin@momentinstitute.org

First published by CNC Press in 2015.
Note: The names and certain details in all of the examples and cases have been changed to preserve the anonymity of the coachee.

978-0-9963563-1-2 (paperback)
978-0-9963563-2-9 (ePub)
978-0-9963563-3-6 (mobi)
Library of Congress Control Number: 2017959780
Publisher's Cataloging in Publication data available upon request.

Cover and book interior design by Yvonne Parks | PearCreative.ca

DEDICATION

I dedicate this second edition to my partner Bärbel, my daughter Hannah, and my dear friend, the late Ann Whyte.

CONTENTS

LIST OF FIGURES AND TABLES

Figures

Tables

ACKNOWLEDGMENTS

In writing the second edition of the book, I came to appreciate all over again the people who have made this journey possible. I acknowledge them here and add a few new people at the end who have played an important role in getting this edition done. I am grateful for all of them; I am a better writer, coach, and person as a result.

I learned the value of resilience and critical thinking from my late father, Bill Drake—both of which have held me in good stead. His untimely death in the middle of my doctoral studies was the impetus for creating narrative coaching. I learned that it is never too late for new stories in watching my mother, Sally (Drake) Murphy blossom later in life—and appreciated her support along the way. I learned that intelligence could be cool and that I could lead from Bob Scarola, my marvelous sixth-grade teacher. I am grateful to Caroline Tompkins for inviting my voice into the world. I learned the importance of defining one's own stories from Wayne Carpenter, a pastoral counselor at my church. I learned to see the world systemically from David Oliver, the chair of my undergraduate sociology department. My lifelong interest in the relationship between grief and growth started when Amy Coffman, a young woman with whom I worked closely in college, was killed in a car accident.

I am grateful to my uncle, James Laurie, for introducing me to Fielding and from whom I have learned about grace. I appreciate Ghost Ranch where I taught my first Shadow workshops and return to be nourished by its magical landscape. I am grateful for Fielding Graduate University—from which the second half of my life, a doctorate and narrative coaching were born. My dissertation chair, Judy Stevens-Long, was a masterful mentor from whom I learned the art of being done. My classmate Wendy Rowe is a kindred spirit and one of the most honestly astute people I know. I am grateful to Dianne Stober for rejecting my first academic paper and encouraging me to present my work in Sydney. The first challenged me to step up my game, and the second opened up the world for me. I am grateful to my core friends in Portland, Oregon—Bruce Hazen, Brian Lanahan, Carolyn McKnight, Alex

Merrin, and Niki Steckler—for their wonderful fellowship and support over the years. You are my home base.

Many of the important steps I took in developing narrative coaching were in Australia. It began at the coaching research conference at University of Sydney, where my work had its real debut. Terri Mandler helped me to see how much I had, was my first champion, and became a lifelong friend. Sandra Bannister was an early supporter who opened some marvelous doors for me. I appreciate the late Ann Whyte for our wine and cheese conversations, her advocacy, and our fierce and faithful friendship. I miss her. I will be forever grateful to the folks in my first Narrative Design Labs in Sydney—it was a raw and generative time without which narrative coaching would not be what it is now. In particular I want to acknowledge Sophie Francis for her keen insights, hard work, and persistent faith and Lucas Finch for his insatiable curiosity and invitations to play. Moya Sayer-Jones has been my muse, continually reminding me (along with Ross) of the importance of the simple things in making people feel welcome. Lastly, I bow to Leora Krowitz, my yoga angel, and to the waters of Clovelly Bay, my sanctuary, for the healing and wholeness they offered.

I am grateful for Bill Randall and the opportunities to present my first post-doctoral papers at the Narrative Matters research conferences in the Canadian Maritime Provinces. I appreciate Ian Wycherley for his friendship and our work on thresholds, Tatiana Bachkirova for our lively exchanges and both of them for providing forums for my work at Oxford-Brookes. People who aspire to great things often have friendly rivals who spur them on to be their best; Reinhard Stelter has played that role for me. I want to acknowledge him for his work on the philosophical foundations of narrative coaching and as a champion for its values-based and collaborative nature. The Four Gateways had its debut with the wonderful folks at the ANSE Summer School in Stavanger, Norway, and its spirit was captured best by the man who soulfully played his saxophone on Pulpit Rock from his heart not his head. I continue to be inspired by Donna Karlin ever since we met at an ICF conference many moons ago.

In closing, I want to acknowledge Ben Croft and the fabulous team at WBECS; I look forward to our new alliance. It has been wonderful to reconnect with Margaret Moore and Carol Kauffman as a Fellow and Thought Leader for the Institute of Coaching at Harvard—and for the utterly fabulous day at the 2016 conference. I am grateful for all that my clients, colleagues, and participants have given me and for the amazing opportunities to share my work all over the world. I am thankful for my marvelous publishing advisor and thinking partner, Janet Goldstein, and the team she assembled to bring this edition to the world. I have appreciated the faith and support of Samir Selmanovic in getting to the next stage of this work as well as the community of retreat hosts that is emerging to help take this work forward.

I offer a big hug to my daughter Hannah who finally got to see me work—and came to understand why I do what I do when she saw the difference it made for people. I continue to give my heart and soul to this work in hopes of making the world a better place for her future. I am grateful for my partner, Bärbel Weiligmann, who has brought such joy and love into my life—starting at the holy bike racks where we met—and from whom I learn daily about the power of choosing our stories. Lastly, I want to thank you for reading this book. May you have a rich and rewarding time as you soak it in, reflect on it, and put it to good use. The world needs you.

PREFACE

Have you ever had that experience of driving down the highway . . . and you suddenly realize you've not been fully conscious for the past few seconds? How is it that we can drive and yet have no recollection of how we got to where we are on the road? I think that our lives are often not too different: We find ourselves further down the road over time, but we are not quite sure how we got where we are. Narrative coaching offers people the opportunity to pause, become more aware of their stories, and make new choices. In the process they can let go of old stories that no longer serve them and develop new, more mature, stories that do. It is about awakening so that we do not fall asleep at the wheel.

My passion for stories began early in life through a love of reading. I still vividly recall the sense of anticipation I felt when the books we had ordered arrived in our elementary school classroom. The smell of fresh paper . . . the eagerness to lose myself in the plot . . . the dilemma about which one to read first. I found respite in the richness of these books and their stories—a love that would take me through thousands of books across the decades that followed. I was particularly intrigued and inspired by characters who "colored outside the lines." In seeing the world through the lens of these characters, I became fascinated by the different ways in which people narrate their experience—and the worlds that form around those choices. Reading was central to the formation of a rich inner life that has served me to this day. I also found insights and a certain solace in these narrated worlds as I compared them with my own. This was an early introduction to the role of projection in learning and development.

My love for stories was enriched through epic tales at church and two teachers who introduced me to the marvelous world of classic literature. There were also influential mentors who helped me start to find my own voice in the process. I went on to get a degree in sociology, in which I was introduced to the novel idea (at the time) that reality and stories were socially constructed. This impressed upon me the importance of understanding the context for stories and the people in them. Next came a graduate degree in theology and an introduction to the field of hermeneutics, the use of stories to witness and awaken, and the value of sacramental rituals. I came to appreciate the various ways in which people make sense and meaning of their lives through my study of different religions—sparking a spiritual journey that continues to this day. I was also involved in peace and justice issues, and I saw firsthand the challenges and opportunities in liberating ourselves and others from limiting social narratives.

Over the next twenty years, I supported people through transitions—as a grief educator and counselor, a rites of passage guide, a facilitator of dialogues on difficult issues, a change consultant and coach, and more. This rich background provided a strong foundation for what was to come with narrative coaching. This book traces the path it has taken since its inception in my doctoral studies in 2002. I developed it as an alternative to both narrative therapy and traditional coaching. While I draw from and greatly appreciate the work of the narrative therapy community (the late Michael White in particular), narrative coaching has evolved to the point where it is a distinct approach and a body of work in its own right.

Over the first decade, narrative coaching served as both my muse and my mantle. It challenged me to grow at many levels in order to keep up with and shape what it was becoming—for example, in opening myself up to work at deeper emotional and somatic levels. It challenged me to be more vulnerable, move more toward the unknown, and deepen my trust in my whole self. In revising the preface for this edition, I feel both grief and joy as that era comes to an end and another begins. I am proud to have established a solid place for narrative coaching (and all it stands for) in our field, grateful for what I have learned from the thousands I have worked with in this space, and keen to see how this work evolves in the years to come.

I know firsthand how powerful this work can be, as I've used it to help myself through a series of major transitions in my own life. Everything I have written here, taught to practitioners, and done with clients I have used for my own ongoing well-being and growth. Many of the most powerful applications of narrative coaching were developed in my living room overlooking Clovelly Bay near Sydney in the wake of a divorce. Out of this proverbial "dark night of the soul," I discovered what this work is really all about. I know firsthand that the thresholds we must cross are not for the faint of heart or the ill-prepared, but are essential for those who are serious about bringing their new story to life. Thresholds call *everything* into question, require us to walk through the doorway of unknowing, and open us in the end to more than we thought possible. I emerged from this time with a much deeper understanding of the power of this work and a commitment to develop its full potential as a resource for anyone seeking to make a significant change in themselves and/or their life.

> Thresholds call *everything* into question, require us to walk through the doorway of unknowing, and open us in the end to more than we thought possible.

My journey with this book served as its own rite of passage and has done so again with this new edition. The first edition was personal, the completion of a long journey. This second edition is professional, as a resource for the next stage of this work and coaching itself. It goes deeper into attachment theory and its links to applied mindfulness, design thinking as a framework for adult development, integrative approaches to change, and transformational development theories to increase our ability to facilitate real change in real time using people's own stories. It shows even more clearly how narrative coaching is a natural human process that is open source by design. In completing this edition, I was struck by how much I have changed even since the first edition and how much the work has matured.

Given that stories are at the core of what makes us human, I believe that narrative coaching clearly has a role to play as we lean into the challenges and opportunities of our time. It calls for more of us to provide leadership wherever it is most needed and support leadership wherever it is most present. It is about extending mindfulness beyond resources that just help us cope to develop new applications that also help people connect, create, and contribute at higher levels. For coaches it is about getting out in front more often instead of standing behind others, cheering them on. This means that we have to do our own work so we can do the same for others. This will require simple things like diversifying our service portfolio and more demanding things like diving deeper into the development of ourselves and our skills to address the complexities of our time.

I wrote this book in the first place primarily for people who coach as their professional practice and who are ready to step more fully into themselves, the moment, and the work to be done. It was a call to reflect on your own stories and a guide on how to *be* with this work as well as *do* this work. What has shifted in the past two years is that more and more of the people in our programs are from related fields and want to incorporate what narrative coaching stands for and offers into their practice. Some have already started to use it to create new forms of practice in their field. They are part of an emerging breed of post-professional practitioners (Drake, 2011e, 2014c) who can work with people and issues in a more holistic fashion to bring about healing and resolution. In the end, there is value here for anyone who uses a narrative approach in their work. For some of you, it will affirm how you have instinctively worked for a long time and give you confidence in knowing why it works and how to take it further. For others of you, this book will be a provocative invitation to expand your beliefs about coaching and give you the confidence to let go of a lot of what you thought you needed to do as a coach.

Either way, I welcome you to this conversation and to the global community of those who are committed to helping people individually and collectively bring their new stories to life. It is an invitation to leave behind what distracts you, drains you, or no longer serves you so you can show up more fully as yourself in doing what matters most in your life and work. Sometimes this even means that "to reconstruct a self, an old self may have to be shattered. Sometimes the world-vessel must be pulverized. To discover who we are, we may have to divest ourselves of everything, go beyond the imagined limits of ourselves. We may have to leap out of the familiar, jump off a cliff, go to the very edge of the world where all the dragons live" (Metzger, 1992, p. 71). The good news is that you will find others out there in those narrative fields, and together you can engage your "dragons" in order to be more courageous in how you live and work with people and their stories. While this book continues to offer an extraordinary and in-depth resource on developing people through coaching, this edition has been written to be more provocative in terms of its challenge to all of us to up our game for these times.

I developed narrative coaching because I believe we need more people who can go to these deeper and more difficult places within themselves and with others. We live in a time that calls each of us to do the real work of our quest and to join with others who are doing the same. This means creating more space for our full humanity; e.g., our pain *and* our suffering, our joy *and* our fulfillment. May this book spark your thinking about how you can help heal the broken narratives that divide us and create new narratives that enrich us. Listen deeply to the silence, the earth, and the hearts of others. Look unflinchingly into your own soul to see what is calling you. Engage the younger generations to see what they are trying to tell us as they prepare to take the mantle of leadership. Ask yourself what the events in your life right now are preparing you for. What do you sense is yours to do? What story do you most want to bring to life? I am heartened that you have chosen to read this book, and I look forward to hearing where it takes you.

A Guide to Reading This Book

This book is not written in a linear or mechanistic fashion as if it were an instruction manual. Instead, it is written as a layered immersion in the foundations and fundamentals of narrative coaching. It is intended to serve as the definitive text for this body of work and approach to coaching. As such, it has more academic elements than many other coaching books. This makes it valuable as a go-to resource on how people change—and it may be a bit daunting for some readers. My suggestion is to focus first on what you find most familiar and useful—and then build out from there. The book is richly dense, yet speaks to a simple way of working. See if you can absorb the spirit of this work; the specifics will sink in with practice. I've added more cases and examples in this edition in order to make it easier to see how you could apply these principles and practices in your work.

You may find that reading the book feels slow at times, especially at the start. Take heart in the fact that it was designed this way as an invitation to slow down in order to have a richer experience, be in a more natural flow and gain more sustainable benefits. Give yourself plenty of time to let the material sink in and find opportunities to experiment with it. The power in narrative coaching is in how you show up to your clients more than the techniques you use when you get there. For many coaches this requires shifts in how they see themselves and their role in coaching. That is why the foundations for working this way are in the first half of the book and the tools and resources come later. The aim, as with the work itself, is to help you become more astute in *observing what is true right now* before trying to change anything.

An example of the simple power in working this way.
It will take you less than five minutes:

1. Find a place where you can be still and silent for a few minutes.
2. Name something that is bothering or concerning you.
3. Close your eyes, relax into your seat, take three deep breaths.
4. Be silent for 2 minutes, noticing your breath as it goes in and out. Observe what happens to your issue.
5. Open your eyes and reflect on what has changed about your issue.

You will notice a number of models throughout the book that look much the same. This is because each of the Narrative Coaching models is based in the same underlying applied Narrative Design framework. It is based in natural human processes of transitioning through change, learning and developing, and telling stories. Most of the models reflect the same fundamental pattern, as seen through the lens of their respective domain. Focus less on how each one works on its own, and focus more on how you can use the four phases in coaching. It is analogous to learning to dance as a couple in that it is less about memorizing steps and more about connecting with the other person and the rhythm of the music. I developed Narrative Coaching over fifteen years ago; this book contains the foundations for this work in its original form. The field has grown over the years to include other approaches to working with stories in coaching.

Learn from what I have discovered along the way, and trust that you will bring to this path your own unique knowledge and experience. Trust yourself and your path as you read this book so that you can find your own way through the material and the practices. As you read these pages: What is stirring inside you? What is it calling you to think, feel and do? Where would you like to apply this work, and how would you like to extend and expand it? If you would like to experience this work and learn more about how to use it, visit us at www.momentinstitute.org. Until then, enjoy the book!

A Parable about a Narrative Coach

One of our Canadian colleagues, Heather Plett, wrote the following to describe her experience with narrative coaching after participating in one of my labs in Toronto. I include it here with her permission because it so beautifully captures the spirit of narrative coaching and the sense of "coming home" this work offers people. Enjoy the parable and the rest of the book.

Imagine you are a pilgrim on a long journey, gathering stories as they appear and stashing them like gems in your backpack.

Sometimes you pull the stories out, dust them off, and share them with fellow travelers. Sometimes you keep them to yourself, afraid that other travelers will find them ugly or unsavory and you will feel shame. Sometimes you roll them around in your hands, reshaping them to better fit with the other stories they share space with.

The stories in your backpack don't look like those in any other traveler's backpack. They have been shaped by the journey through which they've been carried, by the way you've used them to define yourself, and by your assumptions of how other people are judging them.

Now imagine you've been invited by a kind and supportive fellow traveler to sit down on a comfortable park bench along that journey. Your new companion invites you to open your backpack, promising that he will be gentle with the stories inside.

You're a little reluctant at first, but the stories are getting heavy and you'd really like to be free of the weight for a while. Your backpack hasn't been fitting very well on your back during the last few miles, and you wonder whether it might be a good idea to take some time to rearrange the things that are poking you.

Your companion is very good at making you feel comfortable and safe, and it doesn't take long for you to recognize that you trust him. Finally, you sit down and take a few deep breaths. Your companion waits patiently.

Slowly you pull out a story and hold it tenderly in your hand, glancing up to see what response it will elicit. Surprisingly your companion holds no judgment in his eyes as he gazes down at the story. He simply asks you kind and energizing questions about it, helping you to define it and see it through new eyes.

Before long you're pulling more stories out of the bag and lining them up on the bench. Your companion doesn't say much, but asks just the right questions for you to know which stories are important right now. He helps you see the patterns arising as you line up the stories. Sometimes when you shift the story and line it up with another story, it takes on a whole new shape. Sometimes a story shrinks in importance once you pull it out and expose it to the sunlight.

Through your companion's questions, you begin to see brand new things in your stories that you never saw before. There are new colors and beautiful patterns emerging. The light touches them differently, and some that looked like lumps of coal now begin to reveal the diamonds underneath. You see how they fit together, and sometimes you could even swear that you see them dance. The new shapes offer new possibilities for how you will continue on your journey. They're even helping you define yourself in a new way that feels deeply right and true.

When the conversation draws to a close, you pack your newly shaped stories back into your backpack. You brace yourself for the weight as you put it on, but now it feels lighter and fits the groove of your back in a much more natural way. It no longer feels like the heavy burden you placed on the bench when you sat down. You look at the path ahead of you, and though the rough spots aren't gone, you can see a clearer trail through it with a backpack that will offer you tools rather than burdens. You have the distinct sense that your path will be much clearer and your strides much bolder. And so you set off . . .

That companion on your journey is your narrative coach. So, have a seat on the bench, and let me tell you a story . . .

Welcome.

David

OVERVIEW

Narrative coaching is based in millennia of ancient wisdom, a century of social science research, and breakthroughs in new areas such as the neurosciences and design thinking. As a result, it offers an approach to accelerated and transformative development that is fitting for our times. Narrative coaching is unique in that its foundation is systemic, not just psychological, and it can be used and applied in a variety of contexts. To be able to work at multiple levels, narrative coaches draw on: (1) *narrative psychologies* to work with people as narrators in support of their development and performance; (2) *narrative processes* to work with the material that is narrated in support of its reconfiguration; and (3) *narrative practices* to work with the dynamics in the field and guide people across thresholds to new narratives. This is in part why my colleague Reinhard Stelter (2014a) positions narrative coaching as a "third-generation practice" in which "the coach and the coachee (or group of coachees) are dialogue partners and have a mutual relationship as reflective fellow human beings in a relationship that is characterized by varying degrees of symmetry over time" (pp. 118–119).

This book is the definitive text on narrative coaching, and it provides both the academic foundations for this work and its core elements, principles, and practices. It offers a summary of nearly twenty years of my work in founding, championing, and contributing to the growth of this methodology and the philosophy and pedagogy it represents. It has been deeply satisfying, personally and professionally, to weave together critical elements from my studies in sociology, theology, psychology, and systems theory in developing a truly integrative practice. The result is part history, part autobiography, and part professional resource. This second edition feels like the start of a new chapter, in part because it coincides with the launch of Moment Institute and our alliance with WBECS. It celebrates all that narrative coaching has been and all that it will become in the hands of the thousands of people around the world who use this work and will help it flourish even more.

This work is based in a deep respect for people more than rules for how to coach; it honors the human change process that is underway more than imposes a structure to make something happen; and it attends to the "field" more than the formulas in coaching. In the end, narrative coaching is a mindful, experiential, and integrative approach that helps people make real change in real time using their own stories. It enables them to get to the crux of the matter, cross the next threshold in their development, and live their lives more fully as a result. It does this by inviting them to be more present to their reality and more aware of and accountable for their narrative choices. This Overview offers a definition of narrative coaching, the key theoretical influences that have shaped its formation, a comparison of narrative coaching to approaches with a similar philosophical stance, and two basic models we use in this work.

> **Narrative coaching is a mindful, experiential, and integrative approach that helps people make real change in real time using their own stories.**

The following is an experience from my first career that serves as an example of where narrative coaching came from and what it is designed to do. The story I reference may or may not be familiar to you or speak to you, depending on your background. I myself have traveled far on my own journey since this episode took place over thirty years ago, but I am using it now for its narrative implications. My invitation to you is the same I offered to the women that day: Focus on the characters' experience *in* the story more than the content *of* the story.

> I was talking one day with a group of older, upper-middle-class women in a study group at a church about the Old Testament saga of the Israelites escaping slavery in Egypt. I was having a hard time getting the conversation going, so I asked why. They responded that, although they had heard the story many times before, they had always felt disconnected from it because they could not relate to the life of a slave as it was so far from their own. Fair enough. . . . In response, I reframed the question I was going to ask next to enable us to explore the topic from

a different perspective. Little did I know at the time that this decision that day was to become a cornerstone of both my doctoral work and narrative coaching.

I invited the women to shift their focus from the content *of* the story to the characters' experience *in* the story. Instead of talking about slaves, I asked them, "Have you ever felt *enslaved*?" With that question the group came alive. Some told stories about following their husband's career path and feeling enslaved by the assigned role of "wife." Some talked about being the only woman in their fields at university or when they started their careers—and feeling enslaved by the limitations of working in male-dominated professions (or being shut out of professions altogether). Some talked about feeling enslaved to money given the costs associated with living in the San Francisco Bay Area. Others talked about feeling enslaved within the church, their theological insights not taken seriously, since they were *just* a "women's Bible study"—and older women at that.

Through this lens, an all too familiar story came alive for them in a new way. That conversation led to a broader dialogue about their place in the church. It illustrates what can happen for people when they are invited to voice, explore, and transform their stories in a supportive environment.

Narrative coaching is grounded in this same pedagogical stance and offers a practical structure to work this way with people. It draws on Paulo Friere's notion of praxis as a dialectical process of bringing out people's story *and then* the teaching story in a liberating dialogue that fosters a new level of consciousness and action. In narrative coaching, we work in much the same way by using the coachee's own narrative material as the primary resource and catalyst for change. It transcends and includes the individualistic and psychological orientation in most coaching approaches to incorporate collective and sociological considerations. As a result, coachees develop themselves and their own stories *and* their ability to engage with their environments and larger narratives in new ways. We are stewards of a process that offers people a safe and structured space in which they are witnessed in telling their stories, invited to experiment with new ones, and supported to embody and enact them. As the poet David Whyte observed, "Sometimes the best thing to do is to hold a kind of silent vigil beside the part of [us] that is going through the depth of a difficult transformation". Narrative coaches focus on the human interaction and deepen the human process that is already underway. We recognize that stories do not exist as intact objects in coachees' minds, but rather emerge in a co-creative process between a coachee and his coach (see M. M. Gergen & Gergen, 2006; Kraus, 2006) and within coachees themselves.

Getting Started

In this section, you will learn the six core principles that are at the heart of narrative coaching, one of the tools we use to illustrate how this work is done, and a basic version of the narrative coaching model you can use as a reference point before we dive into the foundations of this work. The book is intentionally designed to provide the platform first, then take you on the journey through the process and practices. While there are plenty of examples along the way, I believe it is important to know where this model came from, what it stands for in terms of people and change, and why it works before we look at how to apply it in your practice. Narrative coaching enables people to make profound changes using simple processes, but it is able to do so because of its deep roots in both ancient wisdom and academic literature. As such, the six principles are a good place to begin as they are the lifeblood of this work. They are analogous to the breath in meditation in that you can keep coming back to them again and again no matter what is unfolding in the moment as you work.

Six Core Principles

I developed six core principles that guide this work and allow practitioners to stay focused on what is happening in front of them rather than worrying about whether or not they are doing it "correctly." Principles provide both structure and flexibility; they allow us to stay focused on what is happening in the session, to adapt to the needs at hand, and make faster course corrections. The beauty of working from principles is that they are immediately recognizable and usable for the beginner, and also continue to add value as practitioners gain experience and deepen their understanding of the nuances of this work. They act as memorable reminders to keep us in the flow of the coaching process and the field that is constellated. These six principles emerged from an analysis of the literature upon which the work is based and deep reflection on what I and other narrative coaching practitioners were doing when we were at our best.

The six narrative coaching principles:

- Trust that everything you need is right in front of you.
- Be fully present to what IS without judgment.
- Speak only when you can improve on silence.
- Focus on generating experiences not explanations.
- Work directly with the narrative elements in the field.
- Stand at the threshold when a new story is emerging.

For example, I coached a practitioner who noticed that she is often lost in her head, baffled by the coachee's story, and trying to figure out what she should do. We focused on how she could use the first principle above to shift her mindset and bring herself back into the room and the moment whenever she noticed she was lost in her own thoughts. Working from principles will help you stay focused on what is happening inside you and in front of you as people are telling their stories in coaching. It gives you more freedom to be present rather than multitasking about what to do next. These principles are very much like *simple rules* (Sull & Eisenhardt, 2012) that serve as a clear guide for practice. For example, you can see it in the following practice we use to give clients and students a taste for what it is like and how it works. In both cases, they can then use it with people they coach. It provides both a basic understanding of the largely tacit internal narration process and connects the dots that lead to the outcomes we get as a result. It also demonstrates how we can narrate any experience in new ways, contributing to our ability to make real change in real time.

TOOL

FIGURE I: REWINDING YOUR NARRATION

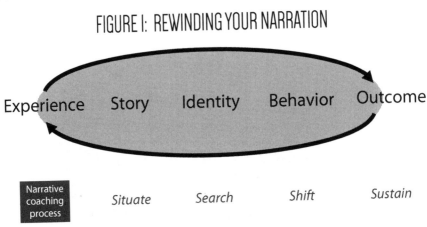

Experience　Story　Identity　Behavior　Outcome

Narrative coaching process　Situate　Search　Shift　Sustain

For both practitioners and coachees, we invite them to first reflect on a recent experience that is emblematic of the issue they are working on. We use the reflective questions in the following list to guide them, and we do so as if we are slowing a movie down so we can see it a few frames at a time. Once they have a clearer sense of what is true now, we use the rewinding questions to support them in constructing a new option for how they frame their experience, what story they tell, who they see themselves to be, what they do as a result—and what outcomes they want to attain as a result. This gives them a visceral experience of how the narrative coaching model and process work such that we can start to work at deeper levels on the issue at hand. People emerge from the process with three benefits: tangible gains in terms of the issue they originally found challenging, a new tool they can use for themselves and others, and an increased sense of agency and efficacy in being able to shift their stories. The instructions for the process are below; take some time to try it for yourself.

Reflecting on a challenging conversation or situation:

1. What did you observe? *(describe it as a reporter would)*
2. What were you telling yourself at the time? *(story)*
3. What does this say about how you see yourself? *(identity)*
4. What did you do as a result? *(behavior)*
5. What happened in the end? *(outcome)*

Rewinding the story to achieve a different outcome:

1. What would you like to have had happened? *(outcome)*
2. What could you have done differently as a result? *(behavior)*
3. What would need to shift in how you see yourself? *(identity)*
4. What could you tell yourself next time this happens? *(story)*
5. What would you observe if "this" were the case? *(experience)*

Narrative Coaching Model

The Narrative Coaching model is not like others that are designed to structure the conversation through a series of steps. In our model, the external process used by the coach mirrors the internal process of the coachee, and the process is centered around the latter, not the former. In addition, in narrative coaching we use the coachee's own stories as the primary resource and catalyst for change—not our methodology or terminology. As a result, you can guide people through the parallel evolution of their story, the transition it is calling for, and the development it will require. Each informs and enables the other. The beauty is that any of the them can lead the way at any point, and each strengthens the others along the way.

In recent years, I have incorporated more from non-dualist paradigms such as Buddhism to balance the Western frames that are dominant in coaching. This supports a parallel effort in the neurosciences to better understand the interplay between how we engage with reality and how we formulat stories. As we shall see, this also plays out in terms of how we define and develop ourselves; e.g., in the distinction between the growth of the self (the focus often in Western approaches) and maturity of the non-self (the focus often in Eastern approaches). One result has been that suffering can now be seen as the result of our attachment to certain stories and, at the same time, they represent the ever-present doorway to our liberation. Given the complexity of the issues people face, narrative coaching is well placed with its multidisciplinary background and holistic approach. It is a layered, spiraling process that is simple *and* powerful, subtle *and* direct.

> Guide people through the parallel evolution of their story, the transition it is calling for, and the development it will require.

Below is a basic version of the Narrative Coaching model you can use as a starting point as you read further. It is based in a rites of passage structure (which we will explore in depth in Chapter 6), and it incorporates the four phases (e.g., Situate), the core question for each phase as adapted from design thinking (e.g., *What is?*), the four developmental thresholds that are crossed as people move through the phases, and the spiral that indicates the circling movement through the process at whatever level is necessary to achieve the desired results. The model reflects one of the paradoxes of this work: it is based in a deep theoretical and evidential foundation yet enables practitioners to work simply and nimbly with people. In part this is because the focus is on their growth and maturation not the material or methodology as the key to success. Let's turn now to some of the theoretical influences that shaped the formation of narrative coaching and how they have enriched this work.

FIGURE 2: NARRATIVE COACHING MODEL (BASIC)

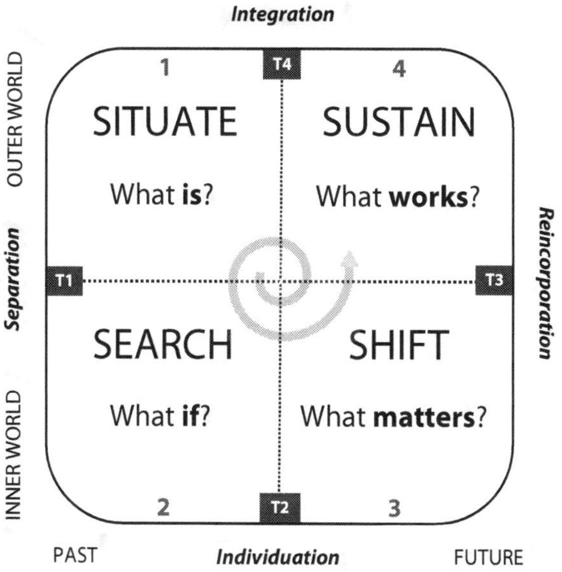

Theoretical Influences

Stories are at the core of what it means to be human, and they touch every aspect of our lives. It is no surprise then that narrative coaching has a more diverse foundation than most approaches to coaching, which enables coaches to think more systemically and holistically about what is occurring in sessions and with coachees. Some practitioners have simply adapted narrative therapy practices for a coaching context, while others like myself have developed new methods built specifically for coaching. I developed narrative coaching as its own methodology from a diverse set of sources and with its own set of practices. It also has become clear to me that narrative coaching is more than anything else a way of being, a mindset, an attitude. It is grounded theoretically and evidentially in the current literature on human learning, development, and performance—and it takes coaching in some exciting new directions. As one example, our training programs have increasingly attracted practitioners who are not coaches but work in adjacent professions and want to incorporate this work into their practice.

I hope that you draw on the bodies of work in which you have expertise (like I do with the list of five influences that follow) so that you can customize this work to meet your clients' needs and contribute to the evolution of our understanding of how to use these principles for personal and social transformation. To see how narrative coaching came to be such a rich resource, let's take a brief look at its history. The groundwork for narrative coaching can be found in my dissertation (2003) and early papers on narrative liminality (Drake, 2004a, 2004b, 2004c, 2005a) and narrative coaching as a psycho-social method (Drake, 2005b, 2007). Two others who contributed to the field early on were Reinhard Stelter (2007, 2009) in Denmark and Ho Law (2007) in the United Kingdom. As the field of coaching has evolved, so too has the depth and breadth of this approach. The result is an interdisciplinary body of work and a holistic methodology. To secure a place for it in the coaching canon, I have written a number of introductory chapters (Drake, 2008b, 2009c, 2011c, 2014b, 2016; Drake & Stelter, 2014).

I have also made the case for a narrative perspective on:

- Coaching as a post-professional practice (Drake, 2011e; Drake & Stober, 2005).
- Coaching as an evidence-based practice (Drake, 2008a, 2009a).
- Coaching across cultures (Drake, 2009b).
- Attachment theory in coaching (Drake, 2009d).
- Formulation in coaching (Drake, 2010).
- Goals and strengths in coaching (Drake, 2011b, 2012).
- Coaching supervision (Drake, 2014c).

While a narrative frame is relatively new in the fields of psychotherapy and coaching, stories have been an essential component of cultures and communities since the dawn of time. People use stories to structure their experience as events and actions in space and as memories and visions across time—in keeping with their brain's primary coordinates (see Schank, 1990) and in forming plausible plotlines that help them make sense and meaning.

Narrative coaching taps into this ancient vein and builds on the postmodern shift in our thinking from "stories as objects" to "stories in context" (Boje, 1998). This is reflected in Barbara Czarniawska's (2004) work in which she makes the case that literary theory, the humanities, and psychology fed into what became narrative studies as part of the broader "narrative turn" in the social sciences over the past fifty years. It shifted our understanding of stories as static, isolated commodities that are *preformed* to seeing stories as a dynamic, relational process that is *performed*. As a result, people can increase their capacity for intimacy (making connections) and agency (making contributions) by telling their stories in new ways (Bakan, 1966; McAdams, 1985). In so doing, they can live more authentic and fulfilling lives.

Five domains that were important in developing narrative coaching:

- *Anthropology:* Stories are embedded in the fabric of our communities and cultures and in ritualized processes—as seen in the work of pioneers such as Gregory Bateson, Joseph Campbell, Victor Turner, and Arthur van Gennep. The four phases of a rite of passage became the backbone for the Narrative Coaching model.

- *Learning and development:* Stories play a critical role in how we see ourselves and how we grow—as seen in the work of pioneers such as Paulo Freire, Tim Gallwey, William James, Roger Schank, and Lev Vygotsky. Their call to the transformative potential for learning and development is mirrored in each phase of narrative coaching.

- *Jungian psychology:* Stories have unconscious and archetypal aspects and their reconfiguration is essential for individuation—as seen in the work of pioneers such as James Hillman, James Hollis, Carl Jung, Ginette Paris, and Murray Stein. Working in third and projective spaces and with the Shadow are key to narrative coaching.

- *Mind and body:* Stories can be more fully accessed through mindful states, somatic work, and mutual regulating relationships—as seen in the work of pioneers such as John Bowlby, Louis Cozolino, Moshe Feldenkrais, Gregory Kramer, and Dan Siegel. Their call to work with the whole person had deeply informed narrative coaching.

- *Narrative studies:* Stories have structures as well as personal and collective functions—as seen in the work of pioneers such as Jerome Bruner, Dan McAdams, Robert McKee, Donald Polkinghorne, and Paul Ricouer. The alignment of narration, transition, and individuation started here and is at the core of narrative coaching.

One of the questions I was often asked, particularly in the beginning, was, "How is this different than therapy?" As coaching psychology has taken hold and more psychotherapists include elements of coaching in their practice, this question has faded somewhat. Still, it is an important distinction as both therapeutic and coaching processes have their place and their requirements. When asked, my answer remains the same: "Done well, narrative coaching is inherently therapeutic for people. Otherwise, why bother?" Narrative coaching uses some of the same techniques as psychotherapy—such as cathartic insight, emotional healing, and issue resolution—to create a foundation for new actions. However, there is more emphasis in coaching on taking new actions toward the future than you would find in most therapeutic methodologies. It is less about analysis of the past and more about awareness of the present and activation for the future. The bottom line: work at the deepest level for which you are qualified and invited and at the appropriate level for the coachee's readiness to learn and the issue at hand. Beyond that, I am less interested in dogmas and labels and more interested in the rigor of our own development and the vigor of the outcomes for those with whom we work.

> The bottom line: work at the deepest level for which you are qualified and invited and at the appropriate level for the coachee's readiness and the issue at hand.

Related Approaches

Narrative coaching has elements in common with other coaching and therapeutic approaches that are mindful, systemic, and "field"-focused. In this section, I will look at narrative therapy as well as two experiential approaches (family constellations and psychodrama) and two psychotherapeutic approaches (Gestalt and ACT). The purpose for doing so is to position narrative coaching, to distinguish it from other transformative development practices, and to identify unique features and grounded base.

Narrative Therapy

Michael White (see M. White, 1988, 1989, 2007; M. White & Epston, 1990) and others in the family systems therapy space led the way by advocating for the externalization of problems, the deconstruction of dominant narratives, the decentering of experts, and the contribution of "unique outcomes" to the resolution of people's issues. They helped us see that a story is just "a story," and the teller, sitting in the protagonist's seat, has more options as a result (Barry, 1997). What was once a totalizing truth could now be seen as simply one of several options to choose from. This involved deconstructing and critically examining people's up-until-then taken-for-granted understanding of life and identity by "exoticizing the familiar" and "familiarizing the exotic" (Turner, 1978) so that a new plot could be formed (M. White, 2004). As a result, people could better understand "dominant narratives" and their impact, explore new territories and possibilities, and renegotiate the relationships between identities and stories as well as between experiences and narratives. The narrative therapists lifted up individual stories as a legitimate and substantive resource in psychotherapy and championed the notion that any given narrative was just one of many potential constructions from which to choose.

I appreciated Michael White's strong philosophical grounding and thoughtful yet playful approach to his work. We were drawn to many of the same sources in formulating our respective bodies of work, and we share a similar contextual view of identity, development, and behavior. Some key terms and insights from the narrative therapy community have been incorporated in this book in recognition of their contributions to our understanding of how to work with people's stories in coaching. They have deeply enriched our capacity to help people liberate themselves from oppressive narratives and have been influential in developing ways to reframe the dominant narratives themselves. You can see their influence in the formation of narrative medicine with its call for a more inclusive approach to our stories about health. At the same time, I see narrative coaching as more than just narrative therapy adapted for a coaching context. It is a more integrative practice that differs in some important ways in both its underlying assumptions and its approach. For example, it shifts the focus from the implications of the past on the present *to* the implications of the present on the future (and the future on the present).

Narrative coaching is distinct from narrative therapy in that it:

- Uses mindfulness and somatic practices to address preverbal issues.
- Draws more from multiple disciplines in social sciences and beyond.
- Uses transpersonal means to access personal and collective unconscious.
- Attends to nuances of and openings for change in narrative structure.
- Focuses more on desired narratives and less on dominant narratives.
- Relies more on silence, presence, and the "field" to support change.
- Sees issues of power through a lens of emergence more than justice.
- Uses directive energies judiciously in support of outcomes.

Experiential Approaches

Narrative coaching relates well with experimental and experiential approaches such as systemic constellations and psychodrama because they are philosophies that stimulate deep change, not psychotherapies (Carnabucci & Anderson, 2012). As with narrative coaching, neither Bert Hellinger (founder of family constellation work) nor Jacob Moreno (founder of psychodrama) were concerned with matters of diagnosis. Instead, they too based their work in the primacy of the embodied here–and–now rather than the verbal abstractions of analysis and in the belief that sustained healing and transformation need to be grounded in experience as well as insight. Lastly, all three modalities take a systemic approach to development in keeping with Moreno's observation that

> the psyche is an open system, constantly influenced and shaped—or misshaped—by the interactional environment in which the human being develops. He knew that to reach this level, words were not enough, that it required action and interaction, that it is in the area "in between" people that demands our attention. (Dayton, 2005, p. xiii)

The Narrative Coaching process is similar to these and other experimental approaches, though it focuses more on the present and future and it takes a naturopathic approach more than an allopathic one. By that I mean that we are systemically working *with* our coachees not *on* them; we are increasing their ability to access their own inner resources. The process consists of the following five phases, cited here with the addition of their respective phase in narrative coaching:

- *Attunement*, which involves resonating internally with the person and accepting the person's here-and-now experience [as seen in the *Situate* phase in narrative coaching].

- *Assessment*, which involves seeking the specific issue or pattern relating to the person's distress and where it originated in past experience [and appears in present experience] [as seen in the *Search* phase].

- *Observation*, which involves offering a safe and careful replication of the . . . dysfunctional adaptation [to understand its dynamics] [as seen in the *Search* phase].

- *Intervention*, which involves a new experience that estimates a shift, release, or other expression of what has never been easy or possible to feel or express previously [as seen in the *Shift* phase].

- *Integration*, which involves incorporating new experience into the person's being and positively impacts the person's life [as seen in the *Sustain* phase] (Carnabucci & Anderson, 2012, p. 20).

Narrative coaching uses the "empty vessel" approach as does constellations in working with what is present in the field[1], and it may use assigned roles as does psychodrama, depending on the needs of the coachee. However, narrative coaching is far less produced or directed than psychodrama or constellation work and is not dependent on expert facilitation in order for it to be effective. This is evident in the fact that I have taught these principles and many of the basic practices to thousands of professionals, managers, and leaders in organizations. A large part of what makes this possible is narrative coaching's emphasis on developing the "field" in support of transformative experiences, not on directing the process in search of transactional explanations. While there is more space for an experiential approach and a greater appetite for the theoretical foundations when I teach practitioners, one of the values of this approach is that it can be used in a variety of contexts because it is based in the natural human process of change.

Family and Systemic Constellations

Virginia Satir (1991/2006) and her ground-breaking role-playing work on "family reconstruction" and "family sculpting" can be seen as a pioneer in this space. Later, with the help of German psychiatrist Gunthard Weber, Bert Hellinger (1998) brought together existential phenomenology, family systems therapy, and elements of indigenous mysticism from his time in Africa to create family constellation work. He emphasized the role of perceptive intuition, the release of our desire to control the unknown, and the importance of moment-to-moment systemic information as the process unfolds in the "field"—all three of which are central to narrative coaching. In constellations work, representatives are investigated and moved around in relation to others who are integral to the issue in order to discern the current constellation, what needs to be resolved, and what new constellation would bring about healing and resolution. At the end, the person whose process is being done replaces her representative to sense how it feels to be part of a new constellation. I know from personal experience how powerful this can be. As with narrative coaching, this involves skills in "reading" the field and knowing what to do with what you notice.

In narrative coaching, characters are literally and figuratively repositioned in people's stories as needed, but the person being coached is active in (and the focus of) the process. In some of our practices—like with our Three Chair work—they are actually guiding the process themselves with peer and facilitator support. The emphasis is on keeping their felt experience and their narration intimately connected in the moment so that both are available for transformation. This parallel process enables people to see a situation in a new way, develop a new story about it, find a new place in it from which to act, and enhance their sense of agency and connection as they try it out. In narrative coaching we work with characters in people's stories as projections, meaning that the resolution of external issues largely involves internal processes. While there are principles that guide its core practices, narrative coaching is not guided by a sense of how things are "supposed to be" in order to achieve resolution, as is the case in Hellinger's orders of love, for example.

Psychodrama

Jacob Moreno, in partnership with his wife Zerka, felt that in giving people the stage, their life stories could emerge in a space where their memories could be reworked and transformed, and their body, mind, and relational ability could heal as a result. They saw it as a safe place and structure where people might freely test out the fears and fantasies that were close to their heart and pressed upon their inner and/or outer worlds. It was a "therapeutic space where we might meet ourselves, including the parts of ourselves that might be held out of consciousness in daily life, even though they powerfully impact and inform who we are" (Dayton, 2005, p. xxix) through their often invisible scripts and illusory logic. Moreno (2008) believed that since we learn and develop in action as we move through life, we must also unlearn and relearn in action. Narrative coaching is based in the same perspective, which is why we work intensively in the moment with what is happening and what people are experiencing. In so doing, you can bring the whole person into the process and coachees can develop more lasting anchors for their new insights and commitments.

To be able to work this way, narrative coaches tend to focus on one thing at a time—usually what is at the heart of the story and its dilemma—and on shifting narrative dynamics rather than on relieving circumstantial symptoms. Narrative coaching has other features in common with psychodrama, such as "spatial mapping," inducing mild trance states, working at emotional and somatic levels, and putting people in touch with their own internal healer. However, there are also differences between the two approaches that are important to note. In narrative coaching, we: (1) invite peers when possible to help one another rather than rely on the expert as the orchestrator; (2) help people connect their body, emotions, and words, but generally do so in the present moment rather than searching for their origins in the past; and (3) work with key elements in coachees' stories as they emerge rather than use pre-assigned roles. Even so, psychodrama was a forerunner to narrative coaching with its use of enacted narration.

Therapeutic Approaches

Coaches owe an enormous debt to the psychotherapists who came before them for the building blocks they developed through their writing and their practices. Narrative coaching draws from many of these early pioneers, particularly those who approached their work using systemic, holistic, and narrative frames. We identify most with those in the psychological community who focus on personal agency and accountability and who are less interested in normative labels. The following are two therapeutic approaches with which we have a special affinity in terms of their philosophical stance and methodologies.

Gestalt Therapy

Gestalt therapy and narrative coaching are both based in a paradoxical theory of change (Beisser, 1970) in which change is seen to occur through fully contacting "what is"—the truth of one's experience—rather than through trying to be different. As with narrative coaching, it focuses on the individual's experience in the present moment, the environmental context in which this takes place, and the self-regulating adjustments people make as they navigate between the two (Bluckert, 2010). It is defined by three core principles (Yontef, 1980):

- *Change Principle*: It is phenomenological in nature and focused on what is happening now rather than what happened "then"; its only goal is relational, present-centered "awareness."

- *Process Principle*: It is based in a constructivist, existentialist position and a process of contact and withdrawal in which change happens in the crucible of the relational dialogue.

- *Holism Principle*: It locates the dyadic encounter in a field of communicative interaction that is shaped by conscious behaviors as well as unconscious projections and expectations.

> **People need to name the truth before they can change it.**

Narrative coaching aligns well with these three principles, though it focuses more on the field and the coachee's experience than on the coach and the coaching methodology. Both approaches focus on working existentially in the present moment with what IS—at both conscious and unconscious levels—so that people can experience and deconstruct their current patterns and be supported as they begin forming new ones. People generally need to name the truth before they can change it. Threshold moments in narrative coaching serve a similar function as Gestalt's "safe emergencies" in which powerful affect emerges or is triggered so it can be worked through toward a new resolution rather than blindly reenacted (see Fritz S. Perls, 1992/1969; Fritz S. Perls, Hefferline, & Goodman, 1994/1951). Unlike most other psychotherapeutic modalities, Gestalt coaches observe and share their subjective experience of their inner and outer world as part of an authentic dialogue in sessions (Bluckert, 2010). While narrative coaches actively participate in the dialogue, they are more likely to keep the attention on the narrative material and the field. If they are engaged in the reconfiguration work, it is as a mirror of the dialogue or a character in the person's narration on behalf of their purpose.

Acceptance & Commitment Therapy (ACT)

The aim of this more recent approach is to increase a person's psychological flexibility by increasing her ability to be present, open up to the reality at hand, and do what matters. These aims align well with narrative coaching's movement from phase 1 (*Situate*) to phases 2/3 (*Search/Shift*) to phase 4 (*Sustain*). Both approaches emphasize contextual and experiential change strategies, the development of more effective repertoires more than singular solutions (Hayes, 2004), and the futility of focusing on symptom reduction. Both approaches help people recognize that "I am not my story," and realign their identity, story, and actions to achieve more of their desired results. This requires what ACT calls "the observing self," clarity about one's core values, and a commitment to act on those values. They both begin with what ACT calls "contacting the present moment," but they differ in some ways in terms of what happens thereafter. In part this is because ACT is expert-driven as a therapeutic modality, whereas narrative coaching is more collaborative and facilitative by nature.

The biggest difference stems from the "glass-is-half-empty" orientation that still lingers in much of psychotherapy as seen in Harris's (2006) article on using ACT to "embrace your demons" and the assumption that "psychological processes [and language] of a normal mind are often destructive, and create psychological suffering for us all" (p. 3). It is true that we are the source of our suffering at a number of levels and we can be destructive of ourselves and/or others. It is called being human. Narrative coaching is no stranger to dealing with challenges from our Shadow and insecure working models. However, I find it more productive to help people release their normative labels, embrace their whole self, tell the whole story, and be more accountable for and constructive with their narrative choices. We help people make room for and be present to *all* of their experience. It is less about measuring how much water is in the glass and more about inviting people to notice and drink what is there—and trust that there is more.

Other Approaches

Gregory Bateson (1972, 1982) was influential in bringing a systemic perspective to psychotherapy and inviting practitioners to think in circles rather than in lines as they approached people's issues. He recognized that problems and patterns were inseparable such that, as Eron and Lund (1996) noted, "serious symptoms could only be alleviated by changing the patterns of interactional behavior that sustained them" (p. 10). The truth in these symptoms—and the problems they are signaling—can often be discerned in the patterns in a person's stories and their relational structure (Mahony, 2003). For example: "Which elements are in the foreground or background? How are the elements in relation to each other? Where is the power situated, how is it being used, and for what purpose?" You can see these systemic principles at work in narrative coaching—e.g., in circling the tree and spiraling through the model; in cycling between the person, the stories and its characters; and in focusing on pattern recognition and sensing the field.

> Help people see the connections between their somatic experience, their stories, and the systems in which they operate—and reconfigure any or all of them as need be.

The systemic orientation in narrative coaching is also reflected at the somatic level in that the four phases of the model mirror the four phases of many body-based learning and healing modalities[2]: (1) listening intently and following the person's somatic patterns as the storyteller until they are understood—and deep trust is gained (*Situate*); (2) allowing the body and the story to unravel the past and unveil the truth in the present (*Search*); (3) supporting emergence toward functional integration by reconfiguring the narrative material (*Shift*); and (4) nudging, redirecting, repositioning, or disrupting the system to speed change in the story and how it is lived (*Sustain*). Narrative coaching helps people see the connections between their somatic experience, their stories, and the systems in which they operate—

and reconfigure any or all of them as need be. As a result, people end up with more touch points to support their growth and more anchors for new stories in their life.

I often invite people when I am working with them to visualize the scene we are exploring as if it is in the room—and at key moments to stand beside me to look at it, and notice what is happening for them as the protagonist and in the broader story. It is often both moving and revealing for people to watch these scenes unfold as they witness themselves in action. This is made even more powerful when we also help them become more aware of what they are experiencing in their stories as the author. Narrative coaching is a spiraling process in which we invite people to (1) move between outside narrator and inside protagonist to deepen their insight into what is going on and what wants to happen; and (2) step inside their experiences to get a deeper felt-sense of their patterns *and* step outside their experiences to gain a larger perspective and experiment with new patterns.

In particular, look for any patterns that impede their inner knowing, outer sensing, or authentic expression. Coachees can more fully embody their existential sense of themselves and achieve more of what is important to them if these patterns are addressed systemically. When they do this well in narrative coaching, their "stories allow the clarity achieved in one small area to be extended to and imposed on an adjacent area that is less orderly" (Weick, 1995, p. 129). Narrative coaching enables you to work with these patterns because the methodology itself incorporates the means to develop people, new stories and resolutions to their issues. The rest of the book offers you a richness of resources you can use to put this work into practice at all three levels.

Implications for Your Practice

What I hope you will gain from reading this book:

- The philosophy and practices that underpin this work, which enables you to see the world and your work in new ways and apply it straightaway wherever you are.

- The embodied sense of what this work feels like and both cognitive and somatic resources to ground you and guide you as you work.

- The permission to let go of much of what you thought coaching was "supposed to be" so you can more easily have transformative human conversations.

- The understanding of narrative function and structure so you can listen for the subtleties of stories in terms of what is being said, not said, and wants to be said.

- The ability and language to address collective narratives, not just personal stories, in helping people make significant changes at whatever level they want to work.

- The freedom to work fluidly with people's stories in the moment in support of their awakening and new actions.

What are your key insights?
What will you experiment with first?

PART I
narrative
PSYCHOLOGIES

CHAPTER I

HOW OUR MINDS WORK AS STORYTELLERS

Without psychotherapy or a crisis as motivation, the past is rarely recategorized. We might from time to time call upon different episodes from the past to justify a present situation or grievance, but it rarely occurs to us to change the way the events or impressions were initially stored. | *Ellen Langer*

As coaches, we are interested in how people's minds compose, remember, communicate, and connect stories in relationship with others. I am using the term "mind" here to refer to all of our cognitive (in the most holistic sense of that word) processing faculties, including but not exclusive to the brain. Our mind is an ongoing neuro-biological process of meaning- and sense-making, and our stories are both a currency and an outcome of that process. In this chapter we will look at the personal and collective aspects of our innate drive to narrate our experiences and share them with others. We will explore the intersection of history, memory and story; how attachment theory sheds light on our working models as meta-narratives; why people need their whole brain to tell the whole story and create new ones; and the importance of neural resonance and dissonance in supporting change.

While the focus is on the brain, our notion of mind is more accurately seen as a whole body system. It is from this system that our stories are formed in the moment and over time. This is why we work to get people out of their heads and into their bodies when we coach.

The capacity and need to tell stories—and to understand and be understood by others in so doing—is part of our evolutionary and cultural heritage. Our ability to tell stories is one of the traits that sets humans apart from other species, and our stories are central to how we identify ourselves and connect with others. In part, this is because both our minds and our stories are organized in terms of time and space (Pinker, 2009) to help us navigate our daily lives. At the same time, they offer the means to transcend our usual sense of time and space in ways that create new experiences and insights. Stories bring together our internal, experiential, and subjective mind with our external, observable, and objective world in an ever-changing kaleidoscopic fashion. At the same time, the stories we keep telling ourselves form memory structures around them and they, not our actual experience in the moment, provide about 80 percent of the neural instructions upon which we base our actions (Graham, 2013).

Narrative coaches invite people to:

- Experience and reflect on their "movies".
- Realize that any story they choose is but one alternative.
- Explore new stories that will enable them to flourish.
- Notice old stories in which they are stuck.
- Reconfigure key elements so they can tell new ones.

That is why in narrative coaching we often slow the proverbial movie down—to frame by frame at times—so coachees can look more closely at whether their responses are based in habituated memories (old stories) from the past or actual experiences in the present (realities). This enables them to be more aware of their narrative patterns as well as to access their prefrontal cortex as a crucial aid for their decision-making. You can support this process through your nonjudgmental presence and use of mindful empathy (Graham, 2013), both of which create more spaciousness and less triggers for the coachee. This makes it easier to bring their attention to the nuances of their narration and to the benefits of greater accountability and adaptability as the narrator of their experiences and their life. This is particularly important for those memories that people select and interpret as self-defining and, thereby, grant privileged status to in their lives and identities (McAdams, 2003).

Connecting History, Memory, and Story

Research by Singer and his colleagues (2005a) determined that self-defining memories have the following five elements: "emotional intensity, vividness, repeated recall, connections to similar memories, and [a] focus on lasting goals or unresolved conflicts" (p. 23). These self-defining memories retain their emotional power because they are generally linked to goals and desires people consciously or unconsciously believe are still important for them. Narrative coaching is designed to help people de-stigmatize these memories, de-energize them as reactive behaviors, and de-couple them from their identity. In so doing, they are deconditioning their neural circuitry to create more space for learning, change, and growth in support of reconditioning it in new directions (Graham, 2013). You can support this process by creating safe spaces in which people can immerse themselves in guided experiences in which they can: (1) stay in contact with their (often intense) emotions without resorting to their usual reactive response; (2) soften their habituated recall and associations through applied mindfulness work; and (3) explore new strategies and stories for their current situation.

In your own practice, look for ways in which coachees are telling the same story and living the same narrative over and over again; e.g., remaining stuck in the same role or response in the misguided belief that *this* time it will get them what they have been seeking. Feeling stuck is often a sign that an underlying pattern has been activated and is, therefore, an opportunity for the coachee to notice the pattern, its trigger, and its alternative. These patterns largely operate at non-conscious and somatic levels, but they can be made conscious and malleable through working with stories in which they are on display. One way to do that is to challenge coachees' unexamined assumptions—the gap between *if* and *then*—in order to open up more room for new stories from which new behaviors can emerge.

EXAMPLE

I worked with a client who didn't feel heard by her team. After surfacing a self-defining memory when she felt small, I invited her to sit on the floor and talk with me as I stood next to her (and notice that experience), stand on a table and talk with me (and notice that experience), then stand in front of me and talk with me (and notice that experience). With the latter, I then invited her to experiment with how much distance she wanted between us and to notice where she felt the most heard.

She acknowledged her pattern of playing small (and what it costs her), her tendency to sometimes lord over people as a compensatory measure, and her desire to relate to people as one adult to another. She began to feel more empowered to make her own choices as well as get an initial sense of what worked best for her. In the process, she befriended postures she typically avoided, such that she now had a larger repertoire to work from. We identified the relationships in which she felt at ease so she had a baseline; talked through how to build on those to redefine the memory and form a new narrative; and experimented to discover her "right size" in relating to others as an adult.

We can see here connections between history, memory, and story—as Freud did with his realization that the stories he was being told were "psychological happenings dressed as history and experienced as remembered events . . . [and, in saying so, he established] the independence of memory from history and history from memory" (Hillman, 1983, p. 40). Freud also believed that these memory traces and associations could be "retranscribed" in keeping with fresh circumstances, but these memories had to first become the focus of conscious attention. As Jung later explored in great depth, our memories are often more easily and productively approached through tangential, indirect means (e.g., dreams, stories, nuances of language, metaphors, shifts in energy or body posture). Otherwise, people's tacit filters and egoic defenses can too easily obscure their awareness and openness. As neuroscientist Norman Doige (2007) noted about Freud:

> By sitting out of his patient's view, and commenting only when he had insights into their problems, patients began to regard him as they had important people in their past. . . . It was as though the patients were reliving past memories without their being aware of it. Freud called this unconscious phenomenon "transference" because patients were transferring scenes and ways of perceiving from the past onto the present. They were "reliving" them instead of "remembering" them. (p. 225)

Narrative coaches tend to sit within view of the other person, though often at an angle, so they can attend to the largely unconscious narrative processes projected into the field between and around them. We regularly invite coachees to immerse themselves in key moments in their stories—rather than just recall and reflect on them—so they can discover the deeper narratives at play. In so doing, they often come across aspects of their memories they had not remembered or acknowledged—but which often are the key to transforming them and their stories. As Seligman and Tierney (2017) note, "The brain's long-term memory has often been compared to an archive, but that's not its primary purpose. Instead of faithfully recording the past, it keeps rewriting history. Recalling an event in a new context can lead to new information being inserted in the memory" (p. 4). This is important because the processes by which their experiences are organized and distinctions are made are largely beyond their awareness (Madigan, 1996; Mahony, 2003).

As a result, people only see and hear what they are open to noticing (Bernstein, 2005), and they unconsciously edit out and effectively forget almost everything else (Kenyon & Randall, 1997). The only way to authentically change a person's story is to alter the underlying and contextual narrative processes that support it. Often this comes through helping coachees make new associations, e.g., between two stories, between two characters in a story, between a problem in one area of their life and a solution in another. This is often quite effective because it bypasses their taken-for-granted associations to uncover other possibilities—which up to that point have been on the margins of their awareness, thinking, and stories. I'm reminded of a conversation with someone who had just become head of her extended family after her husband's sudden death.

EXAMPLE

> She was concerned because this role was new for her and she was not yet feeling up to the task. Early on I asked her what she enjoyed doing in her life outside of work, and her immediate answer was "singing." I was curious about what type of singing she most enjoyed. She answered that she especially liked singing in small groups, such as *leading a small choir*. As someone who sings poorly, I shared my admiration for her gifts. I invited her to talk about what it was like for her when she sang and why she loved it so much.
>
> After she shared, I held out my hands as if one held her story about her family situation and the other her love of singing with small groups. Pausing, I asked her to imagine what it would be like to lead her extended family as if it were a small choir. With that insight, she shed a few tears, then beamed. She realized that it was a role she knew well. She could use many of the same skills, and it would be a great service to her family. She left the conversation with a new clarity and confidence about her role.

The origins of this associative approach can also be traced back to Freud, who noted in 1888 that all of our mental associations, even seemingly "random" ones that appear to make no sense, are expressions of links formed in our memory networks (cited in Doige, 2007). Fast-forward sixty years and Hebb (1949) proposes his now famous axiom, "What fires together, wires together," to which was later added "survives together" (Post et al., 1998), and to which I would add "sires together." What that means in a nutshell—largely in ways we still don't fully understand—is that neurons that are activated together (fired) become associated (wired) over time and are therefore more likely to endure (survive) as a result of their frequent use—and in so doing, attract and spark related associations (sire). For example, a difficult experience in a serious relationship may become generalized as a belief system about oneself and/or others that is triggered while dating and contributes to a more general loss of confidence in other areas. How people respond to events in their lives is based in how they assess the situation, what associations they make, what stories they tell, and what happens as a result.

In general, people are most easily reminded of memories along the neural paths with the strongest impressions, closest ties to core values, and most frequent usage. The stories we most often tell ourselves and others—and manifest in our lives—are testament to our most well-worn neural paths. When emotionally loaded situations or triggers arise, the bigger and more developed neural pathways and their associated "stories" have a significantly greater likelihood of being activated rapidly, with predictable effects (Doige, 2007). As already mentioned, this process becomes habituated over time and therefore less visible, and is often in pursuit of needs that are largely unconscious. Ahead of his time, Orison Swett Marden (1894) described it succinctly: "The beginning of a habit is like an invisible thread, but every time we repeat the act we strengthen the strand, add to it another filament, until it becomes a great cable and binds us irrevocably, thought and act." Our habits are further reinforced by the fact that we tell stories in "shorthand" to express more complex or subtle points. Although this allows us to function in our daily lives, it also obscures the logic (or lack thereof) of our decision-making and storytelling processes.

> The stories we most often tell ourselves and others—and manifest in our lives—are testament to our most well-worn neural paths.

While the patterns in our stories often fall along common and archetypal lines, they also reflect our particular schemas. The latter can be seen as the structures of expectations (Chafe, 1990) we have learned from experience and stored in memory over time. The result is an organized representation, a set of implicit rules, and an accumulated repertoire of tacit knowledge that is used to "impose structure upon, and impart meaning to, otherwise ambiguous social and situational information to facilitate understanding" (Gioia, 1986, p. 56). Russell & van Den Broek (1992) identified three dimensions of schemas that are relevant in working with people's stories in coaching: (1) how events are related to one another, (2) how events and those who are involved are psychologically connected, (3) the style in which the events are narrated—to which I would add (4) the direction in which the events are pointing.

Since schematic representations of events often take narrative form (see Mandler, 1984; Schank & Abelson, 1995), we can access them by unpacking the assumptions implicit in people's formulations about how things are supposed to be, why things are the way they are, and what would make them better. You can also learn a lot about what people notice (and miss), what themes they organize their stories around, and what values they use in making sense/meaning of their experiences. This is important in coaching because, as Polkinghorne (2004) notes, how people interpret significant events can limit or expand their subsequent actions. Their schematic frames shape what is available to them in a given moment and thus influence the rationale, repertoire, and range of available responses. Coaching can help coachees increase their awareness of their habitual narration (including their blind spots), assess how well it is working (and what it leads them to miss), and adopt frames that will yield more of their desired outcomes.

> **Questions to unpack how people see the world:**
>
> - Why this way of seeing things?
> - What do you gain from seeing it this way?
> - What do you lose by seeing it this way?
> - How else could you see it?
> - What other perspectives might you take?
> - What keeps you from considering these possibilities?
> - What might you gain if you did?

As a storyteller, our minds not only help us to make sense and meaning of what we construe happened in the past but, like all complex adaptive systems, it also builds models that allow us to anticipate the world and the future (Holland, 1995). These systems create "frameworks of expectation" (H. Sherman & Schultz, 1998) which affect our choices as we mine the present for clues to anticipate the immediate future and guide our action in the present (Boyd, 2009). This echoes Kelly's (1955) fundamental postulate that a person's processes are psychologically channelized by the ways in which she anticipates events. This is important because the stories people tell about their lives—and the meanings they draw from them—often end up operating as self-fulfilling prophecies. What we are doing in narrative coaching is unpacking the givens inherent in a person's current narratives so that new possibilities become available on behalf of their past, present, and/or future. This can be particularly useful when there is blame or shame involved. We can use narrative coaching tools such as the Rewind process (figure 1) to help them heal those wounds. In so doing, their forgiveness gives those memories a new future (Kearney, 2002).

Narrative coaching is designed to help people externalize their tacit connections and schemas, deconstruct them in slow motion, and reconstruct new neural pathways. This enables them to reframe their memories of the past, have new experiences in the present, and express themselves in new ways in the future. Therefore, invite coachees to begin that journey with a nonjudgmental respect for their current patterns, an honoring of their original purpose, and a release when ready to make room for new narratives. Think of it as though you are working with a coachee to pruning a tree to enable new growth to occur. I find that pruning in itself often has a huge impact because it creates more room for them to breathe more freely and see more clearly. From there they can more easily entertain and envision the possibility of a new narrative. Attachment theory is helpful here because it offers coaches a way to address the preverbal nature of people's narrative patterns such that they can graft new stories onto a more fitting "tree stock."

Understanding Attachment Theory

With . . . states of insecure attachment, the mind is "holding on" to old patterns in an outdated effort to just survive. This inflexible cohesiveness puts the person at risk of chaotic or rigid states. With the movement toward coherence, the system of the person becomes more flexible. | *Dan Siegel*

Narrative coaching was the first coaching methodology to explicitly incorporate the work of attachment theory. It significantly enriched our understanding of the dynamics in the coaching relationship and the preverbal roots of our stories and our actions. Significant experiences that occur when we are young can have a disproportionate impact on our development and identity. In large part this is because we do not yet have the language or a large enough narrative within which to sufficiently process them. It is no wonder, then, that many of our coachees' habits continue unabated when they are only addressed at rational and verbal levels.

Attachment theory provides a strong evidence base and some useful frames that you can use in your practice—within the bounds of your professional capabilities and client expectations—to increase people's relational capabilities. The incorporation of attachment theory in narrative coaching has opened up new nonverbal and somatic practices for addressing people's issues and reconfiguring their stories at deeper levels. It allows coaches to help people re-pattern their narrative and behavioral strategies through small, intentional movements that lead to big changes—similar to other psycho-physiological modalities.

This can be seen in Moshe Feldenkrais's pioneering work (2005/1949, 1972) on differentiation and his discoveries that (1) we can create new maps in our brains by making the smallest possible sensory distinctions between movements; (2) we can learn when we are aware and we can become more aware through slowing down our movements; (3) we learn more when we reduce our effort and thereby notice more clearly what we are doing; (4) making random movements provides variations that lead to developmental breakthroughs; and (5) even the smallest possible movement in one part of the body involves the entire body. Narrative coaching emulates this approach in enabling people to shed what covers them over and be broken open to what matters (Nepo, 1998). Attachment theory has had a significant impact on how I coach and teach coaching. It is operationalized through somatic practices such as the above as they enable us to work at preverbal and granular levels with people and their narratives.

This has coincided with the ongoing work in neural plasticity and its implications for enabling people to release or reconfigure old stories. Michael Moskowitz hypothesized that "in our use-it-or-lose-it brain there is an ongoing competition for real estate, because the activities the brain performs regularly take up more and more space in the brain by 'stealing' resources from other areas" (cited in Doige, 2015, p. 11). We can use this knowledge in working with people's stories to help them access more of their brain (and their body and mind) and free up neural resources to use in developing new narrative patterns. This requires people to consciously (and often slowly) move through their narrative routines so they can notice the nuances and begin to re-wire the circuits that hold them in place.

Some of the practices we use in narrative coaching mirror those based in medical research on stroke patients in that we inhibit coachees' use of a habituated narrative in order to support the development of its under-used counterpart (Doige, 2015). For example, we might invite someone who is used to getting things done by being domineering to practice giving directions while lying on the floor. In so doing, he is quieting the noisy signals in this brain ("If I slow down, I will be overrun") and activating other signals that have been dormant ("If I am more open, others will be too").

One of the best ways we can access these signals is through observing what people amplify and activate as they tell their stories. Narrative coaches pay particular attention to the nonverbal elements and preverbal vestiges in people's stories. This is because the brain is quite adept at deceiving us with its fictions, but the body seldom forgets and often holds clues to greater truths. As Griffith & Griffith (1993) note, "The important life dilemmas are those we feel in our bodies. Closely held, they cannot [easily] be articulated in the functional language of public life" (p. 317). As you coach, notice when insights seem to really settle into a coachee's body as a sign that they are resonating deeply rather than getting seduced by "aha" moments that often rise up only to dissipate quickly.

A strong sense of resonance is generally a sign that their mind is sufficiently aligned around the new narrative, their insights are grounded, and they will more likely act on them. This often requires both parties to pause during the session and attune to what is going on at multiple levels. Listen with your whole body (Mahony, 2003) so you can more fully sense what they are communicating and what is emerging. It is why in narrative coaching we draw people's attention to their experience in telling their story as well as the content of the stories themselves. Often what you pick up in their stories as they are being told, particularly around these difficult issues, are echoes of narrative elements from other people and other times in their lives. What people are seeking from coaching can be seen, in part, as a largely unconscious attempt to redeem and restore what they sacrificed earlier in life, regain a sense of wholeness, and learn more secure ways of relating to others and meeting their needs.

Any reactive strategies people exhibit in coaching are often the result of suboptimal attachment strategies repeated and reinforced over time. These strategies frame their experience; reinforce a familiar set of expectations, actions and rewards; and act as defenses against experiences that re-create a state of anxiety (such as overwhelm or separation). Coachees' attachment strategies can be seen and heard in the way they narrate their experiences, particularly when they are describing aspects that were/are distressing because it is in these places that their defenses are often triggered. Their defenses emerged in the course of their early development to protect their differentiating ego in response to gaps in the attachment process. However, an over-reliance on these defenses interferes with the development of more complex neural networks (Dougherty & West, 2007) and can adversely impact people's working models and capacity for secure relationships. If we can help people lower their defenses, they will be more able to improve their attachment strategies and sense of attachment security.

Attachment theory is based in the study of connection and communication patterns between infants and parents or other primary caregivers, and how these patterns shape a children's cognitive, emotional, and social development (Ainsworth & Bowlby, 1991; Bowlby, 1969, 1973, 1988). Dan Siegel (1999) defines attachment as "an inborn system in the brain that evolves [largely in the first two years of a child's life] in ways that influence and organize motivational, emotional, and memory processes with respect to significant caregiving figures" (p. 67). An infant's developing brain instinctively drives him[3] to seek physical closeness and resonant communication with the people who are the most important to him, usually beginning with the mother.

Attachment is thus an evolutionary imperative designed to ensure that the young infant survives and sufficiently thrives in those early, vulnerable years through anticipating and adapting to responses from her caregivers. The ability of her caregivers to accurately read, sufficiently mark, and astutely respond provides the bedrock upon which the child's sense of self is built. Being able to freely express his emotional state and needs—and have others appropriately perceive and respond—is vital for the development of an infant's brain so he can regulate his internal states; attune and adapt to his various environments; and communicate about and influence his external states (Siegel, 1999).

This is why children will instinctively do whatever it takes to retain a sense of safety and love—even if they have to sacrifice part of themselves to get it. John Bowlby (1969) proposed that the organization of the attachment behavioral system involves mental representations of (1) the attachment figure, (2) the self, and (3) the environment—all of which are largely based on early experiences in a child's life. Bretherton (1991) suggests that these representations result from the scripts formed out of repeated attachment-related experiences. This is particularly evident around issues and episodes related to loss and separation. Bowlby's (1982) seminal study of the behavioral consequences of abandonment and loss also led to his theory of the four phases of normal mourning and grieving: (1) an initial *numbing* phase; (2) a *yearning* phase; (3) a phase of *disorganization;* and (4) a final phase of *reorganization.* These phases represent a typical flow of response to separation and loss for young children; they can also be seen in how adults cope with the same issues in relationships. These four phases mirror the four phases in the narrative coaching process as people seek to develop coherent narratives and mature selves. Part of your work as a coach is to help people recognize their preference (e.g., dwelling on yearning) and move on to the next phase (e.g., be willing to be disorganized in order to find a better way forward).

When children perceive a threat, real or imagined, their attachment system is activated and they seek proximity to and care from attachment figure(s). If the response is satisfying, they gain an increased sense of security, engage in further exploration of their environment, and build working models to suit. If the response is not satisfying, they deploy insecure secondary strategies, engage in less (effective) exploration, and build working models to suit. The behaviors, feelings, and desires that were contained by the caregiver and the relationship will be integrated by the infant in the first instance. Those that were not contained well (or at all) and threaten the attachment bond will be defensively excluded and end up as Shadow in the second instance. Since an infant is unable to regulate himself at first, he learns how to do so through attuning himself with his primary caregivers. His level of success in regulating early in his life often has significant implications for how well he manages himself and relates to others later in life.

The greater a person's ability to self-regulate, the wider her "window of tolerance" will be and the less often her secondary attachment strategies will kick in. Graham (2013) describes a window of tolerance as "our baseline state of physiological functioning" (p. 191). Falling between the extremes of hyper- and hypo-arousal, it is a zone within which "various intensities of emotional and physiological arousal can be processed without disrupting the functioning of the system" (Siegel, 1999, p. 253). Within it, we are grounded and centered, neither overreacting nor failing to act (Graham, 2013). The more secure a coachee becomes, the more she can give herself the space she needs to fully process her experiences and make conscious, self-affirming choices. Therefore, find ways to gauge coachees' window of tolerance related to the issue at hand and provide opportunities for them to experience and explore what it would be like to open it wider. For example, you could invite a person seeking to improve his emotional intelligence to experience and express a wider range of feelings in the coaching sessions so he can allow himself to remain more open when others do the same. How well a child achieves each of the following outcomes—and at what price—has a strong bearing on their level of security later in life.

Three primary outcomes the from attachment process:

- *Safe haven*—enhances self-soothing and empathy
- *Secure base*—enhances self-expression and exploration
- *Working model*—enhances for self-regulation and engagement

---

Young children gain a sense of a *safe haven* from the reliable proximity of, ready access to, and resonant responses from a trusted caregiver when they feel anxious or senses danger. One of the primary ways they develop a sense of a safe haven as well as form attachment bonds and increase their range of tolerable distance is through "contingent communication." This mutual sharing of nonverbal signals and mutual influence through the interactions between children and caregivers forms the basis for healthy, secure attachment (Siegel, 1999). The presence of a reliable safe haven provides children with the sense of a *secure base* from which they can increasingly and confidently explore their world with an ever widening range—and to which they can return as needed. As children grow, they rely less on external figures for safety and more on the repeated experiences they have encoded in their implicit memory as a *working model* (Bowlby, 1988), which they will carry throughout their lives. Mary Main (1995) saw working models as a set of conscious and/or unconscious rules for the organization of information relevant to attachment reflected in patterns of nonverbal behavior, language, and structures of the mind.

Working models have much in common with our notions of the schemas and narrative patterns by which people perceive, organize and navigate their world. A narrative pattern can be seen as the "habitual way of framing one's experience that reinforces a set of expectations, actions and anticipated rewards. "These patterns—and the identities they support —largely operate at non-conscious and somatic levels, but they can be made conscious and malleable through working with people's stories" (Drake, 2016, p. 296). There is a strong link between narratives and working models since both are based in spatial and temporal coordinates. As Bowlby (1973) noted:

> Each individual builds working models of the world and of himself in it, with the aid of which he frames the past, perceives events in the present, forecasts the future and constructs plans. Key features include his notion of who his attachment figures are, where they may be found and how they may be expected to respond . . . and his notion of how acceptable or unacceptable he himself is in the eyes of his attachment figures. (p. 203)

These working models shape how people uniquely situate themselves and others in their stories, what activates their attachment-seeking behavior, what roles they assign to characters (including themselves), and what they perceive as threats and sources of solace. Overall, attachment theory offers a useful frame for understanding the cognitive schemas, somatic reactions, behavioral preferences, and narrative patterns children carry into adulthood. You can also use it to assess people's change readiness in terms of the three key factors—safe haven, secure base, and working model—and adapt your coaching approach accordingly. For example, in coaching someone who is sharing a difficult story for the first time, you may want to pay extra attention to being on time, highly attuned, and compassionate as a way of establishing a *safe haven* for her. In coaching someone struggling to take action, you might invite him to do small experiments during the session to increase his sense of a *secure base* from which he can move forward once he leaves the session. In coaching someone who is stuck in a rut in her stories, you may want to invite her to "circle up the tree" to increase her awareness of the aspects of her *working model* that are holding her back.

Attachment Orientations

Let us look now at the four types of attachment orientations and how they shape our minds as storytellers.

FIGURE 3: FOUR PRIMARY ATTACHMENT STYLES

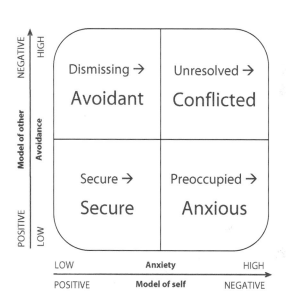

- Children who are seen as Secure generally had caregivers who were Secure: free, autonomous, emotionally available, and perceptive of and responsive to the child's needs, states, and signals. A securely attached child feels safe, understood, and confident that most of the time the parent is a reliable source of nurture, protection, and meeting their needs (Siegel, 1999). They are low in avoidance and anxiety and maintain a positive model of themselves and others.

- Children who are seen as *Avoidant* in their attachment generally had caregivers who were *Dismissing*: emotionally unavailable, imperceptive and/or unresponsive, and perhaps even rejecting of attempts at proximity. As a result, these children tended to avoid dependence by pursuing self-reliance, avoid discomfort with closeness and therefore preserve distance, and avoid their needs by using deactivating strategies (Mikulincer & Shaver, 2007). As Graham (2013) notes, they often develop coping strategies that are stable but not always flexible.

- Children who are seen as *Anxious* generally had caregivers who were *Preoccupied:* inconsistently available, perceptive, or responsive; enmeshed and entangled; and frequently imposing their state. As a result, these children tended to manage their uncertainty about independence by pursuing closeness and protection, and manage their anxiety about their intrinsic value to significant others by using hyper-activating strategies (Mikulincer & Shaver, 2007). As Graham (2013) notes, they often develop coping strategies that are flexible but not always stable.

- Children who are seen as *Conflicted*[4] generally had caregivers who were *Unresolved:* frightening and frightened, disorienting, and alarming. As a result, these children tended to simultaneously approach the caregiver for security and avoid her for safety—resulting in a disorganized or even dissociated state (Cozolino, 2006; Siegel, 2007). As Graham (2013) notes, they often develop coping strategies that are neither flexible nor stable.

These attachment orientations are useful in understanding coachees' mindsets and predominant patterns of relating and behaving. As Holmes (1999) noted, insecure representational models interfere with both *story making* (knitting together the events of one's life in a coherent way) and *story breaking* (examining the events of one's life anew in the light of new insight or information). Holmes (2001) later describes three of these attachment patterns from a narrative perspective: clinging to rigid stories (common for those with an avoidant style); being overwhelmed by unstoried experience (common for those with an anxious style); or being unable to find a narrative strong enough to contain traumatic pain (common for those with a conflicted style). People who are secure are more genuinely agile with their stories, more resilient in the face of ambiguity or challenge, and more able to engage with difficult experiences.

Securely attached adults are generally more able to:

- Self-soothe and mutually regulate so they can learn and grow.
- Constructively (re)appraise situations to maintain self-efficacy.
- Distinguish between their experience and that of others.
- Sense and articulate their feelings and empathize with others.
- Address existential concerns rather than be perpetually on guard,
- Break up their stories and reconfigure them in order to grow.
- Sustain positive yet mature beliefs about themselves and the world.
- Be tolerant of ambiguity and less dogmatic in their thinking and communicating.
- Notice and repair ruptures in their rapport and communication with others.[5]

We can see in this list many of the aspirations people bring to coaching. This is because there is a strong connection between the patterns of response in their early relationships, the patterns of narration that shaped their identity, and the patterns of engagement in their relations with others now. Their attachment patterns are reflected in how they move relative to others (with, against, or away from) in their lives and in their stories, particularly under stress or perceived threats (Horney, 1945). Horney also believed that non-secure attachment patterns emerged in children as a result of their frustrations trying to fulfill their need for both safety and self-expression. She believed that these frustrations contributed to their loss of "an ability to wish for anything wholeheartedly because their very wishes are divided, that is, go in opposite directions" (p. 38). Two good questions to ask yourself when you encounter this in a coachee are: "What frustrated desire is this person seeking to express and fulfill in this story?" "What need, if met, would end this story?" Resolution and transformation in coaching are often the result of putting people back in touch with their wholehearted wish.

> **Putting people back in touch with their wholehearted wish is often what leads to their resolution and transformation.**

Narrative coaching views frustration as a generative and essential driver of growth when handled well. It is often reaches a peak at thresholds as the pressures related to change mount. The good news is that inviting coachees to name and engage with their frustration sheds light on what people and their stories are trying to achieve and what matters to them. Therefore, don't rush to relieve people's frustration, but instead use it as an opportunity to explore their wholehearted wish and what stands in its way. Many of the frustrations coachees express about their current life reflect frustrations they have felt before, often for some time. This is because the unique constellation of influences that shaped their early development contributed to a partial, preferential unfolding of their personality and potential. Complicating matters is the fact that their working models are often stubbornly stable because they were experienced as critical for survival in their original context. These representations and rules are unlikely to be easily relinquished, in part because they are reinforced by the internally consistent logic within the models themselves (Wallin, 2007).

However, if their models are left unexamined, people tend to continue to act as if they are still true. Many of us recognize this when we return home to visit our family at the holidays—and marvel at how differently we see ourselves and act once we are back in the familial context and narratives. These types of patterns impact our affective styles, narrative themes, and patterns of engagement in interpersonal relationships (Siegel, 2007). Coaches routinely encounter vestiges of these long-held patterns in people's stories and lives. Working with them is less about hunting for the sources of these difficulties in the past, and more about experiencing and working with their implications in the present. I have found in my practice as a coach and a teacher of advanced coaching that access to these patterns is often best achieved using nonverbal means. As Wallin (2007) notes, "Given the prelinguistic roots of attachment patterns, and the disavowals and dissociations they may have demanded, we must tune in to . . . expressions of experience for which the person has as yet no words" (p. 4).

Attachment theory is integral to narrative coaching because it equips us to work at deeper levels with people's stories and the schemas behind them. The ability to recognize coachees' attachment patterns and working models in their stories is the first step in helping them to develop a more coherent narrative and attain a greater sense of attachment security. The second step is helping them do the same for themselves so they can mature their working models. With increased security, people can move with more freedom, volition, and efficacy in their lives. Coaching can be very helpful in this quest, especially as a sanctuary in the midst of organizational and civic cultures "with fewer and fewer psychic homes, places and moments, persons and situations where one can take off the armor, put down the defenses" (Paris, 2007, p. 121). It can be both a warm refuge for people (safe haven) and a fiery crucible (secure base) in which to be reborn—and from which their new narratives will arise (working model).

Working with the Whole Brain

I know that most men, including those at ease with problems of the greatest complexity, can seldom accept even the simplest and most obvious truth if it be such as would oblige them to admit the falsity of conclusions which they have delighted in explaining to colleagues, which they have proudly taught to others, and which they have woven, thread by thread, into the fabric of their lives. | *Leo Tolstoy*

To reformulate people's stories through coaching often requires that they first experience themselves as they tell their current story and then experiment with telling their story in new ways. Both processes involve exploring how they put together their stories in their mind. Modern imaging technology has enabled us to begin developing a more nuanced view of our inner universe and how our brain organizes itself, fulfills its functions and formulates stories. As a result, the original emphasis on two distinct and separate hemispheres has been enhanced to focus more on how the various elements of the human brain interact with one another and work together. As Cozolino (2010) points out, "When we speak of functions of the right or left brain, we are more accurately referring to functions that are either represented more fully or performed more efficiently in one hemisphere than the other" (p. 94). However, it is still useful to think in broad terms about the two hemispheres because each affects the way people narrate their experiences, engage others, and work with us in coaching. It is also useful to acknowledge the connections between the brain and the mind, the brain and other neural centers (like heart and gut), the body and the environment, and the self and others. By understanding how the brain functions, you can better understand what triggers coachees, how and why they respond the way they do, and how best to intervene as their coach.

Although both the left and right hemispheres are developing at very high rates during the early years of our lives, the right hemisphere appears to have a relatively higher rate of activity and growth during the earliest years (Chiron et al., 1997). During this time, "vital learning in the areas of attachment, emotional regulation, and self-esteem are organized in neural networks biased toward the right hemisphere. This pattern of asymmetrical growth shifts to the left hemisphere" (Cozolino, 2010, p. 71) somewhere around age three, in large part as a result of the rapid growth in our ability to use language. Around the same time, the prefrontal cortex becomes more able to read and regulate the emotions as largely perceived by the right hemisphere (body sensation, affect) and integrate the meaning of those signals as largely perceived by the left hemisphere (language and thoughts) (Graham, 2013). Stories are useful resources in coaching because they draw on the whole brain and provide a way to understand people's narration style (e.g., which hemisphere's preferences are more dominant in the way they form and communicate their stories).

Although basic language functions are associated with the left hemisphere, recent research is beginning to show considerable involvement of the right hemisphere in the processing of aspects of language such as metaphor—

especially when novelty, creativity, and imagery are involved (Wilkinson, 2010). This lends support for a narrative approach that works not only with the cognitive, logical, and literal processes favored by the left hemisphere, but also with the images, sensations, and impressions favored by the right hemisphere (Fosha, 2003). Stories provide the brain with a resource for emotional and neural integration because they bring together information and interests from diverse neural networks (Cozolino, 2006). Helping people to better access and integrate their two hemispheres enables them to "put feelings into words, consider feelings in conscious awareness, and balance the positive and negative affective biases of the left and right hemispheres" (Cozolino, 2002, p. 29). Therefore, listen for any incongruence between their literal verbal story and their emotional nonverbal communication. For example, "I notice that you slouch down when you talk about how much you like your new role."

TABLE I: SUMMARY OF THE PREFERENCES OF EACH HEMISPHERE[6]

Left Hemisphere	Right Hemisphere
Form	*Form*
Digital (binary choices (i.e., up/down, yes/no)	Analog (integrated map of the body)
Verbal: words, symbols, numbers	Visual/Spatial: images, patterns, maps
Guided by facts, logic, cause-effect, and analysis	Guided by emotions, dynamics, intuition, and nonverbal signals
Processes sequentially, linear thinking, likes lists	Processes simultaneously, parallel thinking, likes big picture
Literal, sees the details to get to the whole	Conceptual, sees the whole to get to the parts
Compartmentalizes, atomizes, categorizes, lasers	Makes contextual, lateral, synthetic connections
Problem defining and solving; goal-directed and solution-seeking	Contextual thinking; embraces ambiguity; can hold multiple realities

Function	*Function*
Later to develop	Earlier to develop
Farther from body, explicit memory, slower	Closer to the body, implicit memory, faster
Factual/semantic memory; story structure; acts as narrator	Emotionally rich autobiographical memory; story material; references self
Biased toward moderate, positive and pro-social emotions; associated with engaging and approaching behaviors	Biased toward negative and/or intense emotions; associated with avoiding and withdrawing behaviors
Appraises opportunity; mediates positive affective states	Appraises safety; mediates distress and uncomfortable emotions
More involved with conscious coping	More involved with self-regulation, self-soothing

Understanding the preferences and contributions of each hemisphere will enable you to adapt your coaching style to meet the differing needs of coachees—especially in drawing out narrative elements from their non-dominant hemisphere. For example, you can help coachees who operate more from their left hemisphere to drop down out of their head and into their body as an important source of information about their inner world and the richer, often more emotional, narrative material there. You can help those who operate more from their right hemisphere to rise out of their body and into their mind as an important source of information about their external world and the more factual structure of the story. In general, your first task in coaching is to help people notice the partial nature of their stories as they tell them; your second task is to invite them to bring more of the whole story into the dialogue. For example, work with a coachee who tends to tell stories that are factual, sequential, and verbal at that level first, and then invite him to explore the emotional, contextual, and nonverbal aspects of his stories.

> Your first task in coaching is to help people notice the partial nature of their stories as they tell them; your second task is to invite them to bring more of the whole story into the dialogue.

What is missing from a coachee's story is often associated with one hemisphere more than the other and provides clues to what they are seeking. It is often helpful for a coachee to first quiet the overactive hemisphere in order to create more space in her narration and in the stories themselves. For example, helping a coachee tap the mental distance and language favored by his left hemisphere can be quite helpful as a regulatory resource if he is feeling overwhelmed by emotions. Conversely, helping a coachee to map the big picture and be grounded in his body as favored by his right hemisphere can be quite helpful as a regulatory resource if he is feeling overwhelmed by details. Working with the whole brain enables people to create the spaciousness they need to access new narrative material or perspectives so they can make more mindful choices in the present and hone new neural pathways for the future. Coaching provides a safe yet provocative space where people can experiment with new regulatory strategies, which then enables them to form new narratives and tell new stories as well as identify and express themselves in new ways. This is important in coaching, especially when you encounter people's self-fulfilling prophecies, because what they see is often what they get.

You can also help coachees develop a greater sense of attachment security by moving between neural resonance and dissonance in keeping with their developmental needs and trajectory, as we shall see in the next section. This flow between the two is what enables any of us, no matter our age, to learn and grow. Again, the more we can do this for ourselves as coaches, the more we can offer this to others. For example, if you have a greater aptitude for and comfort with creating resonance, you may want to look at how to improve your ability to create, stay present to and leverage dissonance. In coaching, you can use this flow between resonance and dissonance to build and repair rapport so coachees increasingly trust you, themselves, and the process. You can use the strengthened relationship to help coachees explore new ways of being, relating, and acting in their world. Being able to access this flow through mutual regulation supports the person being coached to self-regulate and mature as the storyteller of their lives. Dissonance can be used to challenge coachees to get to the core of the issue and to be honest with themselves; resonance can be used to strengthen and resource them to do the real work related to what they discover.

> ## What people see is often what they get.

Using Resonance and Dissonance

Not only can you draw on their hemispheric resources to help people tell more of their story, but you can also use them to help people discover and experience more of themselves. Coaching provides people with an opportunity to become more aware of the downsides to their secondary attachment strategies and experiment with new options that will increase their sense of security, resilience, and meaningful results. The narrative coaching process is well-suited for this because its sequence aligns perfectly with how these strategies are formed in the first place. Rather than trying to overcome or change these strategies—which tends to trigger their egoic defenses—we replicate the process but invite people to narrate their sense of dissonance differently. For example, you can invite them to stay present to the challenge so they become more aware of what it feels like to withdraw. The four phases in the narrative coaching process and the four phases of mutual regulation come together as follows.

- *Situate: Build rapport by matching hemispheres with coachees to create resonance.* This mirroring will generate the neural resonance and sufficient attunement to build trust and elicit more of the story. It will increase people's sense of *safe haven* in the session and dampen unproductive limbic responses. This provides a "holding container," a safe place where they can adopt less defended positions. Most people appreciate right hemisphere-to-right hemisphere resonance at some point early in the coaching relationship and at critical moments, such as when they feel vulnerable.

- **Search:** *Connect with their non-dominant hemisphere to create the neural dissonance necessary for change.* By shifting your attunement, you create the conditions for people to increase their window of tolerance and build a stronger *secure base* from which they can explore openings for development. Help them address the strong emotions that often emerge, experiment with new ways of framing and responding, and develop the inner resources to return to a balanced state. This phase is based in the need for an increased testing and facing of reality as the basis for change.

- **Shift:** *Match their dominant hemisphere again (though now at a more integrated level) as the foundation for a new story and the new actions to bring it to life.* Re-creating resonance enables coachees to operationalize and anchor their gains before moving on from the session and back into their relationships in the world. This is an important step to help them harvest what they gained through dissonance and decide what they would look to do differently going forward.

- **Sustain:** *Invite them to bring the best of what they have gained through resonance and dissonance as well as both hemispheres to be able to operate at a higher level.* In the end, it is about modeling a secure relationship by deepening your empathy for them, sensing their emotions, sharing their states, and imagining the experience of truly being in their shoes while remaining grounded in your own experience, adept at managing your own state, and flexible in your engagement with them.

You can use this process to improve your ability to mutually regulate with more types of people and in more types of states. It is offered as a tool on the next page, followed by an example of a coachee who arrived out of breath and distracted. Over the course of the coaching session, he was able to regulate himself more fully with my support. This enabled him to reach a stronger place from which to make new choices, such as changing his usual task-focused approach to leadership to one that was more relational. This tool connects well with the framework on applied mindfulness that follows.

TOOL

Helping people grow through mutual regulation:

1. **Situate:** build rapport through neural resonance
   → increase attunement *(and provide safe haven)*
2. **Search:** create openings through neural dissonance
   → widen window of tolerance *(and strengthen secure base)*
3. **Shift:** seek alignment through neural resonance
   → integrate learning *(and enrich working model)*
4. **Sustain:** reinforce new narrative through feedback
   → build confidence in new action *(and increase security)*

EXAMPLE

- *Situate:* Attend to his breathing   Neural *resonance*
- *Search:* Elicit his unspoken emotions   Neural *dissonance*
- *Shift:*   Invite him to speak from his heart Neural *resonance*
- *Sustain:* Identify anchors and practice   Neural *integration*

Why This Matters

One of the frameworks I've developed to increase people's awareness and approaches in coaching is *applied mindfulness*— or putting "Mindfulness in Motion." It positions mindfulness as a *relational* activity intended to enable us to live better lives, not just attain higher states of consciousness. As a result, it can be generative at multiple levels rather than just palliative at a personal level. It reflects a theme you will see across the book: Our initial role is to help people become more candidly aware of what is happening now and then to accompany them as they develop new approaches to meet their needs and fulfill their aspirations. Using applied mindfulness in coaching makes it easier for those involved to co-create a stronger working relationship in which both people feel secure enough to be present and proactive.

FIGURE 4: PUTTING MINDFULNESS IN MOTION

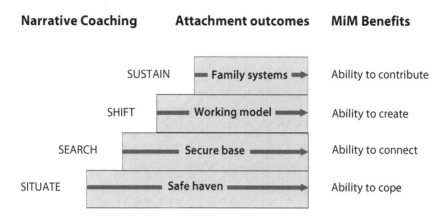

Narrative Coaching	Attachment outcomes	MiM Benefits
SUSTAIN	Family systems	Ability to contribute
SHIFT	Working model	Ability to create
SEARCH	Secure base	Ability to connect
SITUATE	Safe haven	Ability to cope

The diagram above depicts the connections between each phase in the narrative coaching process, the attachment outcome it primarily addresses through mutual regulation, and the applied mindfulness benefit that both accrues and makes it possible. It is based in the observation that more and more of our time as coaches seems to be spent helping people cope better, leaving less time in coaching to help them move on to more generative narratives. There is a direct connection between coachee's level of attachment security, ability to be mindfully in motion, and what they can do through coaching. Each of the levels in the framework is explained below.

1. This phase is centered around helping people *Situate* themselves in the coaching conversation and inviting them to observe how they are situated in the stories and their explanations. This provides them with a sense of *Safe haven*, which enables them to *Cope* with what emerges in the session and be the author of their new stories.

2. This phase is centered around holding space for people in which they can *Search* their stories for what they need to experience and learn in order to resolve the question their story raises. This provides them with a sense of *Secure base*, which enables them to *Connect* with others (and themselves) and be an actor in stories with others in new ways.

3. This phase is centered around giving people opportunities to make a meaningful *Shift* by experimenting with new mindsets and behaviors

that better support their aspirations. This provides them with a more mature *Working model*, which enables them to *Create* new options and be an agent in the narratives around them in new ways.

4. This phase is centered around inviting people to *Sustain* the changes they have made by determining what they want to do differently going forward. This will yield better strategies for engaging the *Family systems* in which they live and/or work, which enables them to *Contribute* to new outcomes and be an activist for better narratives.

Working with *Mindfulness in Motion* will enable you to more quickly and deeply build trust and rapport with your coachees. As a result, through your modeling and interacting they will be able to do the same for themselves. In coaching, we help people increase their awareness and skills; however, our greatest gift is often the experience of a new way of relating based in generative psychological safety. I find that we often under-estimate how novel and how powerful this is for many of our coachees. When you can *be* with people this way, the affects ripple and reverberate through them for longer periods of time and have more impact than most any of the words you say. When you find yourself in moments like this when you are coaching, pause so that the coachee can fully absorb what is happening. There is no need to analyze or discuss what is happening; just allow it to serve as a new starting point for what is possible now. The journey to their healing and resolution are two sides of the same coin, each of which begins in offering them experiences of "being met."

In the end, your ability as a coach to stay in sustained, regulating contact with coachees is a crucial ingredient in their healing and outcomes. Invest in your own development so you can remain compassionate and clear in your reflections to coachees. The more your own security needs are met, the stronger the container you can offer coachees—and the more likely they are to feel understood and have positive experiences associated with secure relationships in working with you. As time goes on, help them build on where they are secure and bridge between what goes on in the coaching relationship and what can happen in other important relationships.

Regulate your behavior to offer coachees the experience of an appropriately responsive, secure relationship. This often involves being resonant enough to be allowed in and make a connection and dissonant enough to break through and make a difference. Make room for experiences their original attachment figures could not sufficiently provide. Suggest assignments to enhance their ability to mentalize, initiate repairs when relationships are ruptured, and stay connected while feeling autonomous. Use people's stories and the relational dynamics in them as a window into their working models and a resource for helping them to shift.

Listen for the defenses which coachees use to stay within the bounds of their implicit beliefs about "what can be known, what can be felt, what can be spoken, and what cannot be contained" (Slade, 2008, p. 773). Help them to recognize how their defenses influence how they form their stories, engage in coaching, and live their life. They can then start to notice their attachment strategies and start to question what else might be possible. Bring their words or experiences into the present moment, activate their defenses so they can be recognized and addressed, and invite them into experiences where they can try out healthier strategies for getting their needs met.

Invite coachees to examine and adjust their often unexamined, taken-for-granted working models. Listen for any tensions in their stories between their need for safety and their need for self-expression. Make room for the feelings, desires, and abilities that a person has denied or inhibited so they are more able to self-regulate and respond from a secure place. In the process, help them resolve any "divided wishes" so they can invest more wholeheartedly in their life and work. For example, what unconscious loyalties or allegiances keep them from venturing forth to a new town or career? Help them recognize that their old working models probably seemed better than the alternatives in relating to sub-optimal attachment figures, but they may no longer be sufficient for meeting the demands of their adult life or fulfilling their aspirations.

People with *anxious* patterns tend to be overly merged with their story and may benefit from externalizing processes that create more spaciousness between themselves and their stories. Help them fill in the gaps in their stories with the factual information they typically dismiss, normalize, or rationalize. People with *avoidant* patterns tend to be overly separated from their story and may benefit from internalizing processes that reconnect them with their stories in new ways. Help them fill in the gaps in their stories with the emotive information they typically dismiss, normalize, or rationalize. One of our roles in coaching is to invest in people's ability to mentalize, initiate repairs when your relationship is ruptured, and stay connected while feeling autonomous—so they can learn how to do so back in their own life and/or workplace.

Implications for Your Practice

- Provide a safe haven and a secure base for people so they can more fully experience and explore what else is possible.

- Position yourself as a "good enough" and available caregiver to help people become more proactive and less reactive.

- Reframe what you perceive as defensive or resistant behaviors in people as their attempt to get their legitimate needs met.

- Bring people into the present moment through either their words or their experiences to foster development and integration.

- Recognize that people need different coaching strategies depending on their attachment preferences, and be willing to adapt your approach to suit.

What are your key insights?
What will you experiment with first?

CHAPTER 2

HOW WE FORM IDENTITIES

*Those who do not have power over the story that dominates
their lives, the power to retell it, to rethink it, deconstruct it, joke about it,
and change it as times change, truly are powerless, because they cannot
think new thoughts.* | *Salman Rushdie*

In the previous chapter we explored the notion that our minds are perpetual storytellers. The stories of who we think we were, we are, and we will be are the most elemental of these narratives. As we saw earlier with the Rewind tool (figure 1), narrative coaching works at the intersections of identities, behaviors, and stories to help people achieve new outcomes. As coaches, we are curious how these three interact—particularly in terms of how they perpetuate people's stories and responses, and where there are openings to disrupt the cycle and create new options. For example, how might they access an under-used aspect of themselves (identity), say spontaneity, to notice opportunities for new experiences in which they feel free (story) to try something new (behavior). While much of the focus in coaching is on changing behaviors, we need to address people's issues at the identity level if their changes are going to stick. The narrative in play is the red thread that connects their experiences to their outcomes. We can gain glimpses of this thread by noticing the stories people tell us in coaching and what they reveal about the person and their assumptions and aspirations. Therefore, be curious about what narratives inform how the coachee sees her experience, how she sees herself, and how she chooses to act (consciously or unconsciously)?

People tap into various identities in the course of their day and across time to keep pace with their internal and external demands and their personal and shared aspirations. You can gain a sense of their narrative identities by listening for the following five elements (see Botella & Herrero, 2000):

- Events they include (or exclude) in their stories.
- Main themes around which they organize their stories.
- Characters they regard as significant (or nonsignificant).
- Voices they privilege or silence when telling their stories.
- Genre into which they place their narrative material.

For example, do they tend to favor positive or negative events? Do they tend to position themselves as above, equal to, or below in relation to other key characters? Do they tend to talk in an active or passive voice? Do their inner and outer narratives tend to match in ways that are healthy for them and those around them?

Narrative coaching involves working with people to reconfigure how they define themselves, narrate their experience, and live their lives. In the process, they develop an increased sense of agency and accountability as an *author* of their stories and an increased awareness and agility as an *actor* in others' stories. In chapter 7 we will look at the other two levels, people's capabilities as an *agent* and an *activist* in relationship with the larger narratives in which they live or work. For now, we will look at the social and narrative nature of our identities and the tensions between how we experience ourselves and how we express ourselves and between how we see ourselves and how others see us. In particular, we will look at the contribution of social constructionism to our understanding of narrative identity; the useful distinction between *I* and *Me*; the role of constructed selves, lived selves, and imagined selves in shaping our actions; a temporal view of identities (figure 5); and the narrative coaching model (figure 7) through the lens of identity. Identities are critical in making and sustaining change because so much of what we do is based on the stories we tell ourselves about who we think we were, are now, and should or could be in the future.

Growth often comes when a core aspect of our narrative identity is challenged and we can open ourselves to new stories and other aspects of ourselves. For example, some years ago I lived for a number of weeks largely from a sensory and emotional place while I recovered from a concussion and rebuilt my cognitive capacities. During that period, I came to see how much I had over-identified with my thinking function. Through this experience I gained a more expanded sense of myself as well as a healthier respect for the long arc of change and what it takes for people to truly heal and develop. We often underestimate what is truly at stake for people in coaching when we ask them—often blithely—to undertake a change in their identity or behavior. We take this seriously in narrative coaching by focusing on one dynamic at a time and ensuring that people have the scaffolding they need to fully leverage the opportunity for learning and development it contains. This enables coachees to sufficiently invest in what is required and extend the benefits from coaching to other areas of their life and/or work.

> We often underestimate what is truly at stake for people in coaching when we ask them—often blithely—to undertake a change in their identity or behavior.

We are guided by a belief that identity is more of a verb in process than a noun in place. While most of us experience a sense of coherence and continuity to our identity most of the time, we are forever engaged in a dance with our environment. Sometimes we challenge the coherence of the status quo and create discontinuities in order to grow, and sometimes we change in response to our environment in order to adapt. For example, we might decide to be the first in our family to earn a graduate degree, yet in achieving this milestone we find that it has changed us and how others relate to us in ways we had not imagined. You can see this in Singer's (2005b) definition of identity as "the psychosocial construct that meaningfully locates us in a sociocultural niche and unifies our lives temporally by finding continuity among our previous experiences, present concerns, and future aspirations" (p. 11). Similarly, Stryker (1987) defines identity as an internalized role designation corresponding to people's social locations in their various networks of interaction. I would suggest[7] that we speak in terms of identities rather than a singular identity because each person is a portfolio of the "individual and the collective, the relational and the volitional" (Bernstein, 2005, p. 25).

Our identities are formed in the continuous interplay between our needs for stability, consistency, familiarity, and continuity as the basis for safety and security *and* our needs for agility, adaptability, novelty, and discontinuity as the basis for exploration and growth (Drake, 2008a, 2009d; Penuel & Wertsch, 1995). The former is informed by our need to preserve and protect who we think we are, and it helps us to retain a sense of a coherent whole with a center that holds. The latter is informed by our need to advance and enhance who we become, and it helps us to increase our capacity to flourish as we push out from the center. Overall, people tend to see themselves largely based on the meaning they (and significant others) give to the events in their lives, and people generally act in ways that are consistent with their familiar or desired identities. The result is that people's behaviors can be seen as efforts to optimize their environments in their favor and their narratives as efforts to construe situations in line with their favored identities.

The more salient a particular identity is to a person, the more often situations will be perceived and structured according to this identity (Cross & Markus, 1991). In addition, the more important an identity element is to her, the more she will seek to have it validated by her significant audiences (Oyserman & Markus, 1993) and the more her behaviors will be in service of confirming these identities (Markus & Nurius, 1986). Again, we can see the interconnections between our realities, our stories, and our identities— and the systemic and self-fulfilling prophecies that tend to keep it all in place. Many of the issues people bring to coaching are related to actions that have not yielded the desired results. In part this is because they have created—"both in their minds and in the actual environment—a social reality that verifies, validates, and sustains the very conceptions that initiate and guide these processes" (Swann & Read, 1981, p. 371). That is why narrative coaches think about people's behaviors as *identity performances* (Mishler, 1992, 1999) in which people are trying to keep a particular narrative going (Giddens, 1991). Openings for growth occur when there is an internal or external interruption in the usual performance and gaps appear between people's expectations and their reality. You can step into these spaces with people to increase their awareness of their current reality and open up possibilities for another way.

What story is worth your life?

It is hard for most people to do this through direct reflection, so it is often more fruitful in coaching to indirectly approach their identities through their interactions, communications, and actions (Ricoeur, 1992). It is about inviting them to be a keen observer of themselves in motion in their lives and in their stories. Stories are perfect for this as they make visible people's largely invisible identity processes and thereby provide access to the narrative mechanisms by which they define themselves. A critical piece of the process is inviting people to see themselves as both authors *of* and actors *in* their performances, recognize that these are just performances, and make new choices about how they want to be present to themselves and with others. A second critical piece is inviting them to see that the stories they tell are embedded in larger narratives that may or may not be aligned with how they want to be in the world or what they want to achieve. Any changes a person makes in coaching are more likely to have a lasting and meaningful impact when their broader patterns, identity strategies, and socially constructed narratives are addressed (Mattingly, 1998). Ultimately, it is about asking this marvelous question from Lisa Marshall: "*What story is worth your life?*"

Constructing Ourselves Socially

By refusing his web of constructions, she also cut him off from his supporting fiction. | *James Hillman*

How do we define who we are? In narrative coaching, identities are seen as historical, social, and contextual processes not just as individual traits. In part this is a result of its roots in disciplines with critical perspectives on identity, including social constructionism. The roots of social constructionism can be seen in Berger and Luckmann's (1966) treatises on the sociology of knowledge and the social construction of reality and in Gergen's (1973) early work, which called for the inclusion of contextual, social, political, and economic phenomena in understanding people. Other sources that advocated for more inclusive and collective ways to think about identities and stories include: Anzaldua (1987) on *borderlands identities*, Frank (2010) on *socio-narratology*, Gilligan (1982) and Sorrell and Montgomery (2001) on *feminist perspectives* on identity formation, and McLaren (1993) on *critical pedagogy*. These writers challenge us to think beyond the usual individualistic theories and practices and consider using instead a contextual and co-constructed frame in our coaching. This is important in coaching because changes in and expressions of people's identities can be thwarted or supported by shifts in the larger narratives in which they are embedded.

As Berger (1963) writes, "Identity is socially bestowed, socially sustained, and socially transformed. . . . Self and identity are not something 'given' in some psychological sense, but they are bestowed in acts of social recognition. We become that as which we are addressed" (p. 99). People define themselves to varying degrees in relation to the views and responses of significant others that are reinforced (Oyserman & Markus, 1993). Over time, our identities are social in nature even if they often feel profoundly personal, and they are constructed in nature even if they often feel profoundly real. As narrative therapists Freedman and Combs (1996) note, "Our prevailing narratives provide the vocabulary that sets our realities. Our destinies are opened or closed in terms of the stories that we construct to understand our experiences" (p. 77). People's most salient stories have a real and tangible impact on their identities and their lives (and vice versa), which is why they are so central to narrative coaching. Social constructionism provides a rich foundation for understanding people's stories and helping them recognize that their stories are not synonymous with their identities.

As coaches, we can use this frame to guide people in exploring the subtle and often invisible ways in which their identities are shaped by their communities and culture over time (Mehl-Madrona, 2010). As a result, they can decouple what was once fused and imagine new ways of being in the world. They can also investigate how their stories and the collective narratives in which they operate influence each other, the consequences of the current configuration in terms of their identities, and the possibilities for re-narrating one or both. As Gergen & Kaye (1993) wrote, "[A] story is not simply a story. It is also a situated action in itself, a performance with elocutionary effects. It acts so as to create, sustain, or alter worlds of social relationship" (p. 253). People are intersubjectively narrated beings who cannot be seen independent of their context—and they must be coached accordingly. In narrative coaching, the social constructionist perspective is augmented with one that is developmental so that coaches can take a more integrative approach and coachees can sustain more of their results.

As Singer (1996) noted, "Theorists who embrace a personalogical orientation . . . emphasize the individual's processes of storying and meaning making within a cultural context, whereas social constructionist theorists . . . are interested in how culture wrote the story of our lives" (p. 452). I agree with Rossiter (1999) and others in seeking a both/and approach to identities, and the term "psychosocial" (McAdams et al., 1997) is useful here as a middle ground (see Drake, 2005b). Identities, then, can be seen as moving feasts, as traveling repertory companies (Singer & Rexhaj, 2006), through which people continually calibrate their internal landscapes and external environments in ways they believe will enable them to achieve what is important to them. They do this by deconstructing, constructing, and reconstructing selves based on the stories told by and about them. If you want coachees to adopt new behaviors or attain new results, help them build identities from which to naturally do so. The results will stick better if they are seen as a logical and natural extension of who they (and enough others) think they are. These new identities are also reinforced by the actions they choose to take over time—and the stories they (and others) tell about them as a result. As always in coaching, start where the coachee is most ready.

Hermeneutics (Heidegger, 1927/1996; Schön, 1983) offers a related and useful frame for doing narrative identity work in coaching. Hernadi (1987) outlined the three classical hermeneutic elements as follows: (1) What does this text say? (2) How and why does this text say what it does? (3) What do I, the reader, think of all this? We can adapt the outline for use in narrative coaching as follows: (1) What does this story say? (2) How and why was this story told? (3) What do I, the coach, hear in this? (on behalf of the coachee). In narrative coaching, we move between all three as we help people to gain a new and deeper understanding of their experience and their expectations. We go beyond what is strictly given and read between the lines; we pay attention to what has been omitted and is in the silence and to what has been so taken for granted that it has not even been questioned (Bergum, 1997). A psychosocial approach adds a fourth element to the hermeneutic process by positioning the three elements (story, narrator, and listener) as a function of the context and discourse in which they are situated (field).

The Narrative Coaching model (figure 2) has four phases, each of which reflects one hermeneutic element in particular:

- *Situate* focuses on grounding the person as *narrator* of the story.
- *Search* focuses on unpacking the *story* and its telling.
- *Shift* focuses on engaging the story in the *field* in new ways.
- *Sustain* focuses on supporting progress as the *listener.*

You can help people to look at their stories from all four hermeneutic perspectives, as we shall see later in the *Narrative Diamond* (figure 24). In general, it is best to start by increasing a person's awareness of her current stories and the identities these reveal (*what is*) before trying to change either the stories or the person telling them (*what could be*). Social constructionism was important in the early stages of the development of narrative coaching, in large part to advocate for a socially critical stance in the profession. As narrative coaching has evolved, it has been integrated with a more fully hermeneutic approach that is experiential, embodied, and integrative. In the end, narrative coaching is a psychosocial process that helps people "come home" to themselves (*Situate* to *Search* in the model) and "go home" to others (*Shift* to *Sustain* in the model) in new ways.

Dancing between I and Me

Every man invents a story for himself which he then often and with great cost to himself, takes to be his life. | *Max Frisch*

Our identities have been epigenetically shaped through our interactions with others since birth. They are forged in the crucible where our internal desires meet our external demands and our need for becoming meets our need for belonging. In many ways, people measure their sense of progress in life by what emerges from that crucible. Two of the scenarios we see often in coaching are people who are living out narratives that bring worth to them but who have lost their connection with others in the process (becoming without belonging) and people who are living out narratives others have deemed worthy but who have lost themselves in the process (belonging without becoming). I find the distinction between *I* and *Me* useful here in understanding these tensions and the social nature of our identities.

> Our identities are forged in the crucible where our internal desires meet our external demands and our need for becoming meets our need for belonging.

Sociologist George H. Mead (1934/1967) developed the term "Generalized Other" as a composite internalized figure that represents the values and the norms of a person's community and is a necessary consequence of normal development. The distinction between *I* and *Me* was central to this process and his social philosophy. Mead described our inner world as a "field, a sort of inner forum, in which we are both spectators and actors. In that field each one of us confers with himself" (p. 401). This resonates strongly with how narrative coaches work with people as authors and characters in their stories. While it is most common to think in terms of ourselves as an *I*, particularly in the West, Mead would argue that our sense of self is largely defined in terms of our sense of *Me*. It is formed, in large part, through the internalization of how others see us, respond to us, and relate to us— particularly in the formative years of our life.

William James, another pioneer in this field, also wrote about this distinction about our identities. He (1892/1927) saw the *I* as the *Self-as-subject, self-as-knower*, and the *Me* as the *Self-as-object, self-as-known*. James (1890/1950) described the characteristics of the *I* as continuity, distinctness, volition, and embodiment, and the *Me* as having material, spiritual, and social characteristics. Others who came along in the field (see Kegan, 1994; Mahony, 2003) echoed this distinction in framing the *I* as the subjective self who is observing and the *Me* as the objective self who is being observed. Much of the work in coaching is helping people to reconcile the two in some new way. For example, this distinction can be used in helping coachees recognize the multiplicity and social nature of their identities and move between telling their story as a narrator and reflecting on their story as a protagonist. In so doing, they can evolve their relationship with the relational and cultural forces that inform their identities.

In general, people develop as a result of a shift in their sense of *I* or as a result of feedback about their sense of *Me*. Sometimes their sense of *I* needs to shift to accommodate a new *Me*, such as when a key contributor at work is promoted to manage her team. Sometimes their sense of *Me* needs to shift to accommodate a new *I*, such as when a person desires to be seen differently by others in his family. Problems often arise when how we see ourselves (*I*) does not match up with how we show up for and/or are seen by others (*Me*). Changing the *Me* is often difficult—not only because it disrupts others' patterns and habituated responses to us, but because it may also challenge their narratives about themselves and the subgroups they represent. For example, the promotion of the first woman as the head of a department may be challenging at first for both the men and women on her team. They will each in their own way need to adapt their narratives about themselves and what constitutes an "ideal leader."

Theodore Sarbin (Mancuso & Sarbin, 1983; Sarbin, 1986a, 1986b) translated the *I/Me* distinction into a narrative frame. He argues that *I* represents the Self as *an author, the self-as-teller;* and the *Me* represents the Self as *an actor or figure, the self-as-tale-told.* People's sense of themselves evolves over time in a dialectic manner in relation to the significant shared narratives in which they are immersed. They tell stories about themselves to retain a sense of continuity for their internally constituted *I,* even as their externally constituted *Me* evolves, in part, through the stories others tell about them. They narrate their experiences so as to accommodate, confirm, and sustain their situated identity and/or to assimilate anomalous events into their identity and restore equilibrium (Block, 1982). People can shift their identities by telling new stories, reframing old ones, or stopping their investment in collective stories that no longer align with their desired identity. In saying this, it is important to acknowledge that *I* and *Me* are useful conceptual distinctions, not realities unto themselves.

Still, you can surface tensions between a coachee's sense of *I* and *Me* by asking questions such as, "What did you want to do at that moment?" (*I*) followed by, "What held you back?" (*Me*). The former sheds light on his instinctive desire (for better or worse), and the latter sheds light on his concerns about how he will be perceived by others. Coaches can help people sufficiently resolve either concern in order to act with greater authenticity, integrity, and efficacy. For one person it might be helping him to mature an impulsive *I* so he considers what others need from him (*Me*), while for another it might be helping her to mature an indecisive *Me* by considering what her *I* truly wants. Look behind coachees' actions to understand the stories that are driving them. What aspect of their identity are they defending or promoting in their stories? How do they distort their experience or sense of reality to conform to their favored identity plot lines? As a result of coaching, certain aspects of people's identities may move more into the background, while others are freed to move more into the foreground. As this work has evolved, the notion of *We* has become increasingly important help us to understand the role of collective narratives and identities in terms of how coachees see themselves and their world and collaborate with others in both endeavors.

I have also come to more loosely hold the distinctions between I/Me and self/other in light of the Buddhist perspective on the illusions of mind and self. It offers a counterbalance to Western views that are often still quite Cartesian in nature. For example, we can help people release their immersion in *non-self* so they can take action as *self* and release their attachment to *self* so they can experience *non-self* (Graham, 2013). I think there is room for both views in taking an integrative approach to identity and development. In the end, it is about helping people grow so they are more authentically aligned with how they want to be in the world and what they want to achieve as a result. For some this will mean gaining greater access to their non-self, and for others it will mean standing more fully in their self. Either way, the net result is greater freedom, authenticity and efficacy for the coachee. This is part of why narrative coaching is often described as "serious play."

The Role of Play in the Dance

Play is a useful framework for coaching because it captures people's need for structure *and* freedom, experimentation *and* consolidation, in order to learn and develop themselves. Play is one of the most significant avenues through which a child figures out who they are and how to relate to others. The child development literature offers a rich resource in support of play as a social process with a social purpose that is also relevant for adults. For example:

- Bowlby's (1988) notion of a *safe haven* that provides infants with a sense of safety and a *secure base* that gives them the confidence to explore (see Ellis, 1973; Mellou, 1994) offers a frame you can use to increase coachees' courage and capability to try new things.

- Winnicott's (1988) notion of the *false self* as a mask which we hide behind rather than risk exposure offers a frame you can use to help coachees' experiment with letting more of their authentic self and their potential selves show to others.

- Horney's (1945) notion of *divided wishes* offers a frame you can use to help coachees explore where they feel torn or stuck, play with new configurations to see what would enable them to free up more of their discretionary energy for the fulfilment of their wholehearted wishes.

- Piaget's (1954, 1962) notion of *imitation/accommodation* and *play/assimilation* offers a frame you can use to understand coachees' tensions between preserving safety and inclusion (follow the rules) *and* extending self-expression and individuation (innovate new strategies).

What children experience through play has a lot in common with what adults' experience in learning new skills and making transitions—two of the most common reasons people seek coaching. Play requires both children and adults to do the following, each of which is particularly present in one of the elements in the narrative coaching process (figure 14):

- Circumscribe activities within boundaries and limits in time and space (Mainemelis & Ronson, 2006)—as seen in the *Situate* phase in which the container is set for the stories to unfold and the work to be done.

- Navigate the threshold between fantasy and reality (Ibarra & Petriglieri, 2010)—as seen in the *Search* phase in which conscious and unconscious elements are explored at the edges of their stories.

- Negotiate between "identities claimed" and "identities granted" (Bartel & Dutton, 2001) and inner and outer worlds—as seen in the *Shift* phase in which coachees make new choices in terms of who and how they want to be in the world.

- Realign identity and role expectations in order to be successful (Hall, 1971)—as seen in the *Sustain* phase in which coachees reenter the world with their new story as a gift to themselves and others.

- Integrate body, spirit, and mind at a higher level, yet in a nonthreatening way (Erikson, 1950)—as seen in the *spiral* in which coachees integrate their progress and the cycle of growth continues.

Play helps people of all ages learn how to interact with their environment, activate more of their whole mind, experiment with new ways of seeing themselves and being seen by others, create their own knowledge of the world, and shape their space in it. Incorporating a safe space for play enables both children and adults to experiment with releasing and rehearsing identities to meet their current or anticipated needs and try out new and untested behaviors (A. Y. Kolb & Kolb, 2010). For children, play is often key in forming their ego structure as they learn; whereas, for adults, play is key in suspending their ego structure in order to unlearn and learn anew. *Serious play* is both an attitude and an activity that can be used in coaching to help people to:

- Experiment and make 'mistakes' with less consequence.
- Have an immediate feedback loop to improve.
- Ask questions that might be risky in public.
- Try out new identities, approaches and stories.
- Engage their whole body and self.
- Challenge the status quo.
- Have more joy and freedom.

The literal and figurative use of play in narrative coaching offers people an opportunity to decouple their habituated associations between means and ends (Mainemelis & Ronson, 2006). However, the notion of play and its potential for adult development is challenging because, as March (1976) notes, the very experiences children seek out in play are the ones that social and organizational norms for adults are generally designed to avoid: disequilibrium, novelty, and surprise. Therefore, a nonjudgmental stance and a commitment to serious play are important in making it safe for people to try out new aspects of themselves, see how those new stories feel in action, and prepare for bringing them into their world. These are increasingly important as coaching as a whole matures and practitioners seek out practices that empower people to address larger narratives not just personal stories. As we shall see in the next chapter, transformative learning and development most often occurs in the fertile space between what coachees knows and what they don't know, who they are and who they want to become, and what they can easily do now and what they can't do yet.

> A nonjudgmental stance and a commitment to serious play are important in making it safe for people to try out new aspects of themselves, see how those new stories feel in action, and prepare for bringing them into their world.

Working with the Past, Present, and Future

We make sense—or fail to make sense—of our lives by the kind of story we can—or cannot—tell about it. | *Joseph Dunne*

Not only can identity be framed in spatial terms related to how we orient ourselves relative to our inner and outer worlds, but it also can be framed in temporal terms related to how we orient ourselves relative to our past, present, and future. It reflects our striving to reconcile our perceptions of "what is," "once was," and "what might be" (Cross & Markus, 1991) in defining and redefining ourselves. Even though the past is given the bulk of attention in conceptualizing identity and development, a clear case can be made that who we are and how we act are as much influenced by our expectations of the future as they are by our explanations of/from the past. People's stories about their lives are as much future-shaped as they are past-determined (White & Epston, 1990). What we strive for and are in the process of becoming is at least as significant a factor in our identity as what we are currently doing (Allport, 1955/1968; Goldstein, 1939; Maslow, 1954). In narrative coaching, we are interested in how people construct their identities in relation to all three dimensions of time (past, present, and future).

Stories are a powerful resource for doing so because they are built around a temporal frame like our minds. People draw on their past, present, and future identities in telling their stories. It is also true that people's stories about the past, the present, and the future shape their identities over time and their experiences and actions in the moment. As such, we can see the past, the present, and the future as a reflexive loop in which each one offers information to and receives meaning in relation with the other two. This means that all three can be accessed in the present moment in working with people and the issue at hand. Narrative coaching builds on the retrospective nature of stories by spiraling through these recursive loops such that the past, present, and future are each available to work with in the moment. I saw this in a recent conversation with a client:

EXAMPLE

He commented that I often seemed to know what he would say next. I responded by saying that it felt like I was getting glimpses of the future (when he was "retired") as it curled back into our present experience—bringing with it our shared memories of working together in the past. All three temporal dimensions were present in that moment. As a result, I could see his current dilemma from all three perspectives at the same time, and he could develop a new plan for what to do next.

As Kearney (2002) notes, "When someone asks you who you are, you tell your story. That is, you recount your present condition in the light of past memories and future anticipations. You interpret where you are now in terms of where you have come from and where you are going" (p. 4). While much of coaching is future-focused, people often end up needing to *restory* their past as part of the process—e.g., shifting the significance and meaning of events, making new connections and associations, repositioning themselves and others (Mishler, 1999). However, narrative coaches work with people's narrative material in the present most of the time regardless of which dimension of time the coachee is addressing (e.g., recollecting a related episode from the past or imagining the future consequences of a pending decision). This is because the present is the only time frame for action, which means that all problems are ultimately problems of the present (Boscolo & Bertrando, 1992). The key is to work with coachees in the present moment, but in relation to whichever temporal dimension would most help them make progress.

For example, one of the core practices we teach in our programs is the Three Chairs. It is used to help people reconfigure the relationship between the past, present, and future as a way to gain greater clarity about their situations and their choices. The configuration of chairs in the "field" can be seen as a three-dimensional representation of the stories about the situation as they are organized in the person's mind. By working experientially with the chairs, people gain access to unconscious aspects of their inner world, which yields insights and resolutions they can apply back in the outer word. It reflects St. Augustine's (400/2009) proposition that there are three times: a present of past things (memory), a present of present things (direct perception), and a present of future things (expectation). Through coaching we can help people make visible, explicit, and conscious the invisible, tacit, and unconscious ways in which their stories are narrated as a means of opening up more space for new narratives and new choices. If their past can become more malleable through coaching, their present becomes more available and their desired future becomes more attainable.

> The key is to work with coachees in the present moment, but in relation to whichever temporal dimension would most help them make progress.

FIGURE 5: A TEMPORAL VIEW OF IDENTITIES

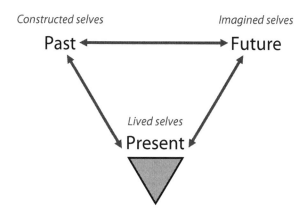

87

As this diagram illustrates, identities can be seen as an evolving prism (Stevens-Long, 2000) composed of the selves we have constructed over time (past), the selves we are living (present), and the imagined selves we seek or avoid (future). The smaller triangle at the bottom reflects the fact that all three sets of selves are available and influential in each moment. The bidirectional arrows reflect the fact that each of the three influences the other two. For example, a coachee feels unfulfilled in his current job (*lived self*) in large part because he has been unable to fulfill his dream of working as an artist (*imagined self*) as a result of having to get a job early in life to fulfill his role in the family (*constructed self*). Help people experience the constraints of their current constellations and then explore them to find openings for new possibilities. These openings can be found where there is: (1) a disconnect between two selves that needs to be rejoined (e.g., I don't see any value in my past self that would enable me to create the future self I want); (2) a fusion of two selves that needs to be uncoupled (e.g., my self as currently lived will automatically lead me to the imagined self I want); or (3) an aspect of their narrative identity that short circuits the whole self (e.g., my negatively constructed self is permanent and will always hold me back).

Because of the forward-looking nature of coaching, we are particularly interested in what Markus & Nurius (1986) called "possible selves" that, for better or worse, beckon us from our sense of the future. They described them as those elements of the self-concept that represent what individuals could become, would like to become, or are afraid of becoming. Ibarra (1999) writes about them as "benchmarks for interpreting and judging [our] behavior . . . helping [us] to decide what behaviors to try again, reject, or modify" (p. 767). They may come as dreams, visions, plans, unlived lives, opportunities not yet imagined or experienced, new statuses, and more. Because they are not yet grounded in sufficient lived experience, they tend to be the most vulnerable and responsive to changes in the environment (Markus & Nurius, 1986). I think of them as "imagined selves" because it is less about all possible selves and more about what is relevant and important for a given person. Imagined selves are shaped by the person's available narratives, often in ways that are significant yet tacit.

As people move through narrative coaching, we invite them to test out imagined selves in order to create what neurobiologist David Ingvar called new "memories of the future."[8] This is important because people with a clear vision of themselves in a future state tend to have more accessible cues that are relevant to this future state and to selectively process information and opportunities that are useful in attaining it. As a coach, you can help people make decisions about which elements of these imagined selves they want to live out more fully in order to achieve more of what they want. For example, a workshop participant was able to temper the righteous indignation that inspired her work with a heartfelt and compassionate imagined self such that she could still approach situations clearly, but now with more openness and warmth. She surfaced a new imagined self that she could access in that moment and in the future. As Kierkegaard argued, it is through the process of choosing our story about who we are and how we will act that we become responsible for our identities, our states, and our lives.

It is important to remember, however, that the pool of choices from which we form our imagined selves largely derives from valued categories and *available narratives* (Drake, 2003, 2005b) in our environments over time. This is why in narrative coaching we attend to the collective narratives, not just the personal stories. Available narratives represent the vocabulary and grammar, plot lines and historical conventions, beliefs and value systems (Polkinghorne, 1988, 1991) that we inherit and internalize from our historical, cultural, and situational narratives. We narrate our identity in large part based on these unspoken, implicit cultural models of what selfhood should be, could be, and shouldn't be (Bruner, 2002). The tension at the heart of both great drama and adult development is found where the forces of continuity as represented by our constructed selves (Past), the forces of discontinuity as represented by our imagined selves (Future), and the forces of reality as represented by our lived selves (Present) converge—as seen in the figure below. For example, a coachee who has been unexpectedly laid off experiences a breach in her constructed self ("I've always worked here") and feels afraid in the moment ("I don't know what I will do next") because she has yet to access a suitable imagined self ("I don't know how to look for work anymore").

FIGURE 6: WORKING IN THE MOMENT WITH IDENTITIES

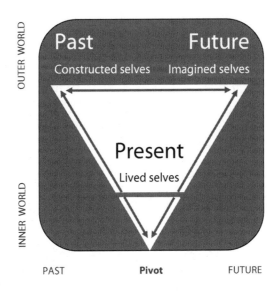

The difficulty for many coachees is that they don't recognize the contours and limitations of their available narratives until they need to narrate experiences or enact selves that are contrary to them. Once they recognize the limitations inherent in these available narratives, they can create a sense of distance from them, see them more clearly, and surface alternative voices (Polkinghorne, 2001). The evolution of their identities can be seen as an ongoing effort to (re)claim an authentic place in their world *and* a sense of right relationship with its available narratives. Maturity can be seen as the ability to self-regulate and more consciously and fluidly choose. As with the *I/Me* distinction, there is an ongoing tension between our constructed and imagined selves. This can be seen most vividly when people are considering major choices in relation to their lived selves. To move into right relationship may require a coachee to shift one or more of these three selves. For example, a coachee may need to prune the number of imagined selves under consideration in order to move on more decisively from his current lived self. A major step in this process for coachees is identifying narrative data from their lives that supports an alternate view of who they are and how they can be in the world. This enables them to adapt their constructed selves in order to pivot toward their imagined selves as seen in figure 6.

People often seek coaching when they realize that certain aspects of their identities no longer serve them well—and the price they have pay to live them has become too high. Conflicts or gaps in people's stories in coaching often signal a parallel conflict or gap in their sense of themselves. Therefore, you can use their narrative material as a proxy and support for the changes that are currently (or soon to be) underway in their identities. For example, a story about a leader's struggles with her boss becomes a conversation about a lack of passion for her current role. This insight that coachees' constructed selves, lived selves, and imagined selves can be brought together through powerful experiences in the present was instrumental in developing the Pivoting process (figure 19) in narrative coaching. What we are often doing in sessions is inviting people to experiment with provisional selves (Ibarra, 1999) as a bridge between how they saw themselves in the past and how they imagine themselves in the future.

Any shifts they make in their identities will be thwarted or supported by those around them and the larger narratives they represent. Therefore, help people find receptive audiences with whom to debut their new story so they can have some early wins, learn from their initial experiences, and make any necessary adjustments. This includes resisting the temptation to tackle their most vexing issue or person first. They need to be able to experience what success looks and feels like so they can solidify the new reference point. We can see this in the following representation of the narrative coaching model that outlines how to guide coachees in releasing old explanations and rehearsing new expressions that are more in line with what they are seeking. Each of these four phases in the process of bringing new identities—and their related stories—to life is an integral part of narrative coaching. They are each important because people can only see as far as their narrative identities will take them, and they can only act as far as their narrative identities will back them.

> They are each important because people can only see as far as their narrative identities will take them, and they can only act as far as their narrative identities will back them.

FIGURE 7: MOVING FROM OLD EXPLANATIONS TO NEW EXPRESSIONS

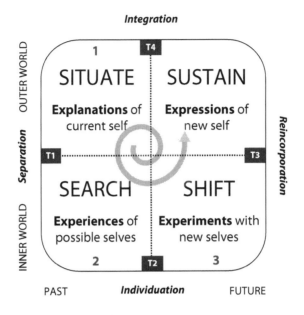

You can help people bring new stories about themselves to life by:

1. Situating themselves in the current *explanations* of who they think they are so they can *separate* themselves from certain aspects of their identity, often internalized from others, and enrich their sense of themselves as the *author* of their stories. *Key questions: How would you* **explain** *the current situation? What is/was your expectation?*

2. Searching their *experiences* for what holds the key to their growth so they can *individuate* through reclaiming aspects of themselves held in Shadow and enrich their sense of themselves as an *actor* in the stories they are in. *Key questions: What are you longing for? What* **experiences** *do you need to allow yourself to have?*

3. Shifting what matters through *experiments* with new ways of being and acting in the world so they can reincorporate what they need now and enrich their sense of themselves as an agent in the related narratives around them. *Key questions: What matters to you about what you discovered? How can you* **experiment** *with it now?*

4. *Sustaining* their new identities through new *expressions* of themselves so they can integrate what works into their identity going forward and enrich their sense of themselves as an *activist* for more generative narratives to support them. *Key questions: How would you **express** what is true for you now? Where would you find support for that?*

In addition to achieving more sustainable outcomes, coachees will develop a greater *narrative maturity*. I coined this term to refer to, "the degree to which people can internally and externally narrate their experiences in order to respond to their environment in an appropriate manner.

Key messages for coachees:

1. Your stories (Explanations) are both the source of much of your suffering and a source for your healing and liberation.
2. If you keep *Explaining* your situation the same way, you will perpetuate the same *Experiences*—and nothing will change.
3. If you allow yourself to have new *Experiences* AND see them through the lens of a new *Explanation* (narrative)—then change is possible.
4. If the desired change remains as an "aha," it will likely wane on its own, like a flashlight with failing batteries. It requires *Experiments* to put it into action and new ways of *Expressing* what is working so that the change becomes real.

Implications for your Practice

- When you are coaching, ask yourself: Does the coachee believe the problem resides in the past, present, or future? The solution? You can often tell by tracking people's body language (e.g., what they are talking about when they have the most energy) and their spoken language (e.g., what verb tense they tend to use as they tell their stories).

- In working with people's stories, pay attention to how they situate themselves in time and how this configuration may need to be adjusted in order to accomplish what they set out to do. As people begin to open up their sense of time, it creates more breathing room in their stories and their identities to explore other options.

- Think of coaching as serious play. Be willing to tackle more serious issues *and* play as an artist would with his materials. Notice when you remain too serious when a freer approach is called for or divert the conversation away from the real issue when a more serious approach is called for. Be willing to compassionately challenge people about stories that no longer serve them and invite them to prototype new ones.

What are your key insights?
What will you experiment with first?

CHAPTER 3

HOW WE LEARN AND DEVELOP

Mostly we learn from reexamination of our own stories. | *Roger Schank*

Narrative coaching is one of the few coaching methodologies with an explicit learning and development component built into it. In addition, it is designed to support change as a natural human process, not to be imposed as a conversational structure. It is an integrative process in which learning, development, and performance are intimately linked and simultaneously addressed to create more sustainable change. It is based in a situated and social view of learning (Lave & Wenger, 1991), and transformative and transpersonal learning theories (Freire, 1970; McWhinney & Markos, 2003; Mezirow, 1991, 2000). As a result, when people finish the narrative coaching process, they are better prepared and more aligned to sustain the changes they have begun. Ultimately, narrative coaching is an experiential and developmental process of awakening—to what is true, what is possible, what matters, and what works. It invites coachees to spiral through the question, "What is yours to learn from this story?" until they break through.

As a result, narrative coaching can be seen as a process which enables people to bring about real change in real time. It does so by bringing together transformative learning and development and design thinking to enable people to make meaningful shifts in the moment.

The first section in this chapter focuses on learning and highlights its transformative potential, the vital role of "mistakes," and Vygotsky's work on proximal development. The second section focuses on development and highlights the importance of working with dreams and projections as well as integrating Shadows and strengths as two unique aspects of narrative coaching. This work is based in a deep respect for the long arc of change and an appreciation for capitalizing on threshold moments where learning and development are accelerated. It reflect the inherent paradoxes in being human and in our stories related to change: We are our stories *and* we are not our stories. We upgrade our stories *and* we let them go. Our stories are the source of our suffering *and* our liberation, our wounding *and* our healing. Narrative coaching is designed to help people learn from their own stories so they can address what matters most to them. The result is a powerful yet graceful process through which people can release what no longer serves them well and welcome into their life that which does.

> Narrative coaching is a process of awakening—to what is true, what is possible, what matters, and what works. It invites coachees to spiral through the question, "What is yours to learn from this story?" until they break through.

Facilitating Transformative Learning

Almost every encounter in life presents possibilities for growth. . . . But these transformations require that a person be prepared to perceive unexpected opportunities. Most of us become so rigidly fixed in the ruts carved out by genetic programming and social conditioning that we ignore the options of choosing any other course of action. | *Mihaly Csikszentmihalyi*

Kolb (1984) defines learning as "the process whereby knowledge is created [and retained] through the transformation of experience" (p. 38). Mezirow (2000) describes it as

> the process of becoming critically aware of how and why our presuppositions have come to constrain the way we perceive, understand, and feel about our world; of reformulating these assumptions to permit a more inclusive, discriminating, permeable, and integrative perspective; and of making decisions or otherwise acting upon these new understandings. (p. 14)

Learning enables us to make new distinctions we otherwise wouldn't be able to make; it enables us to take actions we otherwise wouldn't be able to take. Central to the transformative learning process is the unlearning that is often required to make room for learning at a higher level (Illeris, 2004; Mezirow, 2000). In narrative coaching, we describe it as releasing or adapting old stories to make room for new ones. Otherwise, as in the Zen fable, people end up with more tea being poured into an already full cup.

Over the years, I have found that helping people "empty their cup" is as important to them and their process as adding more or better "tea." What emerges on the other side often arises with such grace once they have put down old burdens and baggage. Many of the issues they once saw as difficult recede by virtue of putting them in a new perspective or softening their absoluteness. Rather than worry about what tea to pour, focus on inviting people to see their world with eyes and ears that are more open, with minds and hearts that are more open. It is my fundamental belief that people learn and develop best in coaching when we start by observing, without judgment, the stories they are currently telling us and living.

This provides them with a more accurate point of reference and departure from which to embark on their journey of discovery. Once they are ready to learn, we can use what we know about transformative learning (Mezirow, 2000) and design thinking (Brown, 2009; Liedtka & Ogilvie, 2011; Martin, 2009) to help them identify how they would like to narrate and live their life differently. This seemingly unlikely combination is actually quite aligned and yields a powerful frame for change that is both personal and practical. The design thinking questions are built into the narrative coaching model and, in many ways, provide the purest expression of this process.

TABLE 2: NARRATIVE COACHING: WHERE TRANSFORMATION MEETS INNOVATION

Coaching Phase	Transformational Learning	Design Thinking
Situate	Become aware of presuppositions	Observe what is
Search	Challenge and reformulate assumptions	Imagine what if
Shift	Test new perspectives and options	Prototype what matters
Sustain	Make new decisions and take new actions	Implement what works

Narrative coaching focuses on awakening people and increasing their "growth mindset" (Dweck, 2008) rather than assessing them, which often ends up reinforcing a "fixed mindset." The result is coachees who not only learn more about themselves and their issues, but who can more readily transfer the learning and development they gain into their life or workplace. One of the ways to do this is by paying close attention for openings in people's stories where transformative learning becomes more readily available. Which presupposition seems to be holding the person back?

Which option or prototype would they be willing to try first? To make the most of these moments, you can use reflective processes to help people nonjudgmentally explore the assumptions about reality inherent in their stories and use experiential processes to help them generate and evaluate new stories and new ways of being. As we saw in the Rewind process, the aim is to increase their ability to notice what is happening in the moment: what is triggering them, what stories are they telling themselves, what is the opening for learning, and what do they want to do (differently) about it?

EXAMPLE

> In working with a team leader, I invited him to pause and notice what was happening for him as a conflict emerged in a team coaching session. He was able to reflect on our earlier sessions in which we discussed his pattern of stepping in to resolve differences on his team rather than developing this capacity in them. Using the Pause and Pivot techniques I had taught him, he used the occasion to notice the tension in his body as he started to respond along the old storyline and then shifted gears to act in new ways that were healthier for him and his team.

Sometimes being "seen" and accepted as they are is enough to dissolve the issue for coachees. For those who require more, don't allow them to settle for insights during sessions with promises that they will act on them later. More often that we care to admit, they don't for any number of reasons. The classic "aha" moment in coaching is like the candle on a birthday cake; it gets most of the attention at first but is not that significant in the end. Instead, craft experiences in the session itself in which coachees can practice, so they can leave with an embodied referent point; and help coachees anchor their learning in real time and, as a result, become more open and confident as learners. I believe this transformative approach to learning is critical in coaching because it is impossible to learn without incurring consequences, making mistakes, and surrendering to the process. As I tell people I am coaching in sessions and in workshops, "It doesn't get any better than this in terms of a supportive space."

The issue for many coachees is that they are afraid of making mistakes. However, everyone is a beginner when they learn something new; a temporary drop in performance is inevitable. Why then do we so often criticize adults when they are attempting to learn? We don't penalize toddlers for the hundreds of times they fall down as they are learning to walk. Instead, we praise them for everything they do that brings them one step closer to walking on their own. Rather than see mistakes as failures to reach the ideal, help people see them as events that did not turn out as they had hoped—but upon which they can build. What coachees deem as "failures" are often their greatest sources for learning (Sitkin, 1992). Therefore, help people realize that they can learn from their outcomes ("Why did the action just taken not result in the outcome I wanted?") as well as in the moment ("What can I learn from what I am doing that will bring me closer to what I want to achieve?"). In her work on bouncing back, neuroscientist Linda Graham (2013) invites people to reflect on mistakes in terms of "this is what happened; this is what I have learned; and this is how I can respond to life now" (p. 244). A famed child psychologist has a lot to offer here in terms of how to help adults learn through coaching.

The Contributions of Lev Vygotsky

For Vygotsky (1934/1987, 1978), play was instrumental in children's learning and development because it enabled them to build on what they knew as they gained new capabilities. Adults who are being coached have the same need, as we saw in the earlier section on serious play. Of particular interest is his notion of "zones of proximal development," which he (1978) defined as "the distance between the actual developmental level as determined by independent problem-solving and the level of potential development as determined through problem-solving under adult supervision or in collaboration with more capable peers" (p. 86). The *actual developmental level* is what the child has already accomplished, and the *potential developmental level* is what the child is capable of— if the appropriate scaffold or support is provided. The contours of any given collaboration are defined by the space between the person's current capabilities, needs, and desires, *and* the environment's demands, resources, and possibilities. It is harder to learn if the gap between the two spaces is too great in either direction—leading to either boredom if the challenge is insufficient or duress if the challenge is too great.

Vygotsky's work fits well with narrative coaching because we are less interested in formal assessments which measure what he called "fossilized" forms of learning and development (e.g., capabilities already obtained) and more interested in experiential processes through which new forms or levels of development emerge (e.g., potential for growth). According to Vygotsky, these zones are based in a symbiotic relationship between development and learning in which development as an individually internalized process always lags behind learning as a culturally mediated process. The process of learning for children awakens a variety of internal developmental processes that only operate when they are interacting with people in their environment and in cooperation with others, especially peers. However, once those processes are internalized, they become part of a child's independent developmental achievement (Vygotsky, 1978).

The same is true in developing adults as leaders: without learning, there is not much hope for development (Day, Harrison, & Halpin, 2009). This is why narrative coaches engage coachees in transformative learning experiences before inviting them to reflect on these experiences as openings for their development. In order to harness the potentiality in these zones as they arise in coaching, it is generally best to focus on one "zone" at a time. That is why narrative coaches focus on getting to the crux of a person's issue and sensing what they are ready to and need to learn in order to move across the threshold it requires. I find that an emergent yet clear focus helps both parties in coaching make the most of opportune moments for learning and development (Greenberg, 2002) and enables them to better track coachees' progress.

A key to learning for Vygotsky (see Chaiklin, 2003) was the role of "scaffolding" in supporting children [and adults] to stretch beyond what they know and can do and incorporate what they do not yet know and cannot yet do. For the scaffolding to work, the task must be within the person's reach such that, with effort and minimal support from others, she can move to a higher level of functioning. This scaffolding is analogous to the notion of "broaden and build" (Frederickson, 2006), in that people are creating a more versatile and mature repertoire one step at a time. Scaffolding prepares people so they make it across their threshold and start out with a solid footing on the other side. A lot of this takes the form of small steps to increase their awareness, focus, and resources as they cross. Otherwise they may end up feeling "in over their heads" (Kegan, 1994), and their subsequent development is diminished as a result.

> **The scaffolding commonly needed at each phase in coaching:**
> - *Situate:* Observing, modeling, and identifying the key elements of what is to be learned in order to separate from what they know.
> - *Search:* Exploring, reflecting on, and articulating new relationships between these elements as the focus for learning in order to step into the liminal unknown.
> - *Shift:* Experimenting, getting feedback and support, and extrapolating the underlying principles in order to apply their learning in the world.
> - *Sustain:* Adapting identity to incorporate new knowledge and capability, generalizing and planning for the future, and integrating what has changed into their daily life.

Coaching is about helping people to identify, scaffold, and leverage the learning that is just beyond their current capabilities yet within their reach and necessary for the next step forward. Having sufficient scaffolding enables coachees to step from the "known and familiar" of their problem experience into the "not yet known, but possible to know" territory of their preferred experience (Carey, Walther, & Russell, 2009) as we saw in the list above. Scaffolding can take many forms: deconstructing issues or aspirations into smaller chunks, asking questions that focus the attention, bringing the whole brain into the narration process to get a more complete picture, experimenting with microelements (e.g., body posture, gestures, key words) associated with what is being learned, and more. Scaffolding often involves creating experiences that give coachees a taste of what is possible through doing it themselves with your guidance, modeling from you, or observing others. The good news is that most of the pieces you will need to help them scaffold their learning and development are in their stories, e.g., current and desired state, preferred modality of learning, pointers to allies and resources, and related social narratives.

The transformation of an interpersonal process into an intrapersonal one is the result of a long series of developmental events (Vygotsky, 1978, p. 57). You can support this process by inviting coachees to engage in specific tasks and interactions in order to support the formation of new functions or the enrichment of existing functions (Vygotsky, 1934/1998). For example, with a coachee whose desire is to become a more confident public speaker, you might help her deconstruct "confidence" by asking her to think of a time when she felt confident, notice what changes come over her body as she recounts that story, identify a verbal or somatic anchor to recall and embody in that stance, and give a presentation right then and there with this in mind.

Coaching provides a structured and experiential space in which people can iteratively deconstruct and reconstruct their narratives as they learn and develop. Coaching sessions can thus be seen as transitional spaces and zones of proximal development where new capabilities and narratives are midwifed. For change to be sustained, the scaffolding for what they have learned there and how they have grown needs to incorporate the structural, objective "pull" from the environment *and* the unique, subjective "push" from the individual. When this happens, what coachees can do with you as their coach today, they can more independently and capably do on their own tomorrow (Vygotsky, 1934/1998).

Fostering Development and Growth

Those who grow old without learning the story that is trying to live through them don't become "old enough" or ancient enough to serve the dream of life. | Michael Meade

One of the unique features of narrative coaching is its multi-disciplinary and developmental approach that enables people to holistically engage with their issues. It is about helping people discern what is theirs to learn in critical moments in coaching and what questions are urgent and essential to answer at this stage in their development and/or life. In looking at growth this way, I have found it helpful to draw on post-Jungians such as Ginette Paris (2007), who laments, "The idea that we 'grow,' as a child grows (or as an economy grows), has come to replace what used to be imagined as the deepening of experience and the lifelong quest for wisdom" (p. 114). A similar sentiment is found in Hillman's (1996) *acorn theory*, which proposes that every person is born with a defining image that acts as a personal daimon; it not only pushes from the beginning, it also pulls toward an end.

This loss of a deeper sense of growth is regrettable even more now that we are living longer and coming to realize with Jung (1967) that "the greatest and most important problems in life are fundamentally insoluble. . . . They can never be solved, but only outgrown when confronted with a new and stronger life urge" (p. 15). Therefore, our role is to help coachees discern the life urge that is seeking to be expressed more than to dissect symptomatic "problems" seeking to be relieved. This requires relinquishing any notions of development as a linear progression or ascension and seeing it instead as a multifaceted ripening of what is already present. It calls for a more inclusive approach in which development is seen as deepening and connecting, not just rising and separating. Bakan's (1966) classic distinction between *communion* (how and why we are in relation to others) and *agency* (how we act and express ourselves) is useful here as a better and more inclusive way to frame people's developmental aspirations (see Singer, 2005b). It ensures that we slow down at times to enable and embed learning rather than always rushing ahead to enact new behaviors.

> Relinquishing notions of development as a linear progression or ascension and seeing it instead as a multifaceted ripening of what is already present.

When I demonstrate this work, some practitioners report that it feels slow and deceptively simple. However, they also observe that it enables people to make important shifts in brief periods of time. They comment that these big shifts seem to happen all at once rather than through a sequence of steps. There actually have been a lot of small steps in the process up to that point, but they are less noticeable because the process is layered rather than formulaic. This reflects the rhythm in narrative coaching that is circling and decisive at the same time. I believe narrative coaching works well because there is something innately human about this work that puts people at ease and, as a result, they can more fully open themselves to learn and grow. It brings together their divergent needs for:

- Knowing where they are (location) *and* knowing what to do (force/movement).

- Having a sense of a safe haven to which they can return *and* having a sense of a secure base from which they can venture forth.

- Being in communion with self and others *and* being agentic on behalf of self and others.

- Retaining a sense of order, coherence and continuity *and* capitalizing on disorder, surprise and change.

Many of the issues people bring to coaching revolve around points of tension within one or more of these pairs. Growth often emerges where there is *narrative friction* (a clash between stories) or challenges to *narrative fictions* (a clash provoked by another story). In working with people's stories, you can help them understand where they are in relation to each set of needs, where they want to productively focus their attention, and how they can increase their capacity to notice and align with their own developmental rhythms.

It is important to remember, though, that these are both/and propositions, not either/or ones. For example, a coachee wants to fit in as the new leader of a team in order to connect with them *and* he wants opportunities to prove himself by taking the team in a new direction. Both needs in each pair above are essential for people to develop. For example, if we focus too much on creating a sense of safety, coachees feel quite comfortable with us but don't engage the real issues. If we focus too much on continually stretching people, they may not have the foundations from which to succeed when it matters. As we saw in the last section, it is about staying within the zone. This also helps coaches deal with coachee's defenses when they inevitably arise, especially when delving into sensitive or critical issues.

These defenses originally formed to protect their differentiating and adaptive ego (McWilliams, 1994) as an intrinsic and healthy part of development early in their life. As Gagan (1998) observed, our defenses "work on our behalf, altering reality by creatively rearranging conflicts into more manageable situations. The resulting distortions give us time to acclimate to life's contingencies until the anxiety of the threatening situation can be borne" (p. 140). People's defenses are an integral part of their psyche and identity, have played a vital role in getting them to this point in their lives, and therefore need to be treated with respect as part of the development process. To bring about change, coachees need to suspend their defenses long enough to try on new stories—and the identities and behaviors that go with them. As part of this process, they will need to upgrade any counterproductive coping strategies (like the overuse of charm) that deny certain aspects of themselves or lead them to cling to others.

When defenses are used repetitively and inflexibly in the face of threats that are perceived as otherwise unmanageable, they become a barrier to people's development and interfere with their ability to self-regulate and respond to others. In narrative coaching, we invite people to experience their defenses in action before exploring alternatives. For example, you notice the coachee uses self-effacing humor when she feels uncomfortable. You can help her notice this is occurring, articulate the story she is telling herself through the defense, identify what is being held back as a result, and explore how else she could respond differently in those moments. What people are defending against is often the very thing they most need in order to grow. Their greatest gifts are often hidden behind their greatest fears. The secret is to ally with their defenses rather than trying to defeat them. This is because their defenses *and* their development, their Shadow *and* their gifts, are two sides of the same coin. As James Hillman (1983) observed, "Where we are most sensitive, we are most stubborn; where we are most exposed, we expend most efforts to conceal. . . . [W]e get closest to soul when we work closely with its defenses" (p. 99). The poet Rainer Maria Rilke put it this way, "Our deepest fears are like dragons guarding our deepest treasures."

Coaching provide a safe space in which people can meet those fears head on and rediscover their lost inner treasures. In so doing, you may run into resistance from coachees—particularly where their narration is taking them into places that are quite new for them and/or they imagine will surface challenging emotions or insights. Since resistance is a natural phenomenon and essential for growth, be respectful of their resistances as you do so because they are likely to feel vulnerable as they traverse their developmental razor's edge. Do what you can to decipher the important information that is embedded in their resistance (Cozolino, 2004) as a key to understanding their defenses and what they are defending against. Resistance is not inherently positive or negative, and it is both oppositional *and* aspirational in nature. *What is asking to die? What is asking to be born?* Meet them in this crucible. Help them harvest the energy trapped in their avoidance. As Steven Pressfield (2011) notes:

> Resistance is the key to your success. Why, because it unfailingly points toward our deepest aspiration, the very thing it most wants to stop us from doing. The more important the calling, the action, the decision is to our true growth, the more resistance to pursuing it we will feel.

Resistance can be seen in Joseph Campbell's notion of the refusal of the call when the person is unwilling to step onto the path to do the work. Like many coaches, I used to try to push past resistance from workshop participants and coaching clients so we could make more progress. However, over time I came to question the value of "pushing," the nature of "resistance," and the meaning of "progress." As a result, I have moved to a "pulling" strategy in trusting that coachees will find their own path, reframed "resistance" as self-definitional boundaries to be explored, and withdrawn my attachments to "progress" to make room for greater clarity and courage. Rather than waging Sisyphean battles with coachees in attempts to change them, I engage them in a process of mindful inquiry about what is true for them and what they really want. In the process, I help them imagine what would become possible if they no longer devoted so much energy to protecting themselves, but instead could use it to increase their openness to experience and their fulfillment in what they do (Drake, 2009).

> **What people are defending against is often the very thing they most need in order to grow. The secret is to ally with defenses rather than trying to defeat them.**

This generally involves moving toward the unknown more than the known and embracing the mystery more than analyzing the history. This is often just as true for coaches as it is for coachees, especially when they find themselves in moments of meeting. The good news is that when coaches can stay in this *not-knowing* position, it invites their coachees to do the same. *Not-knowing* is a natural invitation to dialogue in which "people feel they belong" (Shotter, 1993). In so doing, you can take heart in Wendell Berry's notion that when we no longer know what to do, we have come to our real work; when we no longer know which way to go, we have begun our real journey. For both parties it means relinquishing the need for and illusion of control.

For coaches, it means acknowledging that we are stepping into developmental processes with people that are already underway—and will continue on with or without us. It means not trying so hard to change others and ourselves, but rather to courageously show up as one human to another. It calls for a deeper compassion for humanity, a deeper acceptance of reality, and a deeper surrender to possibility. It is from this place, more so than from our valiant efforts, that new stories are born and new growth emerges. It is about profoundly letting go to make room for the real work to be done. In working this way over the years, I have come to realize that facilitating learning and development is a subtle, organic, and alchemical art.

As Mary Watkins (1976) noted, in order to grow "we must be able to let things happen in the psyche. Consciousness is forever interfering, helping, correcting, and negating, and never leaving the simple growth of the psychic processes in peace" (p. 104). Our role in coaching is to offer the space and the support for the new story that is already unfolding. See yourself as a midwife of a natural process more than an architect of a constructed outcome. Seize the openings in coaching when people are on the cusp of a developmental breakthrough, and work diligently to help them cross that threshold. Help people mature as storytellers so they are more accountable for their stories, their choices, and their lives. As a result, they can act in service of their deepest needs and the common good. Invite them into the possibility of living in a less defended way so that more of their potential is available to them. I treasure those moments when people break through and choose to live this way. The difference is palpable and an inspiration for us all.

Understanding the Shadow

All the life potentialities that we never managed to bring to adult realization, those other portions of oneself are there; for such golden seeds do not die. If only a portion of that lost totality can be dredged up into the light of day we should experience a marvelous expansion of our powers, a vivid renewal of life. | *Joseph Campbell*

I've appreciated coaching's focus on leveraging strengths rather than trying to fix weaknesses. However, over time I saw the need to develop a more nuanced stance on strengths and advocate for the role of the Shadow in development. I soon realized that narrative coaching provided a way to bring the two together. What follows is an introduction to how and why the Shadow is formed and how these hidden aspects of ourselves can be used to help people temper their strengths so they can operate at higher developmental levels. It is about maturing the person, not just achieving the outcomes. The approach as outlined below is based on years of facilitating

Shadow workshops and learning how to transmute what seemed like lead in people's narrative material into proverbial gold. It also connects with Vygotsky's work and attachment theory in that a person's Shadow is a potent resource in making the most of zones of proximal development and developing more robust working models. Narrative coaching is designed to bring forth whole stories and whole people—both of which require working with Shadow material if they are to develop.

In the first years of their lives, children instinctively strive to maintain a sufficient degree of safety and love as they learn to process the outer and inner experiences they encounter (Page, 1999). Young children will do whatever it takes to manage the tension between who they are and who their significant others want or allow them to be—sometimes to their detriment. In the process, they develop what Jung called a "persona" as a mask that was "designed on the one hand to make a definite impression upon others, and, on the other, to conceal the true nature of the individual" (Jung, 1972, p. 192). It expresses how they would like to be seen by their world (*Me*), and it reflects the coping strategies they use to maintain these views (*I*). The persona is a psychological necessity for interacting with the world; it becomes a problem when we over-identify with it and mistake it for the totality of who we are. As with a good story, our Shadow rises up in opposition to our *persona* in an effort to restore equilibrium and wholeness. The Shadow plays a vital role in both this conflict and its resolution.

Psychologist Carl Jung saw the Shadow as composed of the parts of our personality that were repressed or suppressed for the sake of an ego ideal that was largely defined by others in those early years. He (1969) also believed the Shadow contained archetypal ideas and energies from our collective unconscious as well as patterns of thought and pervasive cultural motifs that are universally present in our psyches. It is where we bury all those qualities that don't fit our self-image, the "inferior" part of our personality that we don't deem compatible with our chosen conscious attitude and emerging persona. Kolodziejski (2004) describes the Shadow as containing "that which is feared and suppressed, that which is considered inappropriate and shunned, that which is unbearable to hold consciously and [is therefore] denied" (p. 64). Fitzgerald, Oliver and Hoxsey (2010) conceive of it as censored feeling and cognition where our experience and/or expression is judged to not fit with accepted cultural or group norms. Our individual and collective Shadows contain *all* the elements that make us human but never made it into our conscious life, made it to consciousness but were then suppressed or repressed, or hang around the fringes between the two worlds. As a coach, the Shadow represents a gold mine in terms of energies that are crucial in terms of a person's growth.

The Shadow is:

- A natural by-product of the development of our ego.
- A strategy to secure sufficient safety and love.
- Innate human energy, neither good nor bad in itself.
- Where we bury qualities that don't fit our self-image.
- An untapped reservoir of vital maturational energy.
- Most easily seen in our projections onto others.
- An invitation to keep dying to our self to be reborn.
- A guide for our unique path to maturation.

As with a good story, our Shadow rises up in opposition to our persona in an effort to restore equilibrium and wholeness.

Robert Bly (1988) offers a wonderful analogy to describe the Shadow:
> When we were one or two years old we had what we might visualize as a 360 degree personality. Energy radiated out from all parts of our body and all parts of our psyche. A child running is a living globe of energy. . . . Behind us we have an invisible bag, and that part of us our parents [and other people significant to us] don't like, we, to keep our parent's love, put in the bag. By

the time we go to school our bag is quite large. . . . We spend our life until we are twenty deciding what parts of ourselves to put in the bag, and we spend the rest of our lives trying to get them out again. (p. 17)

Our Shadow is a natural part of our early development, but it tends to become an issue for us later in life as it demands more attention and equal time. Jung believed it does so as part of a primal quest from birth to balance opposing images, feelings, and points of view. The Shadow comes into being because our psyche (particularly the unconscious) is constantly striving toward a greater wholeness and a dynamic homeostasis. It is compelled, if you will, to keep bringing into our lives any elements that remain unintegrated—no matter how uncomfortable we feel about them at the time. Van Eenwyk (1997) put it this way:

If the ego cannot, or will not, embrace the complexity of tensions of opposites, preferring instead to embrace simplistic views of itself and reality, then individuation stalls until the ego can be shaken from its one-sided perspective. Thus the unconscious . . . confronts the ego with the unrecognized dimensions of its existence, often in the form of dream images and daytime life experiences that are deeply symbolic. (p. 163)

EXAMPLE

The presenting issue of a person I coached recently was her partner's best friend whom she disliked and saw as a bad influence on her partner. She continued to position him as a villain in her story and herself as unable to get him out of their lives. As she described the attributes in him that she most disliked, they were largely the opposite of the characteristics in herself with which she most identified and was most proud. I invited her (three times) to consider the possibility that whatever his future in their lives, at this point in time he represented her Shadow. I invited her to consider the even more provocative idea that he was her best teacher in this regard. Once she could allow this in, it unlocked a huge potential for growth for her.

The Shadow is compensatory to the conscious self, always thrusting itself onto consciousness, and it is a source of tremendous untapped potential. The unconscious does not make the distinctions our conscious *ego* does in order to stay within the confines of our self or social definitions. It does not make distinctions between good and bad; it just is. Our unwillingness to face our Shadow often leads us to make unwise choices and generates conflicts in our lives, relationships, organizations, and communities. The Shadow can be seen when people's reactions to a situation seem disproportionate to what actually happened and when people's projections onto others seem stronger than warranted. The more we repress a part of ourselves, the more the repressed part will return into our lives. This is important to remember because the developmental progress people make in coaching often unravels if its Shadow elements are not addressed. You can see this in the coachee who is working on his assertiveness but becomes domineering because he has not addressed the rage or the bully in his Shadow that has been activated.

In working with Shadow material, help people acknowledge the heavy "bag" they have dragged around and reduce any associated shame or blame—as both impede their growth. In so doing, invite them to look at how it has shaped them, what they have gained and lost as a result, what projections they need to take back, and what this would make possible that is important to them. Shadow work helps people reclaim more of their personal vitality and energy as well as more of their diversity and richness as a human. This is especially important during periods of transition when people often need to let go of the very things they have worked hardest to achieve. They come to realize that their efforts to compartmentalize aspects of themselves have failed—and will ultimately always fail—and that the continued repression of any aspect of themselves will lead to an overall diminishing of themselves. As a result, they may need to release some cherished images of themselves and compromises they have made along the way in order to develop a greater vitality and maturity on the other side.

Projections and Dreams

Working with the Shadow is a natural fit for coaching given the projective nature of our stories. In fact, narrative coaching itself was born in an epiphany I had while observing a demonstration at a Jungian workshop on group dreaming: "What if the stories we tell during the day have the same function as the dreams we have at night?" The answer was instantly and unequivocally a resounding "Yes," and in that moment everything fell into place. I realized that stories and dreams are both vehicles for our unconscious to sort through issues related to our identity and development using familiar characters, settings, etc. They have purposes beyond the literal content and they contain seeds of their own resolution if we listen to them skillfully. This supports van Eenwyk's (1997) view that "the unconscious . . . confronts the ego with the unrecognized dimensions of its existence, often in the form of dream images and daytime life experiences that are deeply symbolic" (p. 163). Many of the critical elements in narrative coaching emerged from the "What if the stories . . . ?" question above: (1) the "field" as the primary space and resource for change; (2) the function of the unconscious in narration; (3) the projective nature of our stories; (4) the narrative content as a point of entry; and (5) the story and its search for resolution.

> ## What if the stories we tell during the day have the same function as the dreams we have at night?

All the pieces were now in place. I had already identified rites of passage as the framework for change best suited for a narrative approach to coaching because it addresses both the personal and social dimensions of development and change. I had incorporated key elements from earlier studies of hermeneutics and liberation theology with my doctoral work in narrative structure, critical approaches to identity, and transformative learning and adult development. The final piece was the incorporation of the work on Shadows, dreams and projections. The result was a new way to help people develop themselves, find their authentic voice, and resolve issues that were important to them using their own stories. In particular, it involved looking at people's stories through the lens of the characters—particularly the way in which the narrator, the characters, and the story were triangulated. I came to see that openings for change in a person were often signaled by changes in his narration and that these signals were both conscious and unconscious. The initial models evolved to become the Narrative Coaching model (figure 2) and the Narrative Diamond framework for listening (figure 25) as the two cornerstones of this work.

People tell their stories in coaching through a variety of means, some they are aware of and many they are not. One of our roles is to enable them to discover and tell more of the whole story (in truthfulness, not volume) *as a whole person* so they can bring about lasting change. This includes addressing the unconscious elements in the stories they share and learning from the field of dreamwork. Our psyches use dreams to bypass our need for control, allowing us to retrieve the exiled aspects of ourselves that were left behind so we can become more whole. Dreams often present us with aspects of our personal and collective unconscious that are not consistent with our waking, conscious identities but are seeking resolution (see Boa, 1988; Johnson, 1986; Jung, 1964, 1969). As Jung (1970) suggested, "In each of us there is another who we do not know. He speaks to us in dreams and tells us how differently he sees us from the way we see ourselves" (p. 76) and, in so doing, compensates for places where our stories about ourselves are one-sided. Dreams often contain familiar images, places, and people to aid in our comprehension of this largely unconscious process and reflect aspects of ourselves as the dreamer. Johnson (1986) compared a dream to a screen on which the unconscious projects its inner drama.

Breakthroughs in narrative coaching often occur when people step into their drama—whether from within a story or the material from a dream—so they can experience and experiment with less familiar parts of themselves and ways of being. This brings us back to the insight that helped catalyze the formation of narrative coaching: We can learn a lot about the projective nature of our stories from our understanding of dreams. This notion was echoed by psychotherapist Thomas Moore (2000) who wrote, "[I]t is helpful to approach the narrative as we would a dream; that is, as a composition containing both conscious and unconscious material" (p. 9). In bringing together stories and dreams as projective activities, I kept coming back to the question, "What if the characters in the stories we tell represent parts of ourselves projected onto the 'other' as a means to work through our own development or identity issues?" If so, would not the changes people are going through somehow be evident in the changes as seen in the characters and relationships in the stories they choose to tell? Narrative coaching is based in the fundamental belief that this is indeed the case, and it offers practices to operationalize this process in working with people and their stories.

Given that there are both conscious and unconscious elements in our stories, particularly in a context like coaching, it is fair to assume that many of the latter are projections. I came to recognize that many of these projections were channeled through other characters in people's stories, just as they are in dreams and in everyday life. Therefore, it made sense to think in terms of a projective space in coaching and the need to identify what gets projected onto which elements in the stories and for what purpose. Page (1999) describes projection as the psyche's capacity to "maintain the distorted self-image that results from splitting off aspects of personality and rendering them seemingly invisible, which acts as a psychological and emotional pressure valve" (p. 17). For example, a coachee's anxiety and desire to set a clearer course in his own career gets projected onto a story about a micromanaging boss. As a narrative coach, I invite people to recover these split-off elements through working with the characters in their stories (and sometimes their dreams as well) and the projected Shadow elements these often represent. From there, they will have a much richer palette to choose from in crafting a new narrative.

For example, people's conflicts with others—in their stories and in their lives—are often a reflection of conflicts they have within themselves. As such, many of the issues they ascribe to and project onto others are better seen as characters in their own inner dramas. Their individuation and maturation will, in large part, depend on their willingness to withdraw and reintegrate these projections and take fuller accountability for their stories and their lives. Symptoms which appear in coachees' relationships, dreams, bodies, etc., (Hollis, 2013) often provide openings to work in these projective spaces and increase people's awakening. I know from personal experience that this is some of the most challenging yet most vital work we will ever do. In narrative coaching we immerse people in powerful experiences that bring their projections into the conversational field so the dynamics are more visible and can be addressed in real time as opposed to in abstract terms.

EXAMPLE

A recent coachee felt frustrated with the group with whom she was working because she perceived they were in denial about their lack of progress. The turning point in the conversation was when I asked her to say out loud some of the messages she had given them while imagining that they were sitting in front of her. I then asked her to sit in a chair where she had imagined the group sitting and notice her experience *as one of them* receiving this message from their leader. I asked her what she was feeling while she was looking up front at where she had been standing.

I then invited her to return to the front and talk with me about what story she had been telling herself while she was speaking and how the group seemed to her now. In the end she realized that she had projected her own frustrations as the leader of this important project onto the group and excluded herself in how she talked about it in order to avoid her disappointment in herself. By putting herself back into the story, she was able to take back her projections and move into dialogue with the team to find a new path forward.

> What if the characters in the stories we tell represent parts of ourselves projected onto the "other" as a means to work through our own development or identity issues?

As Jung noted, whatever we deny within, we will seek in the outer world, and what we do not face within our psyche, we will be forced to confront in the outer world. This reinforces Wallin's (2007) insight: "If a person cannot or will not articulate his own dissociated or disavowed experience he will inevitably evoke it in others, enact it with others, or embody it" (p. 4). This often extends into unconsciously recruiting others as "accomplices" (Wachtel, 1991) in the perpetuation of our external life patterns and internal narrative structures. These projective processes are a natural part of our development. They enable us to separate from more challenging aspects of ourselves until such time as we are ready to take them back as parts of ourselves. Narrative coaching offers people a space and a process in which people can begin to take back the work that only they can do. This involves helping them to become more aware of their collusions and projections and more accountable for their authorship and agency in relationship to others. For example, a coachee can take back his projections onto a narcissistic team member in order to access more of the selfish aspects of himself—which he can then use to stand up more often for what he wants. Let us turn now to one of the unique and powerful ways we do that in narrative coaching.

Integrating Shadows and Strengths

I believe that what we do not digest is laid out somewhere else, into others, the political world, the dreams, the body's symptoms, and becomes literal and outer (and called historical) because it is too hard for us, too opaque, to break open and gain insight. | *James Hillman*

Narrative coaching blends the appreciative stance of positive psychology and the deconstructive stance of narrative therapy to offer an integrative approach to working with strengths that I believe is more aligned with how people actually develop. It conceives of people's defenses as a reflection of their lifelong strategies to avoid feeling overwhelmed, alone, and/or powerless. These strategies often compensate for and protect those aspects of their humanity that sit in Shadow—e.g., the person who uses humor to deflect and move away from conflict rather than calling on the suppressed warrior energy in her to step into conflict to resolve it. These strategies may have served us well enough when we were young, but they often represent important thresholds for our development later in life. Coaching involves helping people release their defenses, update their strategies and narratives, and temper key strengths in order to achieve their aspirations. The more that people can leverage their intrinsically motivated strengths, the more likely they are to sustain the gains they make in coaching. The same is true for ourselves as coaches. How would you like to use your strengths differently?

People have evolved their strengths for a variety of reasons, many of which have served them well just as they are. However, strengths are often double-edged swords in that they can cut in our favor or to our detriment. I can think of no better way to make this point than to share what actor Peter Coyote (2014) wrote after the death by suicide of his friend, the actor and comedian Robin Williams:

> Robin's gift could be likened to the fastest thoroughbred racehorse on earth. It had unbeatable endurance, nimbleness, and a huge heart. . . . Sometimes Robin would ride it like a kayaker tearing down whitewater, skimming on the edge of control. We would marvel at his courage, his daring, and his brilliance. But at other times, the horse went where he wanted, and Robin could only hang on for dear life. In the final analysis, what failed Robin was his greatest gift—his imagination.

While we treasure those like Robin who live on the edge, we wish for them and for all of us the space to develop further. When people over-use one of their strengths it often leads to an over-reliance on it that is often reinforced by others. This creates a feedback loop that often keeps them from deeper gifts and opportunities to grow. One of the first steps in coaching someone around their strength using a narrative approach is to determine its nature.

The focus is on the strengths that are most apparent in the stories they are telling and most closely related to what they want to resolve or achieve—not those identified through formal assessments. We do so because we are interested in strengths as they are used in the context of the issues coachees are facing. We are seeking to determine if a person's strength is more intrinsically motivated (*innate* or *acquired*) or extrinsically motivated (*normative* or *compensatory*). *Innate* refers to strengths like physical or cognitive attributes we were born with. *Acquired* refers to strengths we have developed in order to achieve something that mattered to us. For example, I don't have much *innate* strength as a musician, but I have developed an *acquired* strength as a discerning listener to music because it brings me satisfaction.

Normative refers to strengths related to our gender, nationality, birth order, family or work culture, etc. that we have developed because they are expected of us. *Compensatory* refers to strengths we have developed to deal with perceived shortcomings in other areas, either in ourselves or in the systems in which we operate. For example, I developed a *normative* strength in bridging between the thinking world and the feeling world as the oldest son often called upon to bridge between an engineer (father) and a teacher (mother). I developed a related *compensatory* strength around remaining calm in challenging situations, though I see now how often I used it in the past to avoid growing my capacity to stay present to strong emotions and to speak up for what I truly wanted (especially if it rocked the boat).

The secret for working with extrinsically motivated strengths is to help the person tap into the underlying intrinsic motivation that can serve as a more sustainable and valued driver for change. For example, you could coach a person with a strength in organizing any project thrown her way to uncover what she would most like to bring to the world herself—and how she can say 'no' to create more time and energy to do so. As a coach, the better you are in discerning which type of strength you are dealing with, the more effective you will be in working on it with your coachees.

This enables you to better understand what is motivating and resourcing the people you are coaching and how best to approach and support their development. While every strength has its counterpart in Shadow (such as the aggressor to a conciliatory style), it is important to move beyond polarizations and getting stuck in those dualities if we want to support people's development. Thus, strengths and their Shadow are better seen as complementary to one another, two aspects of the same whole. Without its Shadow side, strengths can easily remain one-dimensional, over-used and less productive. Without being grounded in an active strength, Shadows often appear in our lives in ways that are not convenient for us or others. In coaching, you can help people discover their Shadow and the defenses that protect these aspects of themselves. Freeing up this latent energy is an important aim of narrative coaching, in part because it is difficult for people to see either one on their own. For example:

> In coaching someone with a strength in *love of learning*, he came to see how often he over-prepared for meetings (his defense) to avoid his anxiety about being caught off-guard and having to think on his feet (his Shadow). Conversely, in coaching someone with a strength in *improvisation*, she came to see that she kept rewriting the business plan (her defense) to avoid her anxiety about confronting two key associates who had not delivered on their commitments (her Shadow).

By not optimally using their strengths, people often miss out on the opportunity to learn more about themselves and to increase their range, repertoire, and results. To get at this hidden "gold," people need to soften their defenses and temper their strength using its Shadow. Talking about "weaknesses" is not useful here because these behaviors are better seen as over- or mis-applied strengths. The questions I use include:

- What are you avoiding by engaging in this defense?

- What are you afraid might happen if you didn't engage in this defense?

- What might become possible if you didn't engage in it? What would you do then?

- What Shadow element do you need to integrate so your strength is less of a double-edged sword?

- How will that benefit you and others?

TOOL

FIGURE 8: DEVELOPING A MORE MATURE STRENGTH

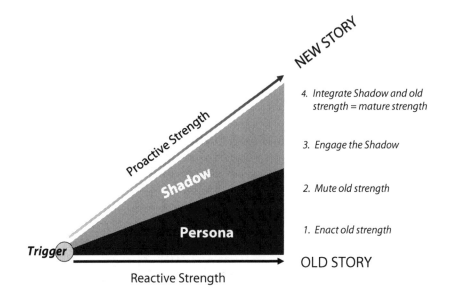

NEW STORY

Proactive Strength

Shadow

Persona

4. Integrate Shadow and old strength = mature strength

3. Engage the Shadow

2. Mute old strength

1. Enact old strength

OLD STORY

Trigger

Reactive Strength

I use this process in coaching—starting with #1 at the bottom—to help people mature a strength using its Shadow. The process is based in the simple yet powerful Pivoting tool (figure 20) used in narrative coaching. The four steps in the process reflect the developmental phases coachees go through as they work on maturing their strengths, each of which is the focus of one of the four phases in narrative coaching (and in the same flow). Stories are useful here because they provide access to unconscious elements of coachees' stories and glimpses of the Shadow elements that may be essential in the process. They also provide tangible examples of triggers that activate coachees' old stories—around which coaches can pause to create the space for the work as outlined above. I find that inviting coachees to free associate in relation to key words that appear in their stories is a great way to enrich this process. You can see this in the example on the following page, preceded by an outline of figure 9 in narrative rather than visual form. The result is a more robust strength and a clearer frame to put it into practice.

How to use the process in coaching:

1. In the *Situate* phase, invite the person to clearly yet nonjudgmentally notice how he is reactively using his strength in line with his old story.

2. In the *Search* phase, invite him to explore the defenses he uses to protect his old story and the value(s) at risk so he can mute the old strength and discover what needs to change.

3. In the *Shift* phase, invite him to engage with the Shadow elements he has avoided but will need in order to mature his old strength and form a new story.

4. In the *Sustain* phase, invite him to integrate his Shadow into his old strength so that it matures and he can use it more masterfully in his life and/or work.

EXAMPLE

Trigger: In *situations* when I feel nervous in a group, I worry about: *"Will I fit in? Will I get it right?"*

1. My old story and typical response (*reactive strength*) is to be **entertaining** using what I see and know.

2. I would like to be more **relaxed** in those situations. Words I associate with relaxed: reserved, insignificant, **intimate**, boring, self-contained, secure, and not self-conscious.

3. I am sparked by the word "intimate" (*Shadow*). If I imagine it as incorporating yet transcending "entertaining" and "relaxed," I think of: focused, dynamic balance, **poised**, and filled with love.

4. I resonate most with **poised**. I can use it to Pivot away from being overly entertaining in situations where I feel nervous. It takes the best of my old strength (e.g., entertaining in example) and tempers it with my Shadow (e.g., intimate).

FIGURE 9: EXAMPLE OF MATURING A STRENGTH

In the end, coaching is not about fixing anything. It is about witnessing and aiding people's efforts to mature so they are more capable and willing to do the work that is in front of them personally, relationally, and/or professionally. Start where people are right now; work with what they have; and build up and out from there. Help them integrate more of their Shadow and its archetypal energies as a source of untapped potential so they can mature their strengths and step into more of their full humanity. You can think of this narrative process as the fire in which steel is tempered to make a sword. It is a process of individuation and maturation.

As Jung described it, this process of individuation is "as much a separation from one's cultural conditioning as it is a unification with the deeper aspects of one's psyche" (Paris, 2011, p. 63). People's most potent strengths and biggest developmental opportunities are both concealed precisely where their weak points seem to be (Carotenuto, 1979). It is also true that many of the behaviors they depend on most to maintain their identities and lives may also be the very things that are holding them back. This is why we bring people's strengths and Shadow into the same process. It is an invitation to coachees to see them as part of the same narrative system rather than as polar opposites.

By bringing strengths and Shadows together, people are able to release old stories about who they think they are—and how they acted as a result—and develop new ones that are more fitting and enable them to flourish more fully. Through coaching, people free up the psychic energy they currently spend on vigilantly keeping watch—making certain that nothing sneaks out and no one can see these hidden aspects of themselves. As a result, they regain energy they can then invest in intimacy, creativity, heartfelt compassion, and growth (Brehony, 1996). I developed the following as a template for participants in my programs they could use for themselves or with their coachees. It covers the same ground, but in a way that is better suited for some people in terms of developing cues and pivots.

A template for maturing one of your strengths in the moment:

1. One of my strengths is. . . . However, I get defensive when . . .

2. Because I. . . . This shows up most often as . . .

3. I would grow by . . . (incorporating this aspect of my Shadow)

4. Therefore, I will mature my strength by . . .

EXAMPLE

1. One of my strengths is *doing whatever it takes to complete a task or project.* However, I get defensive when *I feel others are holding me back.*

2. Because I *am afraid of not being "good enough" and letting others down.* This shows up most often as *impatience and stubbornness.*

3. I would grow by *being more vulnerable* (opening myself to this aspect of my Shadow).

4. Therefore, I will mature my strength by *managing expectations of myself and from others at the start of any project and throttling back when it is better for our long-term success.*

Implications for Your Practice

Narrative coaching is designed to guide people to:

- Experiment as needed; fail well; and learn from their mistakes.

- Take advantage of zones of proximal learning and development.

- Engage with their Shadow so their strengths can mature.

- Get scaffolding and social systems they need to learn and grow.;

- Create new neural pathways so that old ones fade as needed.

- Access both hemispheres in order to integrate the chronological and autobiographical aspects of stories.

- Focus and de-focus in order to widen their window of tolerance.

What are your key insights?
What will you experiment with first?

PART II
narrative
PROCESSES

CHAPTER 4

HOW WE MAKE SENSE AND MEANING

Our stories go deep, into the archetypal realm, into the genetic code, the tribal history, the family of origin both known and repressed, as well as the mythologies we live out on a daily basis. | *James Hollis*

Stories have been integral to human communities since the dawn of time as a means of preserving, transmitting and, at times, imposing or transforming culture. What we believe, to whom we belong, how we behave, and who we become are profoundly shaped by our stories and the larger narratives in which we live. We use stories to remember and organize our past, communicate and negotiate our present, and envision and act into our future. They mirror how our minds develop and operate, and it is through them that we make sense and meaning of our lives. This is why in narrative coaching, we listen carefully to people's stories to gain access to the narrative processes by which each person perceives, frames, and acts on her experiences.

As we saw in the last chapter, stories support our needs for order *and* disorder, stability *and* disruption, continuity *and* discontinuity, and coherence *and* change. The creative tension between the conserving and creating force in each pair is at the heart of both our struggles and our growth. How you work within this tension depends on what coachees need at a given point in their process. A coachee might need stabilizing as they adjust to a sudden change and then might need disrupting if they end up overly ruminating instead of taking action. You can use narrative coaching to address any of these tensions because of its multidisciplinary foundations and its ability to work with stories at multiple levels. It calls us to access and work with the processes by which people make sense and meaning through their stories. As such, this work is as much a part of the rich narrative tradition as it is a part of the more recent coaching tradition.

> What we believe, to whom we belong, how we behave, and who we become are profoundly shaped by our stories and the larger narratives in which we live.

Narrative coaching has benefited from the larger "narrative turn" in the social sciences. Barbara Czarniawska (2004) identified three fields that fed into what became narrative studies and are, therefore, key to understanding this work: literary theory, humanities, and psychology. Each of these reflect one of the pillars of narrative coaching: (1) *narrative psychologies* support us in understanding people's development and performance as narrators; (2) *narrative structures* support us in hearing and reconfiguring the narrated material; and (3) *narrative practices* support us in helping coachees bring new stories to life (Drake, 2008b, 2009c). The Narrative Coaching model integrates material from these three pillars into a unified process of change you can use to deepen your coaching capabilities in working with people's stories. This calls for coaches to make the same narrative turn in terms of how we think about our work and develop ourselves. Not only will this enrich what you offer, but it will prepare you for working in a time where people are increasingly trying to make sense and meaning of what is going on in and around them.

Stories are useful for people being coached because they:

- Engage the whole person, which improves their attention in and retention from sessions.
- Can be accessed at many levels, which increases the number of anchors for their changes.
- Enable them to self-regulate, which increases their resilience and resourcefulness.
- Offer new perspectives, which improves their potential for mentalization and innovation.
- Catch the edge "in-between," which sparks their imagination and generates new possibilities.
- Mirror the mind's time/space orientation, which increases their positional repertoire.
- Contain event sequences and problem-solving steps, which improves their ability to take action toward results.
- Make new sense and meaning from experience, which enables them to let go and move on.
- Surface their values, which increases the impact of their new choices and Pivots.

In this chapter I will provide an overview of the key functions stories serve, a four-phase structure for stories based in the literature (and why it is vital for working with them in coaching), and how to use each phase in working with people's stories in coaching. As my colleague Reinhard Stelter has written about on a number of occasions (see Stelter, 2007, 2013; Drake & Stelter, 2014), narrative coaching has a stronger philosophical foundation than most other approaches because of its focus on the building blocks of human experience and development at individual and collective levels. In narrative coaching, we are accompanying people as they make new sense and meaning of their current situation in order to resolve an issue or achieve an aspiration. By exploring what functions their stories serve, we can get insights into their meaning-making process; by exploring their structure, we get insights into their sense-making process. For now, let me start by defining some of the key terms.

Pekka Tammi (2005) identified three ways to conceptualize narratives in general: (1) as discourse; (2) as speech act; and (3) as cognitive schema. Gergen & Gergen (2006) were similarly interested in the connections between the discursive, dispositional, and cognitive aspects of coachees' narratives as reflected in their stories. You can see this in narrative coaching with our interest in (1) the language people use in their stories; (2) the way in which they tell their stories in the context of coaching; and (3) what their stories reveal about how they see themselves and the world. It is useful to pay attention not only to each of the three conceptualizations, but also to how they are in relation with one another. For example: What is the coachee leaving out of the story she is telling you as her coach? What discrepancies do you notice between how she seems to view herself and the words she uses in her stories? As we look at these three conceptualizations, it is important to distinguish between "narrative" and "story" as the terms are generally used in narrative coaching. At the same time, I acknowledge that the word "story" has a wide variety of meanings in everyday interactions and is used both pejoratively and appreciatively.

I generally use *narrative* to refer to broader patterns and *story* for specific instances, such that stories (for example, about my boss) can be seen as an expression of a larger narrative (about authority figures). A narrative is a socially and contextually constructed communication *structure* marked by temporality and causality, plot, and purpose that enables meaning-and sense-making for those involved. A story is an episodic *form* of communication within oneself or with others that has both conscious and unconscious elements. It has certain culturally defined properties and serves descriptive and/or interactive purposes. Sometimes people form larger stories from a related set of experiences. You can see this in a coachee who vents about a difficult encounter with her boss (a story), which perpetuates her overall view of him (the larger story) and reflects broader issues of gender at work (narrative). Each of these levels is important to address to bring about change in coaching. The stories coachees tell in sessions provide most of the material you will need to help them bring about change and growth in their lives. However, I called this work "narrative coaching" rather than "story coaching" to establish it as distinct from but on par with narrative therapy as a recognized practice modality and to reflect our focus on the larger patterns in bringing about growth and change.

TABLE 3: THE NARRATIVE TURN AND NARRATIVE COACHING

Field	View of Narrative	Examples	Coaching Focus
Literary theory	As speech act	Searle, 1965; Barthes, 1975; Labov & Waletsky, 1967	How stories are formed
Humanities	As social discourse	Madigan, 1996; Berger & Luckmann, 1966; Foucault, 1972	How stories are framed
Psychology	As cognitive schema	Mandler, 1984; Russell & van Den Broek, 1992; Schank, 1990	Why stories are told
Source	(cited in Tammi, 2005)		(Drake, 2009c)

Mattingly (1998) describes a story as a "rhetorical structure that is meant to persuade, to provide a perspective on what happened as part of telling what happened" (p. 26). As such, be curious about who your coachees are trying to persuade and about what through their stories. At the same time, narrative coaching itself is a respectful dialogical practice that is more aligned with the notion of *invitational rhetoric* (Foss & Foss, 2003). This work is not about dissuading people of their current narration or reality, but rather about inviting them to see it for what it is, assess its consequences, and explore what else might be possible. Invitational rhetoric is characterized by five assumptions which align beautifully with narrative coaching: "(1) the purpose of communicating is to gain understanding; (2) the speaker and the audience are equal; (3) different perspectives constitute valuable resources; (4) change happens when people choose to change themselves; and (5) all participants are willing to be changed by the interaction" (Foss & Foss, 2003, pp. 9–10). To make the most of the stories that emerge within an invitational stance, it helps to have a good understanding of the functions and structure of people's stories.

Understanding the Functions of Stories

Leaving home isn't really completed until we create a new center. | *James Hollis*

Narrative coaches are keenly interested in the stories people tell about their lives because "there is an intimate connection between the ways in which people construe themselves and the way in which they are likely to behave" (Novitz, 1997, p. 146). Drawing on my early work in this space, Hänninen (2004) describes this movement between our inner narrative, told stories and lived stories as "narrative circulation." Your role as coach is to notice where the flow is blocked and impinging on the results the coachee is seeking. Central to working this way is to see people's stories as situated processes, not isolated products. In so doing, their actions can be understood as enacted narratives (MacIntyre, 1981). This is why we are interested in the narrator, the narrated material, and their process of narration. Stories are about someone trying to do something, what happens to them and others as a result, and what sense and meaning they make of it. Therefore, in narrative coaching we track the function of stories at four levels: (1) the *identity* (as constructed, lived, and imagined) of the person telling this story; (2) his *intention* (conscious or otherwise) for sharing this story this way in this moment; (3) the *impact* (intended or unintended) of telling this story on himself and others; and (4) the *interpretation* (spoken or unspoken) by himself and others of the impact.

Coaching often involves helping people to reconcile the gaps or tensions between two or more functions, such as the coachee whose leadership intentions are not yielding the impact or interpretations she had hoped for. These narrative gaps and tensions are what most often provides the catalyst for growth (Pearce & Pearce, 2001). This is because when coachees' usual stories prove to be incomplete and/or ineffective, they must face the resulting discrepancy between their verbalized concepts of themselves, their felt awareness of themselves (Fritz S. Perls et al., 1994/1951), and/or their impact on others. Therefore, invite coachees to step into the discomfort of these gaps or tensions in search of deeper truths about themselves, their stories, and their lives. You will likely encounter two of the key functions of their stories in the process: to distance themselves from uncomfortable pieces of their underlying narrative until they were ready to deal with them, and to give them clues about where to find the doorway to their growth (McLeod, 2006).

Understanding the core functions of narratives will help you to better understand what coachees are consciously or unconsciously trying to accomplish with their stories. You can often get a sense for this by noticing what role they are implicitly or explicitly asking you to take up as they tell their stories and/or what emotions or responses they are evoking in you as they do. Sometimes I will take up that role to provide the resonance they need to embark on the journey (e.g., "I care for you") or provide a sense of dissonance by showing them a new way it can be played (e.g., "I will show you I care without having to rescue you"). Sometimes I will not take up a role, but instead invite them to search inside themselves for that character and capability (e.g., "Yes, I've been in that place myself, and I'm more interested right now on what you can draw from in your own experience"). Which stance you take depends on what would help a coachee make new sense and meaning from their stories as a platform for taking new action.

Stories, and the larger narratives they represent, incorporate five primary elements (K. J. Gergen, 1994) as underlined below—each of which serves a vital function (Drake, 2003, 2007). I have paired (and italicized) each of Konstantin Stanislavsky's (1936/1989) essential questions for actors with one of the five functions. These questions are written from the perspective of a coachee as a character seeking to more fully understand her stories and her place in them. This is useful because it takes us deeper into the heart and mind of our coachees as to why they tell the stories they do and what they are hoping to accomplish as a result. This is a critical distinction in narrative coaching, as it is the emphasis is on coachees' understanding of themselves and their stories, *not ours*, that is key to their success. Similarly, in training actors, Stanislavsky believed that characters are always coming from somewhere toward the stage and heading somewhere off the stage when they leave. While we often focus in coaching on stories that are "on the stage," I would encourage you to remain curious about the backstory and the epilogue—and how they are influencing and influenced by what is unfolding in the session. Ask yourself in sessions, "Where did the coachee come from, and where is she headed next?" and "How does this connect with what I am hearing right now?" You can use the five functions below as you listen to coachees' stories and discern where to focus their attention.

The Five Functions of Stories

1. Stable Identities

What are your circumstances (physical and non-physical)?

Stories help people orient themselves in their environment, shape how they interact with others, and address the questions: To whom do I belong? What is the larger narrative?

2. Ordered Events

Who are you as a character?

Stories help people orient themselves in time, bring together the past, present, and future in a meaningful way, and address the questions: Who have I been? Who am I now? Who am I becoming?

3. Valued Endpoints

What is your objective?

Stories help people orient themselves relative to their values, inspire them to move toward what brings them meaning and fulfillment, and address the questions: What am I seeking? How do I decide what is right?

4. Demarcation Signs

What are the obstacles (physical and non-physical) in your way?

Stories help people orient themselves in the midst of disruptions to the status quo, notice and step into the openings for growth, and address the questions: What is being asked of me? Where will I focus my attention?

5. Causal Linkages

Given the above, what do you do (and why)?

Stories help people position themselves in larger narratives in ways that make sense, provide meaning, align with their motivation, and address the questions: Why are things like this? What is the moral of this story?

The following story illustrates one of these functions (valued endpoints) as it played out in a coaching conversation.

EXAMPLE

One of my early questions of Tom was, "How did you come to be a lawyer?" In answering, he shared several stories about Bruce, a lawyer who had been a mentor for him and the other kids in his neighborhood. As a result of Bruce's influence, Tom had carried into adulthood a strong value for justice and fairness, and he eventually chose a career in law himself. As he and I moved from these stories to the present day—and stories of Tom's work in coaching other lawyers and developing new modes of mediation—there emerged a moment when it seemed important for the two sets of stories to meet. I said to Tom, "I bet Bruce would be really proud of you right now." In the profound pause that ensued, Tom was able to recognize for the first time a central narrative thread that ran through his life and was witnessed in that recognition.

The more you understand about the functions of stories, the more you and your coachees will understand what they are trying to accomplish with their stories and what their stories are trying to express on their behalf. Given that form follows function in good design, we turn now to look at how stories are structured and what this means for your coaching.

Understanding the Structure of Stories

The way we describe our lives and understand them is ultimately and inextricably connected to the way we live them. | *Mandy Aftel*

The importance of understanding how stories are structured can be seen in Ted Sarbin's (1986a) notion of the "narratory principle" according to which "human beings think, perceive, imagine, interact and make moral choices according to narrative structures" (p. 9), and in David Carr's (1986) argument that narrative is a "primary way of organizing and giving coherence to our experience" (p. 65). The stories we hear in coaching are often profoundly, albeit unconsciously, shaped by narrative structures formed early in life through a wide array of internal and external influences. They are also embedded in a complex network of narratives that tend to either reinforce or challenge these structures. The working models a person brings to coaching also affects how she tells her stories.

We can listen for her stories' structure to better understand the sense-and meaning-making patterns in her models so that any changes she makes related to the issue at hand can be more readily generalized to other similar situations. You can think of the structure of people's stories as a skeleton upon which the details are hung. These skeletons set the tone and direction for the way in which people narrate their experiences and live their lives. Over time people tend to reinforce their constructed reality by finding the events that fit the skeleton convenient for them to believe (Schank, 1990) and overlook (or reframe) events that are inconvenient truths for them. This is why in narrative coaching we start by helping people to make explicit their implicit narrative patterns so they can then identify how they would like to upgrade them. Most everything we need to do this can be found in the stories coachees share with us in coaching. Pay attention to what they reveal about the current structure and the desired structure.

It is this clash between what the character values and expected to happen and what actually happened that sets the character in motion in search of restoration and resolution (Drake, 2016). According to renowned screenwriter Robert McKee (1997), the energy of the protagonist's desire forms the Spine of a story as its primary unifying force. He and others describe how stories can be seen in terms of a three-act structure that reflects our efforts to: (1) respond to inciting incidents that throw our life out of balance or equilibrium; (2) identify the object of our desire that we believe will restore the balance; and (3) overcome a series of barriers in pursuit of that object until there is a resolution (see also Burke, 1969; Czarniawska, 1998, 2004; Ricoeur, 1984; Todorov, 1971/1977; Vogler, 1998; H. White, 1981). The Spine reflects the clash between the *epistemic stance* (what occurs) and the *deontic stance* (what the protagonist values and/or believes should occur) (Bruner & Luciarello, 1989). Interestingly, protagonists often discover in the end that what they first sought was only a proxy for what they truly desired, and what they sought outside themselves was often within them all along. Be clear yet patient with coachees as they are coming to these realizations about their stories and what they reveal about what they truly want.

> Protagonists often discover in the end that what they first sought was only a proxy for what they truly desired and what they sought outside themselves was within them all along.

Jerome Bruner (1986, 1990) suggested that our stories are defined by a *landscape of action* which answers the epistemic question of what happened (e.g., the scene and setting, what the protagonist and other actors do in a given situation, and the sequential unfolding of the event) and a *landscape of consciousness* that addresses the deontic question of what it means (e.g., emotions, beliefs, and intentions; what the protagonist believes and feels about the situation; and the internal responses of the protagonist and others) (Ochs & Capps, 1996). By integrating the material from these two landscapes, people can construct a full narrative account of their experiences. As coaches, we are curious about how the two landscapes affect each other and how they shape coachees' "storyworlds" (McLeod, 2004).

There have been a number of attempts in the literature to identify the elements and structure of a well-formed narrative (see Burke, 1969; Czarniawska, 1998, 2004; Ricoeur, 1984; Todorov, 1971/1977; Vogler, 1998; H. White, 1981). They have also occurred in fields such as historiography (see Mink, 1969), linguistics (see Labov, 1982; Mandler, 1984), literary theory (see Frye, 1957; Scholes & Kellogg, 1966), and semiotics (see Propp, 1968; Rimmon-Kenan, 1983). The following is the four-act model I developed based on the review of this literature and the needs in coaching.

FIGURE 10: FOUR ACTS OF NARRATIVE COACHING

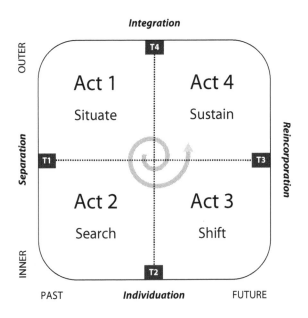

It is not uncommon in books and movies for the story to end when the original narrative arc has been resolved. There is often a sense at the end where the character is heading next—and to pursue it much further would be anticlimactic and require the beginning of a whole new arc. Coaching is different in that where characters (coachees) head next is of the utmost importance to us and ultimate reason we get paid for our work. This is why I added a fourth act to the traditional three-act structure in developing the narrative coaching model. It accounts for the character's need to sustain and integrate the results from the first three acts.

I also added the spiral to acknowledge the fact that narration is an ongoing and iterative process. I've included the four phases in the narrative coaching process in the figure above so you can see the connections between the structure of a story and the structure of the coaching process. It is also a reminder that in the narrative coaching process we are coming alongside a person and her stories as they are searching for resolution. For us as coaches, it is less about "What should I do?" and more about "What are the stories calling for that would help the person make new sense and meaning in this situation?"

In developing the Narrative Coaching model and process, I drew on Burke's (1969) work on dramatism: the search for a person's motive as the driver of their narratives. His Pentad offered five questions you could use in unpacking stories, their structure and their motive: "what was done (act), when and where it was done (scene), who did it (agent), how he did it (agency), and why (purpose)" (Burke, 1969, p. xv). The coda (Bruner, 2002) was added as a sixth element to address the action orientation in coaching and the re-incorporation phase in development (Drake, 2008b). Other key sources for the initial framework included Stein and Glenn's (1979) grammatical structure for stories, Ollerenshaw and Creswell's (2002) problem-solution narrative structure approach, McKee's (1997, 2004) story elements in screenwriting, and Campbell's (1968, 1973) mythological narratives. The next section looks at these four acts in more detail and features a case story to illustrate the Narrative Coaching model in action.

Working with Stories in Coaching

Wherever you are is the entry point. | *Kabir*

It is important to reiterate at the start that this structure reflects how most people, at least in the West, form the stories they tell as well as make sense and meaning of the stories they hear. It is a natural process people are engaged in to achieve *their* purposes, not something we are imposing on the conversation for *our* purposes. You can use this structure as you listen for what is present and what is absent from their narration. For example, "Where is their energy and attention, or lack thereof?" The four-act structure enables coaches to assemble the pieces of the story as they emerge in the conversation into a whole. This enables them to reflect back to coachees what they are hearing, and identify and explore openings for change.

Act 1 is about how the person is *situated* in her story, the world as she sees it and lives in it now, and the coaching session. Act 2 is about the separation from the original state, the *search* for the values at stake in the story, and the desire that will restore what has been lost. Act 3 builds on the individuation that occurs in the process and focuses on what is *shifting* in the person and the story based on what was discovered in the search. Act 4 is about the reincorporation of the person and the new story back into the world as well as *sustaining* and integrating what has changed. Each phase is separated from the one that follows by a threshold, a doorway that marks a shift in attention in terms of what is happening and what is required (Drake, 2016).

Act 1: Situate

Situate incorporates the *setting* (Stein and Glenn, 1979; Ollerenshaw and Creswell, 2002), the *scene* (Burke, 1969), in which there is a protagonist (Stein & Glenn, 1979), and an *agent* (Burke, 1969) about whom we care. A story's setting is "four-dimensional: period, duration, location and level of conflict" (McKee, 1997, p. 68). Other elements and characters are also introduced, often foreshadowing events to come. What turns a routine sequence of events into a story and sets it in motion is often an inciting incident, a disruption in the status quo that upsets the balance of forces in his life. Stories emerge from disruptions and point to desires. This reversal in circumstances—what Aristotle saw as a *peripeteia*—challenges the person to conceive of what will put it back into balance (the object of desire). The story describes a protagonist's efforts to come to terms with the breach and its consequences (Bruner, 1986, 2002; Riessman, 1993) and get the situation back to what he perceives as "normal" (Bruner 2002). The conflict that emerges is the engine of a narrative. It is often in these gaps— where the objective realities of the world do not conform to the subjective assumptions and expectations of the character (McKee, 2004; Ochs & Capps, 1996)— that serve as the catalyst to embark on a search.

Act 2: Search

Search involves an *act* (Burke, 1969), including the protagonist's internal *reaction* or *response* (Stein and Glenn), as she attempts to deal with the situation created by the *initiating event* (Stein and Glenn). It involves a search to determine what she believes will restore the lost equilibrium and put her life back into balance if it is achieved; it defines the spine of the story. Along the way, she will often be challenged to release old attachments for the sake of making progress with the search. As McKee (1997) noted, "The more powerful and complex the forces of antagonism opposing the character, the more completely realized the character and story must become" (p. 317). Trials and tribulations, encounters with individual and collective shadows, the sense of being "in-between," and the appearance of allies and guides are common here. These are important in coaching to help us gauge how deeply we need to work with coachees on a given issue. Once people become clear about their prevailing "attitude" (an element Burke later added to his Pentad to tie the other five together) and what is truly at stake for them, they can move on to explore what new experiences and shifts are called for.

Act 3: Shift

Shift involves what Burke (1969) referred to as the *purpose*, and it reflects the actions taken by the protagonist to deal with the outcomes of the search (Stein and Glenn, 1979; Ollerenshaw and Creswell, 2002). It is about what happens to the protagonist (e.g., his sense of self, mental models, expectations, narrative strategies) as a result of his journey to this point. People often become aware of deeper, often unconscious, desires in this phase and find themselves being led in new directions as a result. These desires are often found where people must face the greatest challenge, answer the most essential question, or make the hardest choice. This obstacle is often the very thing they have feared the most, and yet more often than not it ends up being the doorway to their greatest gift. It is at these junctures in the story that we get to see their true character and if they can convert what they have been through into growth (Yanno, 2006). It is important to remember, however, that the "gift" may or may not be the one they were originally seeking (McKee 1997, 2004). This phase is about identifying what is being asked of the person, and inviting him to explore and experiment with how to put it into action. Once this becomes clear, he can move into the final phase to enact what has been discovered and developed.

Act 4: Sustain

Sustain involves a sense of *agency* (Burke, 1969) in responding to the consequences of the protagonist's actions and the often climactic process by which she reaches a resolution. This phase is marked by the person's return to the outer world bearing the gifts of her journey, during which she will receive support from some and challenges from others. This phase is crucial because it is far easier for people to accomplish and sustain their new stories if they have or can create a supportive collective context (Rappaport, 1995). To be successful, the person will need sufficient scaffolding to support her emerging new narratives. The good news is that a major source of this scaffolding can be found in the raw material in people's own stories (Drake, 2003, 2005; Gergen & Gergen, 2006). "Scaffolding strengthens the space held in coaching so people can learn what is theirs to learn in a given zone, embody it and apply it" (Drake, 2016, p. 298). Providing the necessary scaffolding enables coachees to experience and practice what it would be like to live with their new story and to develop themselves such that it becomes part of who they are. And the spiral comes full circle and begins again . . .

The Spiral

The spiral reflects the moral of the story (Stein and Glenn)—what Bruner (2002) called the "coda." It serves as a platform for new awareness and new action for both the teller of the story and the audience of the story. The spiral is a reminder to not worry too much about which story coachees choose to tell as they begin a session, because most any story they would start with offers a door into the presenting issue. They will start where they start, and your role is to be there to meet them and see where they want to go with it. Openly receive whatever is presented and invite it into the field, trusting that everything you need is already present.

The spiral is also a reminder to maintain a dual focus on the stories *and* the larger narratives they reflect—the issue at hand *and* the patterns they reflect. Lastly, the spiral is a reminder to patiently circle the tree even as you are prepared to step into openings for growth at any point in the process. The deeper the change a person is seeking in coaching, the more often he may need to spiral through the issue in order to get to its core and develop new patterns. The following case story offers a look at how the four elements of narrative structure and the four phases of the narrative coaching process were used in a single session.

EXAMPLE: CASE STORY

Act 1: Situate: I worked with a medium-sized service organization that was experiencing turbulence in the wake of the sudden departure of the CEO. Nancy was a senior manager in her late fifties who was being called on to step up as an interim leader and advocate for the management team and the staff in the midst of this unexpected vacuum. She was resisting these pleas even though she was not clear why she was doing so. The purpose for our session was to help her decide what role she wanted to play in response to the current situation.

Nancy's first story was about coaching a young staff member who felt stuck in not knowing what to do about a client's difficult legal situation. What struck me about this story was her mentoring of her new staff member about how to "get out of the middle." It echoed the sense of feeling stuck that she herself faced as she was caught between those who wanted her to step in and her own uncertainty about what was hers to do.

Act 2: Search: At one level, Nancy seemed to be quite willing to let things drift along as they had always been. However, parallel stories emerged about how she had responded at earlier times in her life when she faced big changes, e.g., stepping into new roles when she divorced and more recently as her children moved away from home. This began to open the conversation to larger themes at play in her life and to what was calling her now.

Nancy spoke about her young adult children establishing their own lives and continuing to evolve a new relationship with their mother. She saw herself at a turning point with them. The poignancy of this phase in her life also came across through a story about her return to her alma mater to take some classes and finding herself talking with young women who "didn't know the history of what went on here."

She also said that she wanted to be able to build relationships at work on her own terms before the "huge stereotype of older women gets in the way." She expressed her ambivalence about this transition "because I'm older than everyone, there's an expectation about knowing things in a way that I don't think of myself as knowing things . . . . I just see myself as somebody at the table, like everybody else at the table, and you're just tossing out ideas. . . . You know, that feeling of just being one of the gang . . . and now that's not true. Now that's not true." This was said with a sense of sadness and loss, as often is the case in this phase as people confront what is ebbing away in order to prepare for what is to come next.

Act 3: Shift: Her "object of desire" emerged through an inquiry about role models she could draw on, which yielded stories about the pioneering women in her family of origin. She saw herself as entering a time in her life and her career that called for redefinition, but she wasn't sure what that looked like. She described herself as "betwixt and between," and "not quite sure what it meant to be fifty-eight." This is fitting for the liminal phase. She became aware that her lingering uncertainty reflected the fact that she was being asked to choose a new place for herself at work at the same time she was seeking a new place in her own life. We returned to the stories of the elder women, who somehow seemed important for her at this juncture.

She remarked at one point, "I have great role models going into old age. We have a very strong connection to the Irish woman across the generations and a strong ongoing community in our family, particularly through my aunts." She regaled me with some of the powerful tales they had told her over the years.

I asked her near the end, "If you were to take these older women as your council of elders, how would that inform what you did at work?" She responded that she had taken them in as her council and they were with her all the time as wise voices even when they were not nearby. She then went back into a story she had mentioned before, but this time she told it in more detail. In so doing, she was able to break through to the heart of her dilemma about what role to play at this critical time of change in her life and in the organization.

> There was a ritual in my family, and I don't even know if it was conscious, but the women in the family would get together and the tea would come out. They would sit around the table, and they would drink tea. That was always the first question when I came in the door, "Would you have a cup of tea? Can I fix you a cup of tea, darling?"
>
> And you knew that you had been accepted, that you had passed from childhood into a new status as a young woman, when you were invited to the table for tea. It was a huge honor for my daughter when it was her turn, though she didn't really appreciate it until she was older. That's one of the family rites."
> *[Long pause . . .]* **"It's my turn to serve tea, isn't it?"**

And with that insight, tears came to her eyes. She realized that while she was not "just one of the gang" anymore as the most senior member of the management team, she still was free to make her own choice. In recognizing that "it's my turn now to be an elder," she realized that all of her life she had been the youngest (for example, she was the last of thirty-six cousins). "I am truly a youngest child and I only know in an academic sense what an oldest does . . . and I am an oldest now."

She realized that the challenge at work was emblematic of a much larger transformation in her life. From this new narrative about herself she could begin to explore what being an oldest would look like for her.

Act 4: Sustain: After the session, she decided not to take on the role as interim leader, but instead to use her experience to help her peers on the management team move through the crisis. While our formal work was done, I stayed in touch as part of a larger project that involved her organization. She remained content that she had made the right choice and seemed to have found a new vitality for work.

The Spiral: You can see in her stories a spiral around the theme of "betwixt and between" in her stories, with each round focused on a different phase. The early story was just about Situate; the final epiphany was about Sustain.

I hope you now have a better sense of how stories help people make sense and meaning in their lives—and how we can use them to help them make the changes they are seeking. You will be more adept at listening to people's stories and facilitating their growth if you understand how stories are structured and what functions they serve. This is why the narrative coaching process mirrors the structure (and function) of stories themselves and is so effective as guide for your formulation in sessions, your approach to change, and your development as a coach. It enhances your ability to (1) track the arc of people's stories *and* notice the often subtle, yet significant, openings for change; (2) notice what is present in their stories in greater detail *and* what is absent yet yearning to be heard; and (3) connect more deeply with those brave enough to bring their stories into the room *and* attend more closely to what the stories are seeking from the conversation. We will close this chapter by returning to attachment theory to understand how to notice openings for change in people's stories, particularly when a coachee's usual sense- and meaning-making is disrupted. This represents one of the most exciting new additions to this work and this edition of the book.

Making the Most of Moments of Meeting

An important kind of healing occurs through meeting and "being met" rather than through insight and analysis. | *Martin Buber*

When the mutual regulation in coaching goes well, coachees can uncover and incorporate information they often overlook in forming their identities and narratives and, as a result, tell more of the whole story as a whole person. This enables them to make new sense and meaning in relation to the past, present, or future aspects of the issue at hand—and therefore make new choices, take new actions and get new results. So, the question then becomes: "How can we notice these opportunities in coaching conversations?" This is what led me back to another important body of work in the attachment literature, "moments of meeting" (see Lyons-Ruth, 1998; Stern, 1998, 2004). These are based on the same two regulatory processes of resonance and dissonance but focus more explicitly on the relationship and the conversation.

The framework was originally developed to understand how (well) caregivers responded to the evolving needs and capabilities of an infant. In particular, what happens at points of disruption in their usual relational patterns? For example, how does the parent respond when her child throws his first tantrum at the dinner table or in the grocery store? Their hypothesis is that the ability of parents to appropriately evolve their style in such moments is critical for the development of attachment security in children. Stern (2004) went on to study these dynamics in the relationship between psychotherapists and clients, and we can draw similar conclusions for coaching in terms of how to develop ourselves and achieve the best outcomes for our coachees.

In narrative coaching, we start by reflecting on our own attachment insecurities, regulatory patterns and abilities to show up in critical moments. What do we experience as a "disruption" and what narratives sit behind that assessment for us? How do we tend to respond to various kinds of disruptions and with what effect? Which kinds of disruptions do we tend to steer conversations around so as to avoid our own discomfort? These are important questions because conversational and relational disruptions provide openings for both parties in coaching to learn and grow. They often trigger old stories and regulatory strategies and, as such, provide opportunities for both of them to develop new strategies and abilities. As with the narrative coaching process, start by noticing if and how you currently engage in each of these types of moments. Then you can move on to explore what you need to show up more fully and effectively in moments where you are not as strong. The key is to remain fully present to disruption and find the thresholds for transformation. This is as true for us as coaches as it is for coachees, though our primary focus is on the latter's outcomes. There are four types of moments related to the attachment process—as seen in the chart below—each with a primary benefit for coachees.

Four Types of Moments in Coaching:[9]

1. *Moving along:* characterized by conversational flow and fosters psychological safety.
2. *Now moments:* characterized by disruption of the flow and fosters critical consciousness.
3. *Moments of meeting:* characterized by transformation of the flow and fosters mutual evolution.
4. *Moments of being met:* characterized by integration of the flow and fosters existential agency.

EXAMPLE

1. *Moving along:* We explore his lack of follow-through on assignments after the first two sessions.
2. *Now moments:* He announces in response that he (one of the first employees) has decided to leave the large start-up company.
3. *Moments of meeting:* In talking through what this means for him, he asked me what it was like to become a parent (why he was leaving).
4. *Moments of being met:* He shifts from making lists to empowering others before he goes (a result of our work).

The first moment, "Moving along," relates to the everyday relationship patterns and implicit agreements between a parent and a child. It is understood and experienced as the normal flow, and it brings with it shared expectations about each other's roles and behaviors. These moments contribute to the child's sense of psychological safety. However, young children are developing rapidly, and therefore their needs and capabilities are changing frequently as well. "Now moments" occur when there are disruptions in the normal flow, and they provide a potential opening for greater critical consciousness for both parties. This disruption is a break in the flow of mutual regulation, even if it is seen to be initiated by one person in the pair. Assigning blame or attribution is generally unhelpful here because it hinders the learning process, the relationship, and the opportunity for personal and relational growth. However, it is up to the parent to recognize the disruption and regulate himself (so the child can do the same to the best of her ability). Children often experience challenges later in life when they take on roles in these instances on behalf of parents and significant others.

If this moment is addressed well, there is the potential for it to become a "Moment of meeting." These moments occur when both parties are able to adjust their participation to fit the new situation—and individually and relationally grow as a result. For example, a parent recognizes she needs to move from taking action herself to inviting the child to do it for herself. In the context of coaching with adults, the developmental potential in these moments of meeting can be championed by either party even if there is the expectation that the paid professional will take that lead. We would do well in this phase to heed the advice from Vincent J. Donovan: "Do not try to call them . . . to where you are, as beautiful as that place may seem to you. You must have the courage to go with them to a place that neither you nor they have ever been before." As you think about these types of moments in your own coaching, what has helped you to step into moments like this? This is particularly important when these moments are difficult for you because they provide such rich opportunities for you to grow as a human being and a practitioner. For example, the coachee who unexpectedly starts crying in the midst of her story challenges the coach to confront his own issues with grieving or with the need to "rescue" people.

When coachees leave a session, they encounter people who have not been on that journey with them and may or may not be supportive of the outcomes. However, what they experienced and learned from any moments of meeting in their sessions—and how their coach handled them—will equip them to be more able to do the same for themselves. They will become more capable of managing any disruptions of the flow that may occur as they live out and speak out with their new narrative. They will also be able to transform and integrate whatever they glean from processing these disruptions, and increase their overall resilience, repertoire and results. What anchors it all for many coachees is if they have had sufficient and significant "moments of being met." These can emerge from a moment of meeting when coachees allow themselves to be met by their coach and to meet themselves in a new way.

This is hard for many coachees (and coaches too) and often needs to be done with care so both parties can soak it all in. The same defenses that kept a coachee from addressing the issue in the past may emerge here again as a way to keep her from receiving the gift and accepting the shift. For many coachees, having the experience of "being met" is often healing in itself, and it helps them to start integrating the change that has occurred. It is what people truly hunger for from coaching, and they are more likely to move successfully through the *Sustain* phase if they can have and internalize that experience. The ability to move through these four types of moments in a coaching session is often significant for the coach's development as well. It helps us become more aware of and address blind spots in our mindsets and formulations, our communication and our actions, and it represents one of the hallmarks of a narrative coach.

Implications for Your Practice

- People make sense and meaning through the stories they tell. The stories they keep telling reinforce how they see themselves in their world, communicate about their world, and participate in their world.

- Listen to the stories you hear not just for what they are saying about the coachee, but also as a witness for the story itself. They are often communicating on behalf of the coachee in ways she cannot see yet.

- Be willing to show up to your coachees as one human being to another, especially in moments of meeting that are challenging. They are doorways to breakthroughs for both of you.

Signs of a Moment of Meeting:

- There is a sudden shift in the intersubjective field.
- Time and space seem to slow down.
- You are both surprised by what emerges.
- You are both at a loss for words and responses.
- There is a pregnant pause, a generative silence.
- There is intimate spaciousness, a call to surrender.
- A new truth and opportunities become visible.

What are your key insights?
What will you experiment with first?

CHAPTER 5

HOW AND WHY WE TELL STORIES

When a great ship is in harbor and moored, it is safe, there can be no doubt.
But that is not what great ships are built for. | *Clarissa Pinkola Estes*

Part of what separates a story from a mere chronicle is the presence of a plot. Emplotment is the process by which we connect events and experiences in such a way that they make sense and provide meaning (Hermans & Kempen, 1993; Polkinghorne, 1988). While some well-plotted stories are linked to self-defining memories and have strong neural ties, stories are not stored in our minds as if they are folders in a filing cabinet. They are assembled from a variety of sources and expressed to suit our needs in the moment. As such, there is not a singular true story, but rather a constellation of situated retellings. Narrative coaches are interested in the nuances of a particular telling and the broader constellation of which it is a part. This applies to both the narration by coachees (the stories they tell us) and the formulation by coaches (the stories we tell ourselves about what is going on, what we think it means, and what should be done as a result—and why).

In both cases, how people act is closely linked to the stories they choose to tell. Coaching is most effective when there is an alignment between their narration and our formulation, though this may include both resonance and dissonance in support of the change process.

> **There is not a singular true story, but rather a constellation of situated retellings.**

The other area of narration that is of great interest to coaches is that of "authoring," which refers to the level of awareness, agency, accountability, and agility with which people form and tell their stories. Do they "own" their stories? Do they feel free to tell their story on their terms? Are they conscious of the impact of their stories on others? Authoring refers to the person who is telling the stories, her experience in telling them and living them, and how the first two affect each other. It involves both the existential act of owning one's stories and the experiential act of formulating and telling them. To be able to make progress in coaching, people need to see themselves as the author of the stories in play and appreciate the ways in which these stories are affected by larger narratives and social discourse. Authoring refers not only to the narration of their experiences and lives from the inside out, but also to take a narrative stance in doing so relative to the outside in.

Coaching is more about helping people to develop new emplotment and authoring strategies in order to achieve better results than doing "story repair" (Crossley, 2002). Your role is to facilitate the formation of new narratives, not fix broken ones. In so doing, ask coachees questions such as: How is your story serving you? Not serving you? What are you afraid will happen if you let that story go? What would a different story help you see or do? The first half of this chapter looks at narration through the lenses of emplotment and authoring. The second half looks at formulation from a narrative perspective in terms of how and why we tell stories, and it offers a framework and a case story on how to use it as you coach. The chapter ends with a brief look at the *Three Windows of Development* (Drake, 2014c) and how you can use to increase your mastery in this area.

Understanding Narration

The moment you have spoken the exact words that describe your distance
from where you want to be, the moment you have uttered the exact aching
dimensionality of your own exile, you have already turned around,
faced the other way and taken the first steps on the
long-awaited journey home . . . | David Whyte

As we've seen, people use stories to situate themselves in time and space. A lot of our work in coaching involves helping people to re-situate themselves in service of new realities and/or new aspirations. Their narration can be seen through two lenses: *emplotment*, the way they organize their stories (structure); and *authoring*, how and why they tell them (function). Charon (2006) described the difference in terms of the "autobiographical gap" between the narrator-who-speaks (authoring) and the protagonist-who-acts (emplotment). Kenyon & Randall (1997) described it as a distinction between the *subjective author* and *objective actor*. People need to address both elements in order to release old stories they no longer find sufficient or satisfying and form new narratives that are more fitting. The first step is to notice and then loosen the grip of the existing narrative as it is emplotted and authored; the second step is to rearrange, replace and/or reframe certain aspects to form a new one. Development can be seen as a progressive alignment along a matured plotline of explanatory narratives (about the past), participatory narratives (about the present), and anticipatory narratives (about the future).

Helping coachees become aware of and address the reinforcing causal loops in their narration is critical to their success in this process. It enables them to get off the proverbial treadmill; acknowledge it will never get them where they really want to go; and drop into the deeper reality and truth where the real work is to be done. However, it is important to do so from a place of respect for their current patterns because, as Mattingly (1998) points out, "emplotments which disregard [their current] narrative sense-making are unlikely to succeed" (p. 74). One of your best gifts is to reflect back to them what you are hearing and observing in terms of their narration (voiced or not) and its consequences. This is important because their explanations, expectations, and enactments all strongly affect one another (S. J. Sherman, Skov, Hervitz, & Stock, 1981) and their overall ability to author their lives. For example, "I see the world like this and therefore expect this to happen, which is why I must do this." We use a process called "If. . . Then . . . Therefore . . ." in narrative coaching to help people create new connections, which makes new plotlines and options more available.

Plots reflect the way people organize the elements of their stories in time (to provide coherence) and space (to provide direction) and the criteria they use to decide which events and interpretations will be included in the story (to further its purpose) (Polkinghorne, 1995). Plots link these elements together by sequencing and situating events in an unfolding movement culminating in a conclusion (Mishler, 2000). In forging a plot, narrators build a "theory of events" (Foucault, 1965), which then guides and justifies their subsequent actions. People selectively recall past behaviors and predict their future responses to make them consistent with their current attitudes. "This can be an issue for people when their past behavior is seen as irrevocable, leaving them with a sense that they cannot undo what has been done" (Ross & Conway, 1986, p. 129). When that is the case, these persistent emplotment patterns tend to become attractors such that similar events are drawn into the same frame and may eventually become self-fulfilling prophecies. However, new emplotments can be developed that reinforce more generative patterns, as is often the focus in coaching.

Narration can also be seen as "authoring" in referring to the person who is telling the story and the purpose for which it is being told. Therefore, pay attention to how the coachee's narration is affecting her, you, and the conversation. Does the coachee:

- Tell his story in the first or third person?

- Portray himself as an active author or a more passive actor?

- Empathize with other positions in his story and reflect on his own?

- Take accountability for his actions in the story and his choices in how he tells it?

- See the connections between his stories, his life and his outcomes?

It is important to note here, as Michael White (2007) did, that much of what goes into people's stories is "absent but implicit" and, therefore, the factors that shape their narration and their identities may not be apparent at first. This notion is based on Derrida's idea that how we make sense and meaning of things depends on the distinctions we make between what is presented to us (privileged meaning) and what is left out (subjugated meaning). For example, a coachee realizes that the posture, voice, and frame he is using to describe his situation are more a reflection of his familial and cultural heritage than his actual experience in the moment. His coach can then guide him to make new choices in terms of the relative weighting of each set of narratives and to find a more authentic voice as a result.

In working with their narration, many coachees start to realize that the development of their lives and the development of their plots as narrated are often two distinct unfoldings (Hillman, 1975a) and their growth often comes at points where there are significant gaps between the two. In my experience, their ability to close these gaps and form a narrative about themselves that is more mature, intelligible, and purposeful (Strupp & Binder, 1984) is dependent on their willingness to be accountable as both author and actor in their stories. This involves critiquing the plots and genres (e.g., tragedy, comedy, drama) by which they narrate their experiences and live their lives, individuate in relation to the larger narratives in which they operate, and experiment with new authoring stances in support of their growth (Hillman, 1975b; Randall, 1995). In this sense, narrative coaching is an existential and ontological practice designed to increase people's ability to claim their authorship and align it with what they are trying to accomplish.

The more that coachees can do this, the more freedom they will experience, the more mature they will become, and the more opportunities to serve they will create. This is true for coaches and their formulation as well. Interestingly, there is often a strong parallel between their respective processes in coaching as each is formed in part by the stories of the other. For example, their stories coalesce around a frame of the coachee as a "victim" in a mutually reinforcing loop. Conversely, the coachee comes to a place where she releases that frame and rebuffs the coach's efforts to continue down that path. As coaches, our aim is not for people to simply replace one story with another, but to invite them to "participate in the continuous process of creating and transforming meaning" (K. J. Gergen, 1994, p. 245). We can help them become more adept and accountable in doing so by mindfully attending to our own formulation. This is particularly important in creating moments of meeting in coaching sessions when the need for mutual regulation and learning is highest.

Understanding Formulation

Beware of the stories you tell yourself—for you will
surely be lived by them. | adapted from William Shakespeare

Formulation traditionally referred to the diagnostic stories that professionals, such as therapists and doctors, formed as *experts at a distance* in the course of their work. However, we will look at formulation as *expertise in relationship* when seen from a narrative and coaching perspective. It is our explanatory accounts of what is happening in coaching, why it is this way, what we should say and do in response, and what we believe will happen as a result. While the focus here is on the coach, formulations are also influenced by the stories coachees tell themselves about being coached, the stories the two of them co-create in and across sessions, and the stories of stakeholders about the process. Formulation is ultimately a shared and symbiotic framework of understanding that has major implications for the trajectory and efficacy of coaching. It needs to be done systemically because the stories they each bring to coaching are inseparable from the context around them (Boje, 1998; Rossiter, 1999). The coachee and the coach are in a co-constructive process in the moment and across the engagement in which their two narrative worlds temporarily intersect (McMahon & Patton, 2006).

Formulation is a process that can be observed in the moment and reflected on after the fact to help us develop ourselves and our practices. As Kierkegaard noted, our life is lived forward—encounter by encounter— but our sense of ourselves and what we are doing and saying is constructed in retrospect. It is only when we tell a story that we "retrace forward what we have already traced backward" (Ricouer, 1984, p. 87). This requires coaches to be critically aware of their own systems of influence and how these play out in the coaching process, to develop the discipline to continuously monitor their internal and external narration, and to be curious about the stories their coachees are telling themselves about what is going on. I find Casement's (1991) question helpful in this regard as a reminder of the collaborative nature of formulation: "Who is putting what into the . . . space, at this moment, and why?" (p. 27). We use the image of a bird circling a tree in narrative coaching to remind ourselves to check in on where we have arrived in the conversation and why.

Before introducing the narrative formulation framework, let's look at the more traditional approach as a point of comparison. Louis Cozolino (2004) identified four tools that are typically used to guide therapeutic practice: theoretical orientation, case conceptualization, treatment plan, and case notes—each of which shapes the one that follows. Case conceptualization serves as the traditional frame for formulation and includes "(1) a description of presenting problems, symptoms, and possible diagnoses; (2) a theory or theories accounting for how and why the problems have arisen and evolved over time; and (3) a general description of how problems are addressed and cured" (p. 35). This classic approach to formulation is useful to a point as a way of structuring one's thinking as a coach, but it focuses too much on the need for the coach to understand as the basis for progress. I would suggest that a more complete model would also account for the emergent and eclectic nature of our formulations, the connections to forces outside the coaching conversations that shape the process, and the fact that coachees are formulating both personally and mutually as well.

This calls for moving beyond the traditional notions of formulation as the detached prognosis of the expert upon which decisions are made about how best to proceed. To be clear, it is about expanding and repositioning the role of expertise, not banishing it from the conversation. A narrative approach to formulation de-emphasizes the coach's analysis and assessment as the primary sources for formulation to make more space for the coachee's experience and guidance from the narrative material as it emerges. Formulation is always a "work in progress." A first step in making more conscious and attuned choices in your formulation as a coach is to recognize your reactions and actions in sessions—and reflect on the stories on which they are based. Where are your comfort zones? What are your habits? Your blindspots? How do you tend to participate in the stories coachees tell you? What we are aiming for with our formulation is to provide enough structure and direction for the coaching conversation without overly imposing our own frames or needs.

Narrative formulation incorporates the same three elements as the case conceptualization method, but it does so with more equity and fluidity. Most importantly, it shifts the emphasis from coaches and their professional discourse and methods to coachees and their psychosocial discourse and narratives. As a result, it helps practitioners to address four of the limitations with traditional notions of formulation and their tendency to (1) privilege professional expertise; (2) overemphasize the past; (3) simplify causality; and (4) take a mechanistic view. It does so by offering an approach to formulation that (1) draws on multiple sources of expertise; (2) incorporates the past, present, and future; (3) presumes various streams of causality; and (4) takes a holistic view. Formulation is a dynamic and mutual process of discovering what seems true and workable in coaching conversations as a platform for change. It is embedded *in* rather than detached *from* the shared experience in sessions; it is a continually and reciprocally co-constructed process; and progress is not exclusively dependent on diagnosis.

> Formulation is a dynamic and mutual process of discovering what seems true and workable in coaching conversations as a platform for change.

Let us look at a brief case synopsis with this view of formulation in mind. Before you read the following description of a brief encounter with a potential coachee, imagine for a minute that it is *your* phone that is ringing. How would you feel? What comes up for you? What would you most likely say and do? Why?

EXAMPLE

Robert, a quiet, middle-aged man, calls your office saying that he may be interested in working with you as a coach. He has tried for six months to get a new job but, even with his credentials, he has yet to find one. Being out of work has created friction with his wife, and he has noticed a lack of energy lately. However, he is also adamant that he doesn't need to "see a shrink" because he knows that all he needs is to find a new job. In speaking with him, you get a sense that he may be somewhat depressed. You ponder whether to take him on as a coachee or refer him to someone else.

As you ponder, the formulation process has already begun. You and Robert are each forming an initial story about the other and already deciding, albeit largely unconsciously, whether or not to work together. However, at this point, what do you or Robert really understand about why he can't find work, what he truly needs, and how best to serve him? What stories have you already make up about him? About how you would coach him? How were these influenced by your background, training, approach, and/or life experience?

In the end, you are left with questions such as:

- Is his issue a deeply personal one—best addressed by a psychotherapist?

- Did his wife stop having sex with him when he lost his job—best addressed by a couples' counselor?

- Is his skill set no longer marketable in his area—best addressed by a recruiter to help him relocate?

- Does he need broader help on vision setting and goal attainment—best addressed by a life coach?

- Is he having an existential midlife crisis—best addressed by a spiritual director?

And this is for just one of the facets of the presenting story; it does not address the possibilities related to what is perceived as depression, for example. Even with this small anecdote, we can see some of the issues related to formulation and a reminder to not rush in with our interpretations as coaches. The aim is to align your formulation as the coach with the process unfolding in the session and the formulation of the coachee—and all in a generative direction.

I use the following formulation model in teaching this work to professionals around the world. It is based in the same four-phase structure as the coaching model to reflect the need for a coach's formulation to stay in sync with a coachee's developmental journey. It requires paying close attention to both people's internal and external narration as well as its impact on the session and the outcomes for the coachee. See if you can focus on what is actually happening in the coaching conversation rather than your beliefs about where it should be going and why. Page (1999) provides a wonderful description of the spirit of this approach:

> The path is one of mindfulness more than a master plan, seeking clarity more than certainty. Formulation is less about providing expert judgment and more about increasing the collective ability among coaches and coachees to notice what is going on, the stories they are telling themselves and others about it, and the possibility for new options at both the narrative and behavioral levels. (p. 58)

Using a Narrative Approach to Formulation

Narrative formulation is as much a call to continuous self-reflection and self-regulation as it is a guide for your professional narration. Your efficacy as a coach is affected by your ability to do both as you make sense of what is happening in sessions and how to respond accordingly. Most coachees appreciate having a clear frame for their sessions because it offers them a sense of safety and a structure to guide them as they tell their stories. At the same time, these frames can interfere with where they and their stories want to go if they are adhered to rigidly. In part, this is why I focus on the relational field rather than a linear process and on patterns as well as particulars in people's stories. As I wrote:

> Many of our challenges in formulation are a result of the tension between remaining stable and compliant within the professional, commercial, and regulatory demands of the systems in which we and our coachees operate *and* being flexible and responsive in light of the evolving demands of the [conversations,] contexts and cultures in which we and our coachees operate. (Corrie, Drake, & Lane, 2010, p. 323)

We are wired as humans to recognize patterns as guides for our listening (e.g., this is a grief story, a bad boss story, a victim story). However, these cognitive shortcuts may or may not match the intent of the narrator or her development needs. This is why formulation is an ongoing process of course correction—a dance of leading and following—in which you are encouraged to be deeply focused *and* profoundly open. Hold your formulations lightly as people's stories begin because you can seldom be sure where they are headed. Otherwise, it is too easy to either get trapped in a storyline that precludes the path the coachee actually wanted to take with their story or prematurely locks in a particular formulation. Notice your formulation patterns in sessions and reflect on them in real time and over time so you can stay fresh and make conscious choices as often as possible. For example, out of your desire for closure, do you tend to seek a resolution for every issue coachees bring to coaching and do so as soon as you spot a potential and viable solution? If this is the case, how can you adjust your formulation process in order to remain more open when that is called for?

Any formulations you make as you coach will inevitably privilege some questions and trajectories more than others. The key is to develop yourself using the *Three Windows* at the end of this chapter so you can be more present, agile, and masterful in using knowledge and evidence in your formulation. Be conscious as you coach and reflect on your choices such that your formulation stays attuned to what is *actually* happening and what is called for next. One way you can become more aware of any unhelpful formulation habits is to observe what happens in moments of silence in sessions and in gaps in coachees' narration. It is in those moments when we are most tempted to intervene in the storyline in accordance with our preferred tales about what should happen. Another pattern to watch out for is smoothing out the rough edges of coachees' stories so as to make the formulation process more manageable for everyone involved. It is similar to the difference between the way we see ourselves in the mirror (smoothed by our brain) and the way we often look in candid photos.

Narrative medicine practitioners (see Charon, 2006; Kleinman, 1988) have wrestled with these tensions between professional discourse and personal experience in their formulation, identified the narrative differences between providers and consumers of health care, and advocated for a more collaborative approach. As Haidet and Paterniti (2003) noted:

> The physician's perspective may exclude crucial patient-oriented data necessary to achieve therapeutic effectiveness. The patient's perspective may miss critical biomedical facts needed for accurate diagnosis. Physicians need a method of fostering efficient sharing of critical biomedical and patient-specific information necessary for both [the] biomedical management of disease and [the] therapeutic healing of illness. (p. 1135)

There is a lot we can learn from their research and practice in terms of seeing formulation as a co-constructed process in which there is continuous interpretation, translation, negotiation, and calibration in both directions. Since most of it is nearly instantaneous and tacit, it is helpful from time to time throughout your coaching sessions to verbalize what you think is going on to make sure that you and the coachee are still on the same page.

At the same time, it is important to remember that there are no "right" or "perfect" formulations. Every formulation captures some portion of the reality of what is happening and yields results of some sort. What seems most productive is when the coachee and coach are working in tandem around a shared narrative about what is happening and where they should head. Sometimes the coach invites the coachee into a new formulation to make the most of a "teachable moment"; while at other times the coachee leads the way by reframing or refocusing the conversation in a direction that fits better for her. Formulation is an ongoing process during and between sessions that creates a sense of shared direction and offers shared markers along the way. It is analogous to the "ducks" that hikers make out of stacked stones to indicate a route through the wilderness where there is no formal trail. In your coaching, balance the need for a coherent formulation that supports safety and security with the need for an emergent formulation that fosters experimentation and adaptation.

> Balance the need for a coherent formulation that supports safety and security with the need for an emergent formulation that fosters experimentation and adaptation.

The key question to ask as a coach is, "To what degree are the stories you are telling yourself about their situations leading to actions that are yielding valued, positive results for your coachees?" The secret is to not get too far ahead with your formulation by assuming you know where coachees or their stories are headed *or* how they could or should get there. You can use the narrative formulation framework below to guide you in the process and gather the knowledge and evidence you will need along the way. It will help you notice more closely how you are tracking and intervening in coachee's stories as they are being told.

You can use this framework before, during, and after a coaching session to create, reflect on, and adapt your formulations. It is also quite handy as a guide for identifying key opportunities for your own development. For example, you might notice that your tendencies sometimes lead you to move toward resolution or action before the issue is sufficiently understood or the coachee is ready. What would you need to be able to pause? You can also use it in comparing notes with your coachees about what is happening or has happened in their session to enhance your working relationship with them. The four phases of the narrative formulation process are listed below along with the classic formulation question related to each one.

TOOL

> ### The Narrative Formulation Process:
>
> 1. *Situate:* What story am I telling myself about this Person and her situation? *(This is what I think is going on.)*
>
> 2. *Search:* What story am I telling myself about the Purpose of this conversation? *(This is what I think caused it.)*
>
> 3. *Shift:* What story am I telling myself about what needs to Pivot or change? *(This is what I think we should do about it and why.)*
>
> 4. *Sustain:* What story am I telling myself about her Progress? *(This is what I think will happen as a result?)*

EXAMPLE: CASE STORY

1. **Situate:** What story am I telling myself about this Person and her situation?

   Sally* was a middle-aged female manager and a long-time supervisor in a program serving low-income families. She had volunteered to be coached in front of the group during an internal coaching skills workshop I was running. Her presenting issue was that she wanted help buying a car after months of no resolution but lots of trips to dealer showrooms.

   <u>Key question for myself</u>: Is my formulation supporting a useful and respectful frame for the conversation?

   <u>Reflections</u>: This seemed like an important personal decision for her. I avoided the temptation to move into problem-solving mode (which assumed she needed my help in making this decision) or focus on the decision itself (that we were there to talk about cars). Instead, I engaged her at the Person level to start our conversation. I encouraged her to be her own expert about herself and a full participant in our formulation of the

Situation. As we proceeded, she gained more clarity about herself and her stories.

2. **Search:** What story am I telling myself about the Purpose of this conversation?

After a few questions, I had a clear sense that she did not need help researching what car to buy (she had narrowed it down to two), how to negotiate with the salespeople (she was quite strong here), or if/how to make this large purchase (she had saved the money). Acting on a sense of what was not being said about why we were here, I asked her what kind of car she wanted to buy. She responded, "A BMW or Chevrolet." I responded that she was considering two very different cars, and I was curious how she came to those two options.

Key question for myself: Is my formulation enabling us to explore in places that seem important and generative?

Reflections: My sense was that deciding which car to buy was not the real story here or the path that would lead to a sense of resolution for her. As a result, I began to formulate a different story that drew on the past (her history), the present (a values crunch), and the future (her desire). I used my experience in working with dualities in narratives to invite her to talk about her two choices—and the stories that went with them—as part of the Search to figure out what was really at stake for her. My sense was that this would lead her to discover what would enable her to choose.

3. **Shift:** What story am I telling myself about what needs to Pivot or change?

I soon discovered that her husband wanted her to buy the Chevrolet because it was practical and it was what they were used to in their lives. However, she let it slip that she secretly wanted the BMW. In unpacking this story, I learned that her kids were now off on their own, and she had driven the same station wagon for a long time to haul them around. She became aware that, for the first time in her marriage, she wanted to buy something just for herself. She had worked hard for a long time and saved the money for the car.

I invited her to unpack the associations she had with the two options. I was able to use my knowledge of her organization and profession in exploring her dilemma and what would help her break through to a decision. The Chevrolet was consistent with the story of her life thus far. I sensed that this decision was ultimately about a turning point in her life, not just a car.

Moving deeper, I asked her why she didn't just buy the BMW. I received some fumbling responses at first. So, I invited her to close her eyes, take a few deep breaths, and then visualize driving the BMW to work. Tears formed in her eyes as she talked about pulling up to visit one of her low-income client families.

She couldn't see herself getting out of the car, so I asked her to close her eyes again and just imagine sitting there for a moment in the gravel driveway in front of their home. In the precious silence that followed, I invited her to consider the possibility that once she could see herself driving up in the BMW and getting out to see this family, she would buy that car.

Key question for myself: Is my formulation aligning to the new possibilities that are emerging for the coachee?

Reflections: She got to a place where she could begin seeing herself as someone who could buy a BMW and stay within her values. I used my awareness of the values issues in play to invite her to Shift her frame by rising above the literal choice of cars to make her decision at another level. Paradoxically, this made it easier for her to decide what car to buy (and why). A big part of this came through inviting her to viscerally experience her desired choice in order to identify and address the key obstacle for her. As a result, she began to see herself as someone who could care for herself as well as she cared for others.

4. **Sustain:** What story am I telling myself about her Progress on the desired outcome?

A few months after our program she wrote to let me know what she had decided. As I suspected, she bought the BMW. She still drove her old station wagon from time to time, but otherwise proudly enjoyed her new car. In the end, it was not about the possession, but the freedom she experienced in putting herself first—for what seemed like the first time in her life. She had worked hard to make that moment possible.

<u>Key question for myself</u>: Is my formulation equipping the coachee to take it from here?

<u>Reflections</u>: My knowledge of the cultural and class complexities at play was useful in helping her find a sense of peace with her decision. If coachees are to Sustain the changes and choices that emerge in coaching, they need to take the "baton" when they are done because it is their race to run not ours. She used the guided visualization in our session as a reminder about what this decision meant to her as she moved forward.

Improving Your Formulation

In narrative coaching, we look beyond the traditional bias for specialized professional knowledge to make room for other forms of knowledge that are essential for a conscious and comprehensive approach to formulation. These include research guidance, practice experience, client experience, local context knowledge, and professional knowledge in working with people (Rycroft-Malone et al., 2004). It is not about searching for the "correct" diagnosis or the perfect formulation, but rather about engaging in a mutual and mindful process with coachees around what to do next and why. Lane and Corrie (2006) made a similar observation that coaching is a "radically unpredictable, almost iterative process in which the next step is informed, in large part, by the conditions immediately preceding it" (p. 155). This requires you to track the formulation as it unfolds, both in each moment and across the conversation, in terms of how well it is serving the coachee and her process. This is why narrative formulation is seen as a collaborative process that guides the stories that coaches and coachees tell themselves about what is happening in a coaching session, what they think that means, what they should do about it, and what they think will happen as a result.

> In the end, it is about their journey, not our jargon.

As a coach, it is a dance between using what you know so you can coach with confidence and moving toward the unknown so you stay attuned to what is emerging. Sometimes this means inviting coachees to explore their stories and use the material in them, and sometimes it means inviting them to move outside their stories to explore the larger narratives or other possibilities. It all depends on which would most benefit a coachee where he is right now in the broader arc of his development and progress. In the end, it is about their journey, not our jargon. Either way, learn to be comfortable with silence and listen into the gaps for what is not being said rather than rushing their narration or your formulation. The reward for doing so is often the discovery of the real agenda for change that will only surface when the "field" and the person is ready. In the end, it is about being fully present to yourself, your coachees, and the narratives in play as well as formulating with a duty of care for people and their stories. People tell us stories in coaching in hopes that we will "meet" them, heal them, and enable them to make the changes they are seeking.

Implications for Your Practice

To be aware and disciplined in your formulations, ask yourself:

- "What story am I in?" (Mattingly, 1998, p. 72). What role(s) am I playing and how are these affecting the coachee's narration, interaction, and action in this session? What assumptions do I unconsciously make as a listener that may alter people's storytelling? What do I miss or disallow as a result?

- "In what ways do I steer their storytelling into my preferred frames and language in an attempt to reduce my own anxiety, stay within my loyalties and cater to my strengths? What are the acceptable shapes of a life that I . . . find myself promoting?" (Phillips, 1994, p. 70).

- "To what extent do my formulations remain within the confines of the 'received view' of what is acceptable, and to what extent do they challenge prevailing ideas about legitimate explanations?" (Corrie et al., 2010, p. 325).

- "What factors in the session inhibit certain selves and certain versions of a life story and activate others?" (M. Gergen & Davis, 2005, p. 243). What are the constraints from the environment, our working relationship, the construct of 'coaching' itself?

What are your key insights?
What will you experiment with first?

CHAPTER 6

HOW WE CHANGE AND TRANSITION

In performance training, first we learn to flow with whatever comes.
Then we learn to use whatever comes to our advantage.
Finally, we learn to be completely self-sufficient and create our own
earthquakes, so our mental process feeds itself explosive inspiration without
the need for outside stimulus. | *Josh Waitzkin*

Sometimes we change because our stories change. Sometimes our stories change because we have changed. The two processes are deeply interwoven, which is why this chapter has been moved into this section for this edition. In either case, narrative coaching is designed to guide people through the transitions that are required. People come to coaching because they want to change something in themselves, their life, and/or their work. Sometimes they think they know what they want, but often they are surprised by what emerges as important to them in the course of coaching. One thing that is certain is that it will inevitably involve change and transition.

A transition is an internal process related to, but neither synonymous nor necessarily concurrent with, change as an external event. Either of them can be the trigger for the other, and it is often our stories about them that matter most in terms of how we fare. For example, the same change can happen to a group of people (e.g., their team is disbanded), but they may have very different experiences of the transition and responses to the change. In this chapter we will look at the rites of passage framework and how it is used in narrative coaching as well as the centrality of thresholds in the narrative coaching process. In so doing, we will highlight the fact that the Narrative Coaching method is unique in that it is organized around the change process not a coaching structure.

Narrative coaching is a semi-structured process in which you can use people's own stories to help them move through transitions and bring about desired changes. It involves both parties slowing down in order to move ahead and not trying so hard to change in order to actually change. The focus is on their presence in the here and now—to themselves, each other, and the narrative process—with a clear intention but no agenda. At first this may not seem like it is enough. However, in due course people come to realize they can make more progress by focusing on one shift or decision at a time—after which they will have a much clearer line of sight on what is next. This focuses their energy and enables them to self-regulate more readily so they can learn more fully and notice more readily any opportunities for practice. Narrative coaching works because it mirrors the phases that people naturally go through as they change and transition. It is a parallel process, though not always concurrent or linear, in which the experience itself is often as healing as the content. The narrative coaching process is designed to serve as a rite of passage to guide people from one story to another in order to achieve what is being asked of them or sought by them.

Understanding Rites of Passage

Those who do not regularly shed their psychological skin in order to become new again become old before their time. Death-rebirth rituals allow us to reemerge in the present, free to perceive without the veil of personal history that may dull your perceptions and keep you from detecting the road ahead. | *Mikela & Philip Tarlow*

The roots of narrative coaching's approach to change and transition can be found in van Gennep's (1960) work on rites of passage, Turner's (1969) work on applying this model more broadly, and Campbell's (1973) work on the hero's journey. Arthur van Gennep studied a number of communal ceremonies accompanying people's "life crises" (e.g., birth, initiation, marriage, death), and he came to call them *rites de passage*. One of the primary functions of a rite of passage as a cultural practice was to guide people through important and/or cyclical transitions in their personal or communal lives using ritualized processes and resources. He distinguished three phases these practices had in common: separation, transition (from a French word meaning "margin"), and incorporation. The three phases involved both external changes (e.g., state, role, status) and internal transitions (e.g., identity, orientation, attitude) in ways that were both complementary (ensuring continuity) and contrary (enabling challenge). These rites codified natural processes of life, death, and rebirth that were present everywhere. As Turner (1979) later noted, "The first phase detaches the ritual subjects from their old places in society; the last installs them, inwardly transformed and outwardly changed in a new place in society" (p. 149).

> Narrative coaching is about slowing down in order to move ahead, and not trying so hard to change in order to actually change.

Early on Van Gennep (1960) used territorial and spatial terms in developing his framework; it is from this perspective that the view of passages as crossing thresholds took hold. The thresholds in the model below (separation, transition, and reincorporation) represent the movement from the outer world to the inner world and back as people leave behind one role or status and prepare to take on a new one. The term "liminal" is used to describe the transition phase as "betwixt and between," and it comes from the Latin "limins" in referring to the threshold or boundary between two separate places. In this case, it speaks to the fact that the person who is being guided through a rite of passage has left the profane space but has not yet re-emerged in the profane space—having been transformed by the liminal experience in sacred space. I have placed the elements of his framework in the following classic depiction along with Eliade's (1959) distinction between profane and sacred spaces. It is important to remember here that each phase in the process is essential and none are more privileged. As Moody (1997) notes, "Breakthrough is not the goal of spiritual journeying. It is simply one of the stages" (p. 335).

FIGURE II: RITES OF PASSAGE MODEL (CLASSIC)

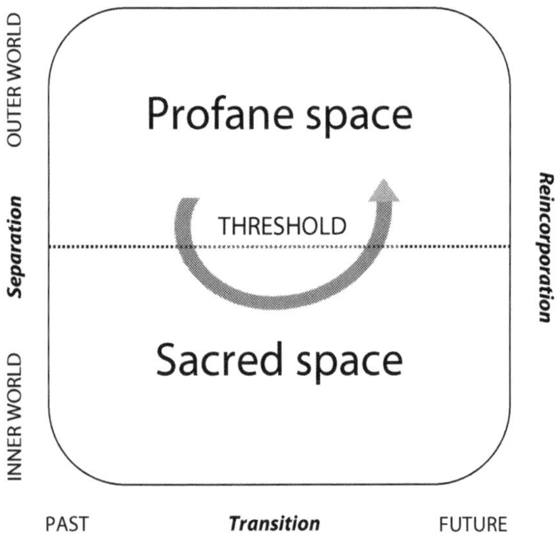

Zadra (1984) offers a clear description of what happens in a rite of initiation or passage:

> In this first phase, which is one of separation, symbolic behaviour demarcates the sacred from the profane and indicates the detachment of the ritual subjects from their previous social statuses. During the next phase of transition or limen, the ritual subjects pass through a period and area of ambiguity with reference to the social structure, in which few of the features of the preceding and subsequent profane statuses or cultural sates are present. The symbolic phenomena and actions of the final

phase of reaggregation or reincorporation represent the return of the subjects to newly defined positions in society. (p. 84)

Victor Turner (1967) recognized that these rites and practices were not confined to culturally defined life crises but could also be used to describe any significant change from one state to another. Turner (1969) also observed that decisions to perform a rite or ritual were often connected with a crisis in the social life of a village and served as a container for the structural and anti-structural energies that were stirred up as a result. Rites of passage provided the means to manage the paradoxical requirements of individual and social development: structure and anti-structure, elevation and subversion, transition and continuity. However, they only had power as long as they were vital and imbued with a current mythology as a coherent system of narratives that is shared and meaningful within the system (Petriglieri & Petriglieri, 2010). This is why it is important to place people's aspirations and stories in a broader narrative context if they are to bring about change. For some people it entails a deeper connection with a broader narrative (e.g., reclaiming part of their heritage), while for others it entails a looser connection (e.g., redefining their relationship with their heritage).

Rituals of passage reflect the larger rhythms of nature (Gluckman, 1962); they make visible the natural pattern of dying, chaos, and renewal that operates everywhere in the universe. Van Gennep (1960) saw this regenerative flow as a law of life in which the energy in a system runs down and must be renewed at intervals. One of the challenges many of us face in moving through change and transitions now is that we have lost touch with these natural cycles. Another issue is that these ceremonies were designed to "enable the individual to pass from one defined position to another which is equally well defined" (van Gennep, 1960, p. 3). We frequently coach people who are seeking to make passages into positions that are not yet known and/or defined. This is part of a larger issue we face in coaching in that more of life feels liminal, traditional passages feel less stable, and the future is arriving with greater uncertainty but at a faster pace. Narrative coaching seeks to address these issues by providing a safe passage for people seeking to make changes in their life and/or work. We often end up inviting people to "stop their habitual ways of seeing life and open the[ir] psyche to a greater view of the world and their place in it"(Meade, 2006, p. 147).

Narrative coaching is a developmental methodology through which people can make shifts in their identities and perspectives using their own stories and, as a result, resolve their issues at a number of levels. Because narrative coaching is seen as a rite of passage, we work with both sacred and profane spaces, personal and collective narratives, and conscious and nonconscious dynamics in people's stories. Carotenuto (1985) intimately describes why this type of work is essential for these times, particularly for those people who are seeking transformative change:

> Anyone who undertakes [this journey], even or especially if he has been driven to his knees by suffering and necessity and initially unaware of what awaits him, chooses the path of deep awareness, which in itself is already a heroic act. . . . A withdrawal of energy from the outside world is also necessary, and for this a certain price must always be paid. (p. 45)

Narrative coaching has deep roots in disciplines related to critical consciousness and, as a result, is designed to help coaches, coachees and coaching itself to address important issues related to change and development, such as:

- Developing post-professional practitioners who are not identified by a singular profession—e.g., they can work across boundaries in an integrative manner (Drake, 2014).

- Defining adult development in more relational and collective terms— e.g., separation is not the only path to individuation (O'Reilley, 1998.)

- Understanding gender differences in how we conceptualize narratives—e.g., both connection and conflict are emphasized (Nicolopoulou, 2008).

- Developing contemporary rites of passage using more inclusive and ecological frames—e.g., growth is no longer only seen as the result of a crusade (Bynum, 1984).

Coaching as a Rite of Passage

All changes, even the most longed for, have their melancholy; for what
we leave behind is part of ourselves; we must die to one life before we can enter
another. | *Anatole France*

For most of human history, our survival has been dependent on an intimate understanding of our environment. It is no surprise, then, that many of our rituals are patterned after the rhythms in nature. With the increasing presence of technology in our lives, many of us are less attuned to the environment and our place in it. Instead, we live more of our lives through our screens. Part of the impetus for developing narrative coaching was to provide a way for people to reconnect with their humanity and these larger rhythms of life. It provides a powerful frame for doing so and brings together ancient wisdom with postmodern realities. However, I realized that some finer distinctions were necessary if I wanted to get the most from rites of passage as a framework for coaching. In particular, there was a need to add a vertical axis to the classic framework as a way to acknowledge:

- The movement through time between the past and the future.

- The changing needs as one moved through the liminal phase.

- The fact that transitions were occurring in each phase, albeit in different ways.

- The thresholds between each of the four phases, each with its own role in the passage.

- Sacred spaces are brought into play in relation to a particular situation not just to address collective issues.

- We return "home" a different person on a different mission than when we began.

- Integration and consolidation are vital parts of the process, without which the change/transitions are less likely to stick and have impact.

FIGURE 12: RITES OF PASSAGE MODEL (ENHANCED)

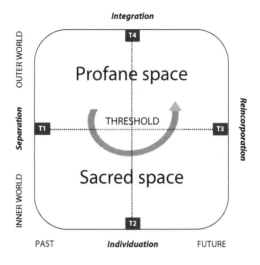

This addition provides an enhanced perspective on the rites of passage framework, a useful way to map where people are in terms of their transitions, and the skeleton for the narrative coaching model. Each of the four Ts in the figure above indicates a threshold between two phases. Individuation is now positioned as a liminal process in which we are moving from one narrative to another as we grow. Development and change are seen as a natural human process of evolution, and coaching is seen as a useful resource for guiding people through change, particularly in periods of "punctuated equilibrium." Narrative coaching is designed to enable people to make real change in real time through adapting their relationship between their inner and outer narratives. It provides a process within which they can address both their profane and sacred issues as they move through the cycle.

This aligns with work by other writers on transitions, such as William Bridges (2001) who identified four types of natural endings people often experience in a change process: disengagement, disidentification, disenchantment, and disorientation. In the midst of change, a person may *disengage* from the world as she knew it in order to *separate*, *disidentify* with whom she thought she was in order to *individuate*, become *disenchanted* until she breaks through the spell or veil in order to *reincorporate*, and feel *disoriented* until she can settle into her new story in order to *integrate*. Change often brings with it the loss of an old identity, an in-between time that is neither here nor there, and the formation and integration of a new identity. Rites are important here because they provide a safe yet challenging structure for the energy that is in motion so people can successfully complete their passage. Narrative coaching is designed to guide people through the ritual actions they need to bring about the change they are seeking using their own stories. This works because stories that are located and shared in ritual actions take on special therapeutic powers (Mattingly, 1998), particularly at thresholds in our lives.

Rites of passage involve movement through four phases, marked by the crossing of four distinct thresholds:

- *Separation* from the outer world to embark on a journey into the inner world to undergo a transformation in one's identity and narrative.
- *Individuation* as one overcomes obstacles to transit the inner world in search of what will bring restoration and maturation.
- *Re-incorporation* as one leaves the inner world to return to the outer world with what has been gained through exploration and experimentation.
- *Integration* of the transformation into a new identity and narrative in the outer world, often with subsequent changes in relating to the environment.

As we will explore later in the chapter, thresholds represent powerful developmental moments and processes for people. It is here they can release *from* what no longer serves them and release *into* what is possible now in terms of how they see themselves, tell their stories, and live their lives. Thresholds 1 and 3 in the model are important for people's development in relation to the world, with a focus at T1 on their internally focused deconstruction and a focus at T3 on their externally focused reconstruction. Thresholds 2 and 4 are important for people's development in relation to themselves, with a focus at T2 on their internal authenticity and a focus at T4 on their external accountability. T1 is often a release of who others think we are (in order to separate); T2 is often a release of who we think we are (in order to individuate); T3 is often a release of how we think we need to be (in order to reincorporate); and T4 is often a release of what we think we are supposed to do (in order to integrate). The following explores in more depth what happens for coachees as they separate, move through liminal space, and reincorporate. The chapter closes with a look at thresholds in the narrative coaching process, how they contribute to change, and your role as a guardian to ensure a safe passage.

Separation

Transitions, just like stories, begin because something has changed or wants to be changed. Separation marks the departure from one's current situation (with its identities, roles, status, narratives, etc.), and signals the intent to seek out a new one. These points of separation can be chosen intentionally (e.g., a marriage or a new job), emerge disruptively (e.g., a break-up or a layoff) or happen biologically (e.g., a coming of age or a retirement). At the start of a rite of passage, initiates would traditionally be ritually separated from the social group that had defined their cultural role and identity; taken to a special and usually secluded place (Turner, 1967); and the loss would be literally and symbolically marked. The purpose of this phase was to accentuate, sometimes quite starkly, the boundary between the two worlds such that it was undeniably clear there was no return. Unfortunately, many people these days lack sufficient support structures for this phase or clarity about what is next. To paraphrase Tennessee Williams, the *Separation* phase is still a time for departure even when there's not yet a certain place to go.

This first threshold marks the departure from the profane space as the person knew it and the entry into the unknown of the sacred space. This space is collectively sacred relative to the person's profane world and individually sacred relative to the profane aspects of the person. This crossing often includes the dissolution of old stories and senses of oneself —often through a ritual wounding or engaging with existing wounds. As Michael Meade (2006) has written, "Initiation leaves certain wounds and scars that mark a person specifically as who they are and where in life they have been. . . . the wound that makes him limp a bit is his passport for crossing between the daily world and the otherworld" (p. 305). We can see the connection between our wounds and our healing in the fact that the word "blessing" comes from *blesure*, a French word that means "wound." The doorway to what we seek is often in a place we might otherwise avoid. "We each seek a blessing exactly where a wound waits; we each become wounded exactly where we seek to be blessed" (Meade, 2006, p. 60).

A key role for coaches is to help people increase their window of tolerance so they can *be* with their anxiety long enough to imagine there is blessing in the wound. In the process, the coachee begins to let go of the "attitudes to which he clings for safety, of the perspectives which these attitudes give him on the world, and of the familiar labels for what he sees in the world" (Schachtel, 1959, p. 195). Critical questions for coachees at this juncture include: "What am I leaving behind? What is it time to let go of ? What in me is dying or must die to make room for what wants to be born?" When people separate from their familiar patterns of self-organization—and their tidy distinctions, such as "I am this, not that," come apart—they are often left wondering who they "really" are.

The ties of meaning that once linked them with everyday life—and to which they were accustomed—are now stretched or even severed (Deegan & Hill, 1991). Separation is often marked by breakdowns and a sense of regression as people step back to reconsider their identities and their lives. As with all thresholds, this work brings coachees into contact with internal and external forces that are often greater than they expect. In moving beyond the comfort zone of their familiar narratives, they encounter elements of their personal and collective Shadows, their own divided wishes, and countervailing narratives around them. However, it is through this proverbial fire that the true nature of the transition crystallizes and the direction of the work to be done becomes clear.

Your role as a coach is to strengthen the working relationship and the quality of the "field" so that coachees feel safe enough to embark on this journey. Once they can quiet the grasping of their egos, they will be able to attend to the essential inner work ahead. This enables them to develop greater trust in themselves, the process, and the allies they will meet along the way—and, ultimately, to take more existential responsibility for their own choices (Raff, 2000). As a result, they can more unflinchingly yet compassionately see the truth and reality that is before them. The less willing they are to surrender, the less they will see—and the more they will continue to suffer. As the knights discovered in their search for the Holy Grail, each coachee must enter the "forest" at a point where it is darkest for her and with the recognition that there is ultimately no map. Even if there was a map, they are only useful "if (a) you are able to locate your position, and (b) if you have a sense of your destination" (Paris, 2011, p. 63)—neither of which is often the case as people start on their journey. This is why, as the great myths have shown, people will go astray if they attempt to follow someone else's path. As James Hollis (2004) once said, "Their individuation task has already been accomplished. Our duty is to risk living our lives as fully as they have risked living their truths" (p. 61).

In understanding the role of suffering in *Separation,* it is important to remember Jung's view that our psyche is by nature continuously moving towards wholeness. For example, when our psyche calls out for a change, it often takes away something we truly value to force us to go in search of fuller consciousness. Therefore, "sit" with people as they begin their descent rather than rushing to make it all go away. As Paris (2007) observes:

> Moments of great suffering usually signal that the old self needs to die, and because it is painful, we are tempted to look for quick solutions, buying into the common illusion that every psychological "problem" calls for a positive "solution." Yet, this well-intentioned approach increases the suffering because it ignores one of the great paradoxes of psychological wisdom: the activation of the death principle has more power than anything

else in the psyche. The destructive impulse can be crucial if we are to get rid of what oppresses us. (p. xii)

Once people move through these "deaths" in the process of *Separation*, they find themselves in the liminal phase—and the search begins to restore what they have lost and awaken to what they most desire.

Individuation (as a Liminal Process)

A mode of entrance is crucial. A door. A window. A chink in the otherwise unbroken surface of what we consider real and proper. | *Thomas Moore*

The work on rites of passage emerged from the fields of sociology and anthropology. By using this frame in narrative coaching we can align these fields with psychology and adult development to form a unified process of change. Nowhere is this more pronounced than in connecting the liminal state (in which the person undergoing a social rite of passage has left one status but has not yet reached the new one) with the process of individuation (in which a person has left behind one level of maturity and capability, but has not yet settled into the new one). These parallels are important in narrative coaching as they provide the foundation for working with people and their stories to make the desired changes. This section builds on the work in chapters two and three, but focuses on the role of liminality in a rite of passage to offer insights you can use with your coachees as they seek to grow. It will increase your understanding of how to guide clients through this in-between phase in their development such that they emerge on the other side with clarity about what they want.

Arthur van Gennep saw the middle phase as the transition between the profane and sacred worlds (and back again), and he portrayed it as both a process and a state of its own. It is the ultimate "both/and," an extended and ambiguous state of "in-between-ness" (McNamara, Roberts, Basit, & Brown, 2002). Carson (1997) described the liminal state as a "place of sacred time and space, set apart and separated, the locus of revelation" (p. 11). It can be seen as a container that holds the primal energies people encounter in this phase (Ramsay, 1997) and offers them a new perspective on lives and stories once taken for granted. T

This container must be strong enough to hold all that is stirred up without getting blown away or over-inflated and discerning enough so the purification process is focused on what is real and essential. Other characteristics of this in-between space include: a profound sense of ambiguity, confusion, and uncertainty; a loss of power, status, and/or role; a loss of normal relations but a gain of temporary *communitas*; a designation as "contaminated" yet connected to divine energy; a subversive challenge that also provides continuity; an encounter with death and a dark night of the soul; and a feeling of depression and despair. Overall, it is generally an uncomfortable yet unavoidable experience that is at the heart of any transformation.

Liminality is paradoxical in that it is defined in contrast to the clearly defined states on either side of the threshold in the original model and yet is marked by a fundamental lack of clarity in itself. A person in this space knows that everything is different now, but they typically cannot say why at first. This is why it is critical for people to stay in this space long enough to discern what the passage is truly about. Liminality is an ambiguous period in which their hold on a particular reality loosens and "the past is momentarily negated, suspended, or abrogated, and the future has not yet begun, an instant of pure potentiality when everything, as it were, trembles in the balance" (Turner, 1982, p. 44). The structures of their former identity are dissolved and new structures are constellated (B. C. Alexander, 1991; J. O. Stein & Stein, 1987; Turner, 1967), often with instructions from ritual elders (Moore, 1987) who ensure there is sufficient structure and guidance for people as they pass through these uncharted territories.

Moving into, through, and out of the in-between spaces also exposes and scrutinizes the basic building blocks of a culture (e.g., its norms, values, axioms, traditions) in ways that are not generally available through people's everyday experience (Turner, 1969). As a result, liminality creates a frame within which people can experiment with the familiar categories of culture by isolating these elements and recombining them in new ways (Turner, 1967, 1974, 1982). Sometimes these experiments are built into the social processes in order to maintain some boundaries around them (like with court jesters of old), and at other times they emerge on the margins of the society and its rituals. It is a place where expectations are challenged, unspeakable subjects discussed, and new roles tested. In the process, people are not only attaining a new status, role, or identity in relation to their social systems, but there is also a change of being itself, an ontological passage (Carson 1997). Their previous certainty gives way to new possibility, though in true liminal fashion the former often recedes faster than the latter becomes clear. This is what leads to the profound sense of being "betwixt and between" and calls for guardians such as coaches.

This aligns with Vygotsky's work on zones of proximal development in that people generally cannot go directly from an old state or story to a new one, but require an intermediary step that is neither old nor new (T. Barrett, Cashman, & Moore, 2011). As he pointed out, this requires carefully stewarded boundaries, a sense of containment to manage people's vulnerabilities in this in-between phase, and access to scaffolding to support their learning and development. This is critical because, in this phase, people can become strangers to themselves, feel empty and drained, lose their sense of certainty and solidity (Ashton, 2007), question what they know and who they are, feel afraid and outcast, and become anxious as their ego resists the requisite surrender (Miller & Miller, 1994). People in liminal space are "both weak because they are outside the group and the profane space, and they are also strong because they are in the sacred space relative to the group" (van Gennep, 1960, p. 3).

It is challenging work to persevere as a *liminar* (Turner & Turner, 1978), a *liminal self* (Deegan & Hill, 1991), in large part because people's ego generally experiences a sense of loss as they move through this phase. Old habituations dissolve and possibilities for a new direction resolve into focus—as with the acorn that gives up its life to become a mighty oak or the phoenix that rises from its own ashes. Finding our way to a new attitude and a new story, necessitates an acceptance of and surrender to the descent, the depressive state that often accompanies it, the release of what must be left behind, and the work that must be done (Tarrant, 1998). When this occurs, a person's pretenses and compromises fade away as she is confronted with stark truths that have become more visible and accessible during this period. As a result, she can challenge old narratives to make more room for new stories, and she can release energy that was once trapped and channel it in new directions. She can then bring more of herself to her life, particularly aspects that had previously been put aside or underdeveloped but would now come in quite handy.

Many people describe moving through liminal spaces as like trying to pilot a rudderless ship through a thick fog. In part, this is due to the temporary lack of referent points in their inner and outer world. The good news is that if a person is able to endure this disorientation, he begins to find and hone his own internal compass. There is a delicate balance in this for coaches as there is for parents who realize they cannot protect their child from everything and, even if they could, much of the resilience and confidence the child will need for the rest of his life is born from these challenges. Therefore, focus on holding a safe space for coachees to do *their own* work. Help them tap into the literal and symbolic resources that typically appear in this phase. They often appear in forms they would not normally recognize or expect, but frequently turn out to be essential for breaking through this phase and on to the next (Shenk, 2005). It may take a while for the fog to lift, and coachees may feel lost at sea or crashed on the rocks at times. However, in the process, you can help people develop a better feel for the boat, the sea, and themselves as sailors so they can find their bearings, do their work, and move forward again.

Given the absence of rites of passage for many of us, coaching can play an important role in helping people do their liminal work as the individuating bridge between separation and reincorporation. This is particularly important at T2 in the Narrative Coaching model because it is here that people are called to make clear choices and step into new narratives and actions. One of our challenges as coaches is to deal with the commercial and professional demands that pressure us to move quickly toward outcomes and, in so doing, short-circuit real growth for coachees and those around them. Growth requires this descent, this voyage of discovery, and this shedding of old skins so the new story and the renewed person can emerge. While the liminal process can be intensified and focused to enrich people's awakening, there are no shortcuts. Instead, it requires the courage of coaches and coachees to immerse themselves in this unknown and sacred space. We can take comfort in the fact that at the *nadir*—the darkest point at the proverbial, and often literal, bottom—the person is also closest to the divine. It is the place where the veils are removed so people come face-to-face with the part(s) of themselves most in need of surrender, and in so doing, they begin to glimpse what is waiting to be born on the other side.

> While the liminal process can be intensified and focused to enrich people's awakening, there are no shortcuts.

By walking with coachees on the liminal portions of their journey, you can help them make sense of and find value in this phase as an "occasion of fruitful darkness . . . and the ground of renewal" (Halifax, 1993, p. 19). This passage often requires people to:

- Go as deeply into the darkness as is called for, and deal with whatever must be faced in the chasms of their fear and self-doubt (Hollis, 2004).

- Name the pain and truth they find there, and emerge on the other side with greater permission to name their reality from their own point of view (Feinstein & Krippner, 1988).

- Accept that they don't need permission from anyone to live their lives, feel what they feel, desire what they desire, or pursue what their soul intends—they must seize it and decide to show up (Hollis, 2013).

- Stop struggling to escape the emptiness and darkness which is theirs in the end (Miller & Miller, 1994), and rest in it until a resolution emerges (Tarrant, 1998).

Your role as a coach is to help them navigate these depths where "obscure resistances are overcome, and long lost, [and] forgotten powers are revivified" (Campbell, 1973, p. 29). It is from here that the person prepares to return to the world, transformed by the process thus far.

Reincorporation

We would rather be ruined than changed.
We would rather die in our dread
Than climb the cross of the present
And let our illusions die. | *W.H. Auden*

The *Reincorporation* phase is an important one as the person rejoins the profane world—but does so as a changed person. In more traditional settings, the return would often be as stark as the initial separation to emphasize the significance and unidirectional nature of the transition. While in many ways it is the culmination of one journey, it is also the beginning of another as the person takes on a new identity. That is why it was a time of both celebration and further initiation. There was a need to keep people focused on the tasks at hand and sufficiently supported as they entered the new role as a novice. Then, as now, this was rarely as easy as it first seemed because there were many facets of their life that needed to be adjusted to align with their new identity. What they had gained often seemed clear and compelling to the those who had come through the process, but that was not always the case for those around them. While rites of passage have evolutionary value to the community as a whole, they often surfaced the tensions between reaffirming and challenging the status quo. They both provide opportunities for growth, the first related to fitting in and the other related to standing out.

This is significant because people need others around them to support the new narrative if it is to take hold. For example, a new manager who wants to move away from micromanaging when her anxiety goes up will need others to step up and play a bigger role in order to get the work done. When I am coaching someone at this stage in their process, I will often ask the team members what they will change in themselves to support their leader's success. It reflects the need for the community to receive the new person as they are becoming, *not* as they were. In addition, many of the coachee's gains will be lost if he does not pay sufficient attention to embedding the shifts he has made in his everyday life. It is also true that many people experience a sense of deflation after the "high" of the liminal (individuation) phase and need to be reminded to address the demands and details that await them as they reincorporate as a new person, with a new story. This is why, as we shall see in the next two chapters, the final phase in narrative coaching is so critical.

At this point in the process, people get much clearer about what they truly want to do (or do differently), and their intrinsic motivation tends to increase. This generally culminates in identifying and claiming the key lesson, insight, or offer that grew out of the fires of their liminal experience—and developing themselves to be able to carry it forward. It is a time when people start getting ready to bring it back to their world and, with that, bring their journey full circle. The irony is that at the end of their great search, often to faraway lands, they discover that the gift was right in front of them or inside them all along. Regardless of where the gift is found, it can be tricky for the person to bring it back to her world for a number of reasons, including:

- Getting caught up in the thrill of the epiphany and, as a result, not reconnecting with reality.

- Feeling bored or impatient and, as a result, forgoing the hard work to bring it to life.

- Rushing to take action and, as a result, losing sight of the true nature of the gift.

- Communicating ineffectually the new reality to others who have not been on their journey and, as a result, failing to get their support.

- Underestimating the power of narratives that will challenge them and, as a result, failing to adequately prepare.

Traditionally, rites of passage were seen as occurring in relation to singular events (e.g., entering manhood/womanhood, marriage, death). However, we can extend Turner's sense of rites to any transition by looking at them developmentally. Each of the three phases (separation, transition, and re-incorporation) signals an opportunity for a significant shift in a person's development. In this case, re-incorporation is both the completion of one cycle and the start of another—albeit at a higher developmental level. Perhaps you have experienced this in your own life: you sufficiently resolved an issue—only to discover that in addition to enriching your life, it also revealed the next layer to be addressed. And so, the bird circles the tree once more . . . though hopefully with greater wisdom and ease. Therefore, focus on fewer things in your coaching sessions to keep the person's reincorporation process manageable, and use powerful Pivots to help people nudge themselves toward their new narrative.

Crossing Thresholds

The breeze at dawn has secrets to tell you.
Don't go back to sleep.
People are going back and forth across the doorsill
where two worlds touch.
The door is round and open.
Don't go back to sleep. | *(Rumi in Barks, p. 36)*

In the enhanced Rites of Passage model (figure 14), there are four thresholds (up from one in the original version). This reflects the need to make finer distinctions about the change process. Turner (1986) noted that "the word 'threshold' derives from a Germanic word which means to 'thrash' or 'thresh,' a place where grain is beaten from its husk, where what has been hidden is thus manifested" (p. 92). To cross a threshold is to literally or figuratively leave behind the husk and arrive at the grain (O'Donohue, 2008). Eliade (1959) described the threshold as "the limit, the boundary, the frontier that distinguishes and opposes two worlds—and at the same time the paradoxical place where these worlds communicate" (p. 24). A threshold is a noticeable crossing between one phase and the next as part of a broader transition and change process. As John O'Donohue writes:

A threshold is not a simple boundary; it is a frontier that divides two different territories, rhythms, and atmospheres. . . . It is a real frontier that cannot be crossed without the heart being passionately engaged and woken up. At this threshold, a great complexity of emotions comes alive: confusion, fear, excitement, sadness, hope. This is one of the reasons such vital crossings were always clothed in ritual.

Thresholds represent a time and place when the limits of the self are recognized and a territory is entered where the boundaries of the self are tested and broken. Thresholds can be found wherever there is an in-between zone in which passage from one sphere or way of being to another is made possible. Thresholds both divide and bring together significant "regions," such as inside and outside, sacred and profane, psyche and matter, self and other, conscious and unconscious. Thresholds can be seen both spatially as a doorway, a *place* of transition; and temporally as a movement, a *process* of transition. Sometimes thresholds appear as singular and momentous moments in time, like when people make major decisions. At other times, they act as cascades, rippling out from the first step. Either way, they are significant in that you cannot return to where you were because you're no longer the one who crossed over (O'Donohue, 2008). If you can help people approach their decisive thresholds with reverence and attention, the crossing will bring them more than they could ever have hoped for. Each of the thresholds in the narrative coaching process has a unique and significant role to play in developing people and their stories.

> Thresholds can be seen both spatially as a doorway, a place of transition; and temporally as a movement, a process of transition.

Thresholds are a powerful place of communication between the opposing worlds that lie on either side of them—for example, the sacred, metaphysical world of soul and psyche can be found on the other side of the profane world of history, human affairs, and events (Eliade, 1987). As a place, they mark the boundary between two opposing regions; as a process, they hold together the tensions inherent in the duality. Thresholds provide a stable center that mediates between and holds the tension of the opposites; they are "a place of possibilities where both sides have the potential to be seen and where energy has the opportunity to flow in either direction" (Buck, 2004, p. 3). They provide an opening and a beginning to a state or action, and they offer a third space with a changing combination of attributes of the two bordering spaces (Muller, 2001) at the edge, the frontier, where they intersect. Paying attention in these spaces demands commitment and endurance; "simply to keep oneself there, in open and honest relationship, requires a fitness of soul" (Kaplan, 2002, p. 67). Otherwise, the person attempting to cross is often defeated and turns back (or is turned back)—and the necessary communication and transition between the worlds is thwarted.

Thresholds are also a process in time. It is often the case, however, that while the distinction between "before" and "after" is often experienced as pointed and stark, the complete transit is often extended and blurry. Sometimes a threshold becomes clearly visible only once you have crossed it. Either way, crossing a threshold marks a point in time that serves as a new referent point going forward in terms of the person's plotline and identity. It has been my experience in coaching over the years that there is something palpably different in the moment when a person approaches a threshold. Many times it is a subtle energetic or somatic shift that comes over the person that can only be described as an *urgent calm*. It feels urgent because there is a readiness to make a big move and big issues are often at stake, and it feels calm because there is a clarity and a certainty about what is to be done (and why). Overall, thresholds are both the culmination of a longer process and a very distinct moment in time.

In the classic Rites of Passage model (figure 11), the threshold was crossed twice—once as a person left the world to embark on a journey through the "lower" world and once to return from liminality into the "upper" world. In more contemporary contexts such as narrative coaching, people cross the horizontal axis of space twice and the vertical axis of time twice. Each of these represents a critical point in the process where coachees often need to make developmental breakthroughs and important decisions in order to move through to the next phase of their transition. Each one involves moving from the known to the unknown in order to do the work at hand. In crossing a threshold, people gain a new vantage point from which to see the world and a new starting point from which to discover what is next. To move through the passage, coachees need a safe container, a robust and experiential process, and a guide to accompany them. Timothy Carson (1997) offers an insight that helps us see why the notion of thresholds fits so well with coaching: "Rather than merely attempting to return a person to a past state of equilibrium, their approach is oriented toward the future. . . . Liminal categories construe crisis in terms of progress rather than regression" (pp. 89–90).

Guardians

At the threshold of each hour
To open the gates in the underworld
One must know the names.

While thresholds get the most attention, there are other aspects of a doorway which make the crossing both recognizable and possible. Thresholds represent the moment of choice and lintels represent the structure that keeps it open. Buck (2004) uses the entrance to Carl Jung's Kusnacht home in Switzerland to talk about the lintel's role:

> 'Called or not called, the gods will be present.' Everyone who walked down the path saw this enigmatic message [on the lintel] as they approached. . . . The lintel is the weight-discharging horizontal piece above the door and directly over the threshold. . . . In partnership with the grounded threshold, the lintel above creates the opening between two places. This doubling reinforces the entrance as a power place. (p. 4)

Moving across thresholds requires strength of character to contend with the polarizing energies of the opposites that are crystallized there and to deal with the ambiguities in the unknown on the other side. That is why it is important to ensure there are "lintels" for every threshold. For those on the journey, it is imperative to not take these passages lightly. They are not for the ill-prepared or fainthearted as they can often challenge our core constructs about ourselves, others, and life itself. This is why the guardians at thresholds are so important; they ensure that the person is prepared for dealing with the powerful forces in play there and on the other side. Once people are at a threshold, it is incumbent upon them to know what it will take to cross it. Their crossing may involve a single bold act or a series of major moves, though either way there is almost always a moment of reckoning when it all becomes very real.

This requires the person to address the forces at the doorway— "threshold guardians" as Joseph Campbell (1973) called them. They are symbolically and literally there to remind people to not take thresholds lightly, to fully appreciate what is truly at stake, and to challenge them to be ready. These guardians are often either close allies or people deemed as enemies because, paradoxically, each is especially well-equipped to point out the truth of the situation and what is called for. Psychologically, these guardians can often be seen as projections of the fears and aspects of our Shadows that are critical for the crossing of this threshold. Terms such as "good" and "bad" are not relevant here because every guardian serves the same purpose: to lift the veil that has kept the person from seeing what was there all along and help him cross the threshold of his truth. Every guardian essentially asks the same questions:

- "What do you need to confront to gain access to what you are seeking?"
- "What projections do you need to withdraw so you can bring that energy into yourself to support your growth?"

> Your role is to support coachees to stay open yet conscious, firm yet fluid, throughout the ordeal; and to foster the courage they will need to complete their passage.

Guardians can play many roles in the process, such as helping a person to see a situation more clearly, providing her with aid, or testing her to make sure she is ready. Not only are guardians protecting us, they are also protecting the thresholds themselves. Their task is to maintain those places where the sacred and the profane meet in an enlightening moment of awareness or where the past and the future meet in a critical moment of choice. They are charged with keeping the boundaries in good repair and the center fresh and strong. Part of our role as a guardian in coaching is to challenge people to sink deeper into the truth of that moment. In so doing, they discover the real name that will unlock the potential of that threshold and enable them to cross it. This enables people to release stories that no longer serve them so they are no longer trapped between an old world they are struggling to leave and a new world they are afraid to enter (Brown, 2004).

Guardians matter-of-factly stand at these doorways because they recognize the potency and power that reside there. As a recent student of this work reflected:

I am too often a "nice" guardian. Which, I think, often makes me an ineffective guardian. Guardians are clear, they know what they are protecting and they stand firm in their role—they are challenging and reassuring all at once. As I thought about my own journey and what it takes to actually cross a threshold, I realize I need to be tougher as a guardian.

That is why guardians challenge people to be prepared and to face the threshold with both fierceness and surrender. Guardians play an important role here because, "when some part of us dies, there must be a time of mourning, a period of withdrawal and introspection, a period of allowing the tears to fall. Tears connect us to our hearts, our real values, our own inner Home" (Woodman, 1987, p. 211). Guardians are stewards of these vital crossings and of the deep grief and deep joy that often are found there.

As such, your role is to support coachees to stay open yet conscious, firm yet fluid, throughout the ordeal; and to summon the courage they will need to complete their passage. They will need this support, especially when the work gets hard (e.g., in the betwixt-and-between places where powerful forces are afoot and important choices need to be made). It is in these liminal places where people often come into closest contact with their most honest self-awareness, their most potent questions, and their deepest hopes and fears. What they discover there often precipitates the biggest shifts in them because they ripple out through many aspects of their lives. To serve well as a guardian in the coaching process requires a sense of sacred leadership (R. L. Moore, 1987), strong cultural and spiritual awareness, physical and emotional resilience, and personal and relational maturity to guide people through these fiery yet precious spaces. Narrative coaching facilitates change at a transpersonal level, brings together transitions and development in the same process through a rite of passage, and helps people heal old stories and bring new ones to life.

Use the space below to explore the next threshold in your life or practice. It is a process we do regularly in our retreats and labs to give people a visceral experience of the crux of their issue and what it will truly take to address it. Write down your responses to the four questions and see what emerges. Your threshold can be between any two phases in the change process; the template below is based on the movement from Shift to Sustain. If you want to really go for it, place a threshold on the floor, stand before it and notice your experience, and cross it when you feel ready. It is important to recognize in so doing that when you cross a threshold with purpose, it takes you to a new space, a new story, from which there is no real return.

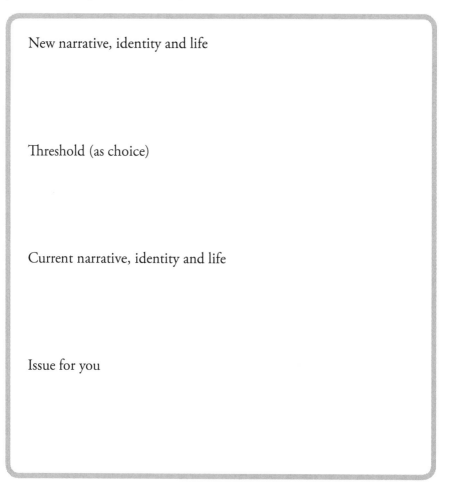

New narrative, identity and life

Threshold (as choice)

Current narrative, identity and life

Issue for you

Implications for Your Practice

Principles for serving as a guardian at a threshold:

- Be fully present to what is unfolding rather than thinking about what to do next.

- See time as malleable rather than, for example, seeing the past as fixed.

- See space (and the items in it) as malleable rather than, for example, staying in one position.

- Be fiercely compassionate and compassionately fierce; thresholds are not for the ill-prepared.

- Be willing to sit with dissonance and the unknown rather than succumb to or collude with "narrative smoothing."

- Move between the external change issues and internal transition needs as required.

- Move in and out of stories as needed rather than asking sequential questions.

What are your key insights?
What will you experiment with first?

PART III
narrative
PRACTICES

CHAPTER 7

HOW NARRATIVE COACHING WORKS

Aborigine trackers are the best in the world, able to follow a man even years after he has walked through a dry desert terrain. An anthropologist asked one of these expert trackers how he did it. The tracker responded, "Oh, it's easy. We walk with him." He does not look for clues; he enters the time and space where the journey occurred. He knows how to walk in the same world as the event he seeks. | Mikela & Philip Tarlow

The first half of this book provided the foundations for a narrative approach to coaching. It began with a look at three of its unique features: using attachment theory to deepen the coaching relationship, working with identities to deepen the outcomes from coaching, and incorporating transformative learning and development to deepen the coaching process. We then looked at three other features: understanding stories to deepen what they offer, observing patterns of narration to deepen our awareness of what is unfolding in sessions, and using a rites of passage frame to deepen the impact. In the second half of the book, we will focus on the application of the narrative coaching process. We will first explore the Narrative Coaching model as a way to reconfigure stories and two of the key processes for doing so (externalization and unique outcomes) and its integrative approach to change. A fuller version of the Narrative Coaching model (figure 18) is offered in the next chapter as we look more closely at how it is used in coaching. While narrative coaching has deep roots in psychology, it draws on other disciplines to enable you to work with people's stories at multiple levels simultaneously for more sustained results.

The model can be used not only to help people resolve specific issues in their life and work, but also to help them develop themselves as more mature storytellers of and in their life. It does so by addressing their personal stories in the context of interpersonal and collective narratives. As a result, you can use it to coach people to address their issue today *and* to shift their narrative patterns and identities so they can better address issues like this tomorrow. As Ricoeur (1992) noted, our destiny is profoundly shaped by our stories, and our stories are profoundly shaped by the larger narratives about our destiny. Narrative coaching is fairly unique as a methodology in that it addresses the socially constructed nature of our discourse, identities, and behaviors. We recognize that while each of us is personally responsible for our own narrative choices, our ability to bring a new story to life is impacted by the narratives around us. That is why this edition of the book includes more on narrative activism not just authoring.

The first step is helping people become more aware of where their stories come from and more accountable for the stories they choose to tell. In so doing, they become more agile in working with the narratives around them. Marshall Edelson (1993) has a wonderful description of this progression:

As he becomes able to identify what evokes his telling or enacting a story on each of many occasions, he increasingly understands its value to him—the purpose it serves. Typically, he begins by viewing himself as passive victim. He attributes causation to the external situation. Eventually, he comes to see that what he has attributed to external reality stems from what he carries in his own mind, and what he does, through imagination or action, to make external reality conform to it. (p. 298)

The stories we work with in coaching include elements that are conscious and unconscious, which is why narrative coaching works so much at the nonverbal level. The stories people consciously know, or believe they know, are seldom the whole story that is actually unfolding within them (Rennie, 1994). Therefore, a critical role in narrative coaching is to draw people's attention to what their psyche is trying to bring forth through their stories. It is almost as if it is leaving a trail of bread crumbs, hoping they will notice and follow it to discover what it is trying to reveal. In the same vein, you can help people see in their stories the ways in which the narrative they are living—or think they are living—clashes with the narrative they want to be living. By working with their stories in coaching, people have the opportunity to surface and address their largely unconscious narrative patterns and processes. This gives them significantly more material to work with in the coaching sessions.

Sometimes a change in a person's life calls for a new narrative, and sometimes a new narrative calls for changes in his life. Sometimes an increased level of awareness leads him to take new actions, and sometimes the new actions he takes increase his level of awareness. My suggestion is to start with the one that is most familiar to the coachee and then bring in the other. For example, with an introverted person, I might invite her to access her awareness and then explore what new action she would like to take. For an extroverted person, I might invite him to replicate the action and then explore what he notices about his internal experience. Either way, change is a dance between what is and what could be, what is inside and what is outside.

This reflects the use of resonance and dissonance we explored in chapter 1, and offers opportunities to ask questions such as: (1) What has been your story about your issue up to this point? (2) How is that working for you? (3) Do you want to continue or change your story? (4) If you want to change it, what pieces can you bring forward to help you? (5) What are you hoping the new story will do for you? (Singer, 2001; Yalom, 2000). The Narrative Coaching model is quite useful in this regard because its flow mirrors the process by which people narrate their identity and experience *and* the process by which they develop themselves and new behaviors.

> Draw people's attention to what their psyche is trying to bring forth through their stories.

In developing the Narrative Coaching model, I was drawn to:

- Freire's (1970) critiques of the traditional banking methods of education and the over-privileging of the dominant narratives at the expense of personal narratives.

- Jung's (1969) insights into the collective and unconscious influences on the self and the search for a means to connect the two worlds.

- Clandinin & Connelly's (2000) use of Dewey to create a three-dimensional narrative inquiry space (personal and social interaction, temporal continuity, and situations as place).

- Tillich's (1965) notion of a third area where one can stand for a time without being tightly bounded—a concept that was later explored by Schwartz-Salant (1998) as an imaginal vessel in psychoanalysis.

- Oldenburg's (1989) work on "the great good place" where he talks about the important role of a third place outside home and work.

Each of these sources speaks to the four phases of narratives, transitions, and development in the model; the interplay between personal and collective narratives as found in rites of passage; and the importance of third spaces in bringing about change. We will look at the latter in chapter 11 on listening.

Understanding the Model

Let me fall . . . for I will be caught
by who I am becoming. | *Cirque de Soleil, Quidam*

In the beginning I found kindred spirits in Kenyon and Randall's (1997) work on "restorying, as it too was based in both narrative structure and narrative psychology. I shared their appreciation of: (1) the actual words people use in narrating their experience; (2) the genres and points of view they habitually use; (3) the importance of finding their authentic voice amid the cacophony in and around them; (4) the interpretations they and others rush to make; (5) the need at times to change their narrative environments if they are to flourish; and (6) the untapped value of the material that they have overlooked or left untold. However, I opted to speak of narrative coaching as a "reconfiguration" process rather than as a "re-storying" or "re-authoring" process because I wanted a more integrative term. It invites coaches to approach change systemically because neither changing the story nor one's sense of authorship are sufficient in themselves. For example, you could work with a coachee to shift from "I failed, like I always do when it comes to speaking up for what I want" to "I see now that I can make new choices when people challenge me." What gets reconfigured includes elements of identities; relationships with others; perspectives on the past, present, or future; the sense or meaning attributed to an event; and their assumptions about what they want.

> Change happens when people make shifts in who and how they are as Author of their stories, as Actor in stories with others, as Agent in the narratives around them, and as Activist for better narratives.

Through the work with attachment theory, I came to see the need for stronger ties between our abilities to work with the narratives within us and the narratives around us. I identified four roles that are central to our narrative maturity (e.g., Author). They align with the work on applied mindfulness that was introduced in Chapter 1, in which I identified four capabilities (e.g., Cope) people need to develop to be able to mindfully and generatively enact these roles. They function as a hierarchy in that a person's success at any level is dependent on their success with the one(s) prior. If people are using a significant amount of their discretionary energy coping, they will be much less able to connect with others—let alone create and contribute. These roles and the associated capabilities are generally addressed in this sequence in the narrative coaching process. Instead of imposing a coaching structure on a conversation, we come alongside a person and the conversation to note where they are, what they may need to address next, and how they might get there. People's success in moving through their change process depends on how (well) they enact the following roles and capabilities.

TOOL

People change as a result of shifts they make as:

1. *Author* of their stories so they can *Cope* at new levels (*Situate phase*)
2. *Actor* in stories with others so they can *Connect* in new ways (*Search* phase)
3. *Agent* in narratives around them so they can *Create* new options (*Shift* phase)
4. *Activist* for better narratives so they can *Contribute* to new outcomes (*Sustain* phase)

EXAMPLE

How a coachee stepped into each role to get a better outcome:

1. *Author:* I realize it would serve me well if I would stop telling my story as if I am a victim (in order to cope).

2. *Actor:* I need to have an honest conversation with my manager about my role in the project (in order to connect).

3. *Agent:* I will ask others on the team if they are having a similar experience right now (in order to create).

4. *Activist:* I will talk with my manager and suggest a session to address what is going on (in order to contribute).

As you can see from the example above, the beauty of narrative coaching is that it is experienced as a natural human process rather than a mechanical intervention. It shifts the emphasis from coaches and their methodologies to coachees, their stories and their journeys to change. It empowers people to address the larger narratives in the course of working on their personal issues. Each reinforces the other. This can be seen in the model itself, which depicts people's movement between their inner worlds (e.g., identities, beliefs, attitudes) and their outer worlds (e.g., states, roles, statuses), between their past worlds and their future worlds, and between their constructed selves and their imagined selves. The Narrative Coaching model aligns the four acts of narrative structure, the four phases of development, and the four phases of transition in an integrative process in which change is occurring at multiple levels. As a result, people can do transformative work in the session *and* develop themselves at the same time. The result is that what they experience and accomplish in coaching can more readily be applied and integrated when they return to their life and/or work.

FIGURE 13: NARRATIVE COACHING MODEL (STEPS TO RECONFIGURE A STORY)

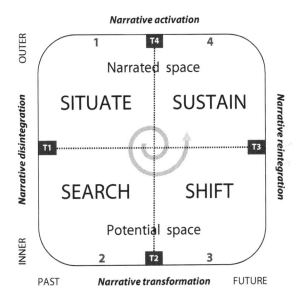

This version is built on the enhanced rites of passage framework (figure 12) and adds narrative and coaching components. The details of the model will be fleshed out in the next chapter, but here are the key additions:

- The spatial-temporal coordinates for the four quadrants remain the same, but the upper half is now the "narrated space" and the lower half is now the "potential space" to reflect the shift from an anthropological frame to a coaching frame.

- The four Ss are now used to indicate the four phases in the Narrative Coaching model. The process begins in the upper left quadrant and spirals counterclockwise. The spiral runs in this direction to reflect the disruptive nature of transitions and change, which moves in a different direction than the status quo.

- What was labeled "Transition" in the liminal phase is now "Individuation" to reflect the fact that the entire process is a series of transitions and that maturation is the focus of this phase. Also, "Integration" has been added as its counterpart at T4 to reflect the need for people to embed the new story in their life and environment.

- We can see the links back to the Narrative Rewind tool (figure 1) in that *Situate* helps people assess their Story, *Search* helps them assess their Identity, *Shift* helps them assess their Behavior, and *Sustain* helps them assess their Outcomes.

- The path to reconfigure a story is depicted around the outside: (1) The quest begins with the disintegration of the current narrative in the wake of internal transitions and/or external change; it is then (2) transformed through liminal experiences; (3) reintegrated in a new configuration that reflects both what has been discovered and what is now desired; and (4) activated as part of a new identity.

  For example: (1) I did not get the promotion I was hoping for and thought I deserved; (2) I realized I was trying so hard to please others that I lost my own voice and beliefs; (3) I have shifted my focus from getting promoted to being a better leader; and (4) I have put a plan in place with my coach about how to put this into action to be ready next time.

Taken together, the model reflects the phases that people go through as they reconfigure elements in their stories to create a new narrative.

Reconfigurations generally come sooner and have more impact when coachees frame them in language and images from their own stories and in terms of aspirations they are seeking, not problems they are solving. This requires coaches to be expansive in holding space in the field and laser-focused when it comes time to zero in on openings for change. If the process is only expansive, changes dissipate into the wind because they are ungrounded; if the process is too laser-focused, they often wither under the glare because they are unsupported. Reconfigured stories are like new shoots in the garden in that they need care and time to grow. This supports the emphasis in narrative coaching to get to the crux of the issue, focus on it, and ensure there is sufficient scaffolding to bring the new story to life.

In process, let any new stories that emerge breathe until they settle and feel rooted. This requires the person to first empty the proverbial tea cup by releasing any old stories that are in the way to make room for new ones as part of the reconfiguration process. In the end:

- Some stories will lose their relevance and/or influence.

- Some stories will take on new relevance and influence.

- Some stories will come more to the foreground and are "thickened" (Geertz, 1978).

- Some experiences will be "de-narrated" and allowed to drop back into the sea of life.

Reconfiguring Stories

There is only one problem, ever:
your uninvestigated story in the moment. | *Byron Katie*

Early on in developing narrative coaching, I moved away from the term "re-authoring" (Epston & White, 2005; White, 1995, 2004; White & Epston, 1990) that was made famous by the early narrative therapists. I appreciated the phrase for bringing attention to the need to foster greater agency and autonomy in people in the midst of dominant social and professional discourses. However, I came to the conclusion that the word—

like "re-storying"—was not fully representative of what I saw happening in narrative coaching. I found it limiting to (1) focus solely on the author or the story when it comes to bringing about change; (2) assume that change and development emerge primarily in opposition to dominant narratives; and (3) minimize the existential and developmental need for accountability for one's narrative choices.

As noted earlier, change requires shifts at multiple levels. Narrative coaching helps people to shift narrative patterns through reconfiguring elements in representative stories in order to attain what they are seeking. It starts with helping them be mindfully present as a foundation for taking multiple perspectives on what they are seeking to shift as noted below. It also involves coachees developing themselves and remaining agile in terms of how they resolve their issues. In order to understand more about why this is the case and how to use this in your practice, let's look at a more enhanced version of the Narrative Coaching model.

FIGURE 14: NARRATIVE COACHING MODEL (ENHANCED)

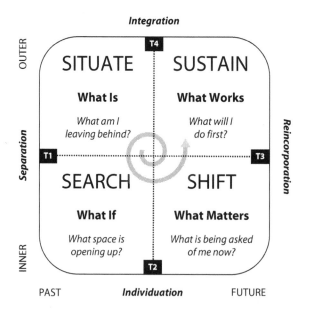

Each of the 4 Ss (*Situate, Search, Shift, Sustain*) in the model reflects a phase in the coaching process, which, in turn, reflects and a phase in the journey of the person being coached. The following additions to the basic model (Figure 2) offer more insights on how the model works and how to use it in your practice:

- In temporal terms, the first two phases (*Situate, Search*) are defined by what is; the latter two phases (*Shift, Sustain*) are defined by what could be.

- The primary area of focus for each of the four phases is now listed so that the objective for each phase is clearer.

- The influence of design thinking on the model is evident with the addition of the four "What . . ." questions and speaks to the nature of narrative coaching as structured emergence. It also shows that there is lasting value in each phase of the process, not just in the outcome. This is particularly useful for people who coach in organizations.

- Each phase is characterized by a different degree of change readiness, so listen carefully for changes in people's language as signs that they are ready to move on. The key is to match your actions with their level of readiness—e.g., what helps people get started is generally not what helps them get finished (Prochaska & Norcross, 2002).

- The spiral—the fifth S if you will—becomes more prominent to remind us that people often need to "circle the tree" more than once to break through in developing themselves, crossing thresholds, and making decisions.

Each of the small black boxes indicates one of the four thresholds in the process and marks the transition from one phase to the next. Thresholds have both internal and external aspects in terms of what is required to cross them. For example, a coachee has started thinking about leaving his current role (outer world) to find one that is more aligned with his skills and passions. In crossing the first threshold (T1), he starts to gain a new clarity about his values (inner world) that will help him understand what he wants. Crossing a threshold enables and enriches the work of the next phase (e.g., the more a coachee allows the old story to disintegrate, the more material becomes available for its reconfiguration). You only need to go as deep as is necessary for what the coachee is trying to achieve and ready to address. At the same time, it is not uncommon for people to make significant changes based on what seems at the time like a minor issue. The key is to notice when threshold moments appear—no matter whether they are big or small—and help coachees cross over to what is on the other side. As we've seen, this involves shifts in how they see and carry themselves as the *Author, Actor, Agent*, and *Activist* of new stories and new narratives.

EXAMPLE

In a recent coaching session, the coachee told me a story about being the victim of an unfair partner in which he has the following realizations. His key insights in each phase are included as well as actions he took (which are in brackets).

- **Situate:** I notice that my language is mostly in the passive voice, as if all this is just happening to me. I wonder why I am telling it this way. I think I have a belief that I have to take whatever is given to me—and make the best out of it somehow. As a result, I feel tired most of the time, with little energy to do what is important to me. *As the Author: I need to create a new narrative about who I am and what I deserve.*

- **Search:** This often leaves me feeling like I am trying to catch up—and a bit resentful. However, the story feels incomplete, like there is so much more. . . . I wonder what would happen if I changed my story into the active voice. [He retells the story from this place . . .] *As an Actor: I can change how I see myself and give voice to my needs in relation to others.*

- **Shift:** It was hard to stay in that voice at the point in the story when something was asked of me. [He practices with the coach, moves through his fear, and feels a new sense of power in so doing . . .] I need to be clear about what I need in order to be at my best and what I am willing to offer so I can respond differently in those moments.

[He creates a Pivot for himself . . .] *As an Agent: I can advocate for a new narrative about how we relate and what my role is in this context.*

- **Sustain:** I notice that my voice is quite shaky as I practice asking for what I want in this new way. But it feels good too. It helped me when I planted my feet firmly on the ground and paused to give myself time to think. In this moment, it feels like you are taking me more seriously now. [He makes commitments about whom to try it with first when he leaves.] *As an Activist: I will continue to advocate for this new way of relating and offer feedback to my partner as part of that process.*

This example illustrates how you can help coachees release or reconfigure narratives that no longer serve them and/or are less functional in current circumstances. Like a masseuse who presses into a muscle to release its tightness, you can do the same by entering into coachees' stories to help them release any narrative tension. For example, you might challenge a person when she declares she "had to do what she did." In so doing, you could help her see that the story she have chosen to tell herself and others is one of many fictions available. You can also help them see that their personal stories are developed in a social context—with its preferred discourse, histories, and expectations—and serve social as well as personal functions (Rappaport, 1993). It helps to think in terms of situated identities (Ochs & Capps, 1996) as well as Gergen and Gergen's (2006) request for "an account of human change understood in terms of relational action" (p. 119).

Reconfiguration can also be seen as a rebalancing between what we see as given, what we see as possible, and what we see as desired (see Bruner, 2002; Maddi, 1988). Narrative coaching works because it invites people to move between direct experience and narrative formulation in the same process, each informing the other. The need for change is often triggered when people recognize that what once provided them with a sense of protection has now become constrictive or perhaps even destructive. What was once the mask they wore, the artifice of their persona, has now become a self-imposed prison (Hollis, 2013). Ironically, both their incarceration and their liberation are a function of the stories they choose to believe.

As we shall see in the next chapter, narrative coaching is a process through which people can learn to (1) more nonjudgmentally experience reality (*Situate*); (2) put down their masks in relating to others (*Search*); (3) live in the world new ways that are more satisfying (*Shift*); and (4) get more of the results that are important to them (*Sustain)*. The aim, as Boyd (2009) observed, is to support transformative narrative work that "helps us not to override the given, but to be less restricted by it, to cope with it more flexibly and on something more like our own terms" (p. 50). Before I share how this is done, let's look at two familiar tools from psychotherapy and how they are re-conceptualized in narrative coaching.

Externalization

Externalization is a well-known concept from narrative therapy. It has a place in narrative coaching, but it is conceived of and used differently in some important ways. Externalization is a process in which a quality or problem that is seen to be subjective and internal to a person is objectified and moved outside the person. Fox (2003) offers a couple of examples of how this would be done in narrative therapy: "I am weak" becomes "you get overwhelmed by a feeling of weakness"; or "she is anorexic" may become "a fear of food has taken control of her life." By casting the problem as outside of the person it becomes easier for her to see and enter into a relationship with the problem and revise it (White, 1989). Otherwise, she can only attack the problem by attacking herself. Externalization can be helpful when a person first engages an issue, particularly if it is stigmatized and/or she would benefit from a sharper distinction between her own experience and others' narratives. The narrative therapy community has done great work in this regard.

There are three differences in how externalization is used in narrative coaching. Firstly, we would agree that externalization interrupts the habitual formation and performance of our stories by allowing us to stand back from them and separate our identities, stories, and performances from each other. In narrative therapy, the person and the therapist would then assume a united stance *against* the problem (Brimhall, Gardner, & Henline, 2003, p. 406) which is outside the system, whereas in narrative coaching the coachee and the coach would assume a united stance *with* the problem which is part of the system. The focus in narrative therapy is on what people had interjected (internalized from others), whereas narrative coaching is more focused on what people have projected onto others to avoid their own inner work.

Secondly, while externalization in narrative therapy thankfully reduces the experience of blame, it can also reduce the level of accountability and what Mahony (2003) saw as the person's existential responsibilities. Narrative coaches think in terms of third spaces in which people gain some temporary distance from their issues and stories without replacing one binary frame with another. The aim is to soften the fused "narrative grip" while acknowledging that whatever they are dealing with is still part of the same system and subject to the same expectations of existential accountability for their stories.

Thirdly, I sometimes find the way externalizations are described in narrative therapy to be awkward and overly problematized. For example, to translate the phrase "I am weak" (Fox, 2003) as uttered by a client into "You get overwhelmed by a feeling of weakness" seems awkward, passive, and presumptive. "I am weak" does not have to be a declarative statement of a person's identity that needs to be amended. Instead, it may be a truthful description of his current state or an opening for an exploration of that phrase. In a narrative coaching session, this phrase might be reframed in more natural terms by the coachee; for example, "When you say that, I notice myself feeling weaker," or "I frequently position myself as weak in my stories about my team." We would then explore "weakness" as a character in his stories to see how this aspect of himself (and potentially larger narratives as well) could be reconfigured to generate new options. In this way, the person is no longer conflated with his stories yet retains a sense of accountability for them.

Narrative coaching is about helping people recognize that what they once saw as a natural and inevitable reflection of their world is actually a construction, and their suffering stems from an adherence to that construction—particularly when it contrasts with reality (Fulton & Siegel, 2005). So, ask yourself as you move through your coaching sessions, "Where is this person right now and what does she need in terms of her stories about reality in order to move forward?" The focus is less on determining why things are the way they are and more on accepting things as they are. It is about defining the results the person wants to attain instead, and developing a way to bring them to life. This often requires coaches to use both internalization and externalization, depending on which would best serve the developmental needs of the coachee at that time. Sometimes this means matching where they are right now (e.g., letting the painful story element they have externalized stay there until they are ready to address it), and sometimes it means challenging where they are (e.g., inviting them to consider the role they played in creating the situation they experienced as painful).

This requires coachees to stay actively connected to and engaged with whatever has been externalized as they work with it. By keeping it within the field, they can more freely move in and out of relationship with it until such time as they can reclaim it and/or resolve it. This is why there is so much emphasis in narrative coaching on attention to the field and holding space there. Elements in people's stories and larger narratives as well as aspects of themselves can be temporarily suspended in the field as part of a reconfiguration process. People can then separate what has been projected from the other person (Fraser & Solovey, 2007), externalize it into neutral territory to see it more clearly, and take more responsibility for their narrative construction as they internalize it as their own. I find this blended approach is also useful for coaches because it lessens our need to "make something happen" by keeping the focus on coachees' accountability for their own stories.

> **We can work openly with the narrative material because we trust that a more desirable reconfiguration is already present.**

We can work openly with the narrative material because we trust that a more desirable reconfiguration is already present. Sometimes it is discovered by inviting the coachee to "circle upwards" through externalization to more astutely observe her story from above, while at other times it is discovered by inviting the coachee to "circle downwards" through internalization to experience her story from within. Externalization can be quite useful when there is a need for greater awareness and acceptance, and internalization can be quite useful when there is a need for greater accountability and action. Either way, it calls for a deep curiosity as you help people explore new ways of relating to their stories. Narrative therapy tends to focus more on deconstructing external and dominant narratives as a requirement for liberation from others. Narrative coaching tends to focus more on deconstructing internal and embodied narratives as an opening for a fuller expression of ourselves. These are both important processes; the secret is to use whichever meets the unfolding needs of the coachee and his journey.

Unique Outcomes

Another resource from narrative therapy that is useful in reconfiguration is that of *unique outcomes*. Following Erving Goffman (1959), Michael White referred to the contradictions to the dominant narratives within people's stories as "unique outcomes" (White, 1988; White & Epston, 1990) and saw these "sparkling moments" as the gateway to alternative territories to be explored in terms of ways of being in the world (Epston & White, 1992). Other narrative therapists have described them as "unique experiences" (Bird, 2000) in referring to newly noticed behaviors, or as "exceptions" (de Shazer, 1988; Hewson, 1991) to establish them as behaviors that are consistent with the person's unwritten history. In general, narrative therapists use questions to elicit, clarify, and enhance descriptions of times in the past when the "problem" was not influential in clients' lives (Chang & Phillips, 1993). One of the values of eliciting alternative stories that reflect these exceptions is that "other sympathetic and previously neglected aspects of the person's experience can be expressed and circulated" (White & Epston, 1990, p. 17).

In narrative coaching, the notion of "exceptions" resonates; however, we frame these outcomes in terms of a person's past behaviors more than in contrast to dominant narratives. They are framed in terms of what people are "standing for" more than what they are "acting against" because the former is more actionable. We also shy away from making normative evaluations of identities, stories, or actions as "positive" or "negative," "good" or "bad," as these judgments tend to shut down learning and perpetuate a dualistic way of thinking. Instead, we focus on increasing people's candid awareness of their stories, the impact and consequences of those stories, what they want to be different, and how they can make that happen. This is in keeping with the core principle in narrative coaching that everything you need is right in front of you. We invite people to externalize in order to separate what was once fused so they can better articulate the dilemma. We invite them to internalize when they are ready in order to reconfigure the elements at stake and attain a resolution that brings healing and strength (Raff, 2000).

In the end, narrative coaches don't invest in trying to fix "problems," but recognize instead that "every expressed concern can be construed as an attempt to solve a problem, and every presenting complaint can be construed as a problem-solving effort gone awry" (Mahony, 2003, pp. 10–11). We are interested in how people have construed the problem, why they believed their attempt would resolve it, and what caused it to go awry. What coachees discover in exploring these questions points to the elements that need to be reconfigured in order to achieve more of their desired result. Therefore, invite your coachees to take greater accountability for their own awareness, attitude, and actions as they work with you to reconfigure their underlying narratives. In the end, narrative coaching is an iterative and developmental approach in which the focus is on identifying the crux of issues, learning and growth are central, and both short-term and long-term needs are addressed. All of this reflects the importance of reconfiguring people's stories through integrative processes such as those used in narrative coaching.

Using an Integrative Approach to Change

One of the unique features of the narrative coaching model is that it weaves together three separate processes (narration, transition, and development) into one. As a result, people who are coached using these methods are developing themselves in ways that are directly related to what they will need in order to resolve their issue. Thus, by the time people get to the *Sustain* phase, they are better prepared to successfully implement what they decide. In large part that is because they have already experienced what it is like to be or act in that way and have experimented with how they might bring it into their life and/or work. The narrative coaching process is used to not only identify the critical factors related to the narratives being explored in coaching conversations, but also to identify what scaffolding people need to successfully embody and enact the changes they begin there. In taking a more holistic approach to change, we use the four integrative elements from applied Narrative Design (the foundation for narrative coaching). They are mapped onto the Narrative Coaching model as follows:

FIGURE 15: INTEGRATIVE ELEMENTS IN NARRATIVE COACHING

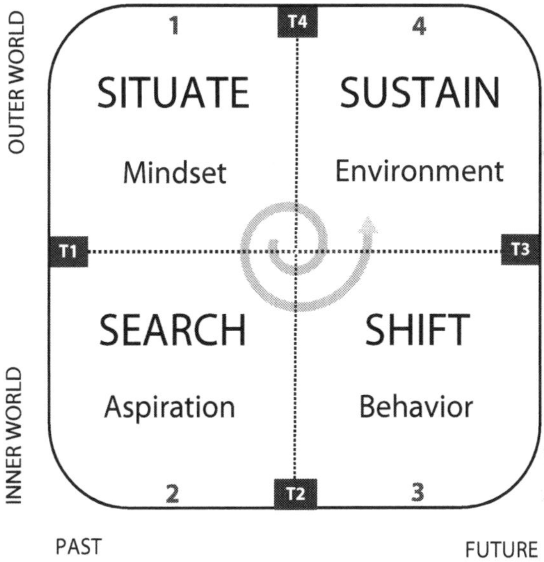

It is important in viewing the figure above to not confuse the map with the territory. All four of these elements are available at all times; it is just that the work in each phase of the narrative coaching process tends to focus on one of the BEAM elements more than the others and in this order. *Mindset* is about how coachees see the world and themselves in it; *Aspiration* is what they believe will bring a resolution; *Behavior* is what they will do differently to fulfill their *aspiration;* and *Environment* is what would need to be different (internally or externally) so they and their aspiration can flourish.

The first movement through the spiral in narrative coaching is often about uncovering what is actually happening now. This takes place prior to making any efforts to bring about change. The second round through the spiral then focuses on what the person wants to change and for what purpose. Aspiration is listed second because it is almost always the case that people only discover what they really want from coaching after they have been more honest about their current situation and have seen it through the lens of a new mindset. Let us look at the four BEAM elements in more detail.

Mindset: In my experience, helping people develop and sustain a new mindset is often the most significant contribution I make to their growth and success. Mindsets are important because people can only see as far as their stories will take them, and they can only act as far as their stories will back them. They must be able to see themselves as the new person they are becoming, even if only in glimmers in the beginning. New mindsets and new behaviors must co-evolve if coachees are to sustain the changes they begin in coaching. Each one must be experienced as a natural by-product of the other.

Aspiration: A common challenge in sustaining change is that people lose sight of their initial aspiration and, as a result, the insights and enthusiasm from the coaching experience wilt under the pressures of returning to the "real world." To help with this, narrative coaches focus on fewer things in coaching sessions, identify strong and authentic leverage points, ensure that coachees have a very clear purpose, and offer them the four reconfiguration tools to keep the aspiration front of mind. Aspirations reflect the desire that is at the heart of all narratives and point to what the person is seeking.

Behavior: New narratives and stories must be both believable (e.g., linked to existing life conditions as the coachee understands them) and actionable (capable of being put into daily practice) if they are to be enacted. Coaching sessions provide a safe space where people can experience and experiment with new stories—and the behaviors that go with them—before they have to try them with others. In so doing, they will build up the neural pathways and muscle memories associated with their new narrative such that they can more fully embody and enact it once they move back out into their world.

Environment: Any new story told in a coaching session—even if it has served as a transformational vehicle for the coachee in that setting—must survive the retellings that will occur in other contexts if coachees want to sustain change. There is little value in sending a changed person back into an unchanged environment. Narrative coaching looks beyond the individualistic psychologies as found in many coaching methodologies to address the social and contextual issues that shape people's narratives and lives. This enables coachees to be better prepared as they reincorporate into their world. As they do so, they will hopefully be able to support others to evolve as well—leading to shifts in the environment that will make it more supportive of further changes.

Taken together, the narrative coaching process is about breaking vicious cycles in which people feel frustrated and creating virtuous cycles in which people can flourish. A key piece in that process, and narrative coaching more broadly, is to release any stories that are not aligned with reality or in service of people's well-being and purpose. This work challenges us to mature even as it invites us to trust; it challenges us to serve as a witness even as it offers us deep rewards. Narrative coaching works because it blends together ancient wisdom, natural processes and contemporary scholarship to create a truly integrative practice modality. In the next chapter we will look at the process in more depth to assist you in incorporating it in your practice.

> **Mindsets are important because people can only see as far as their stories will take them, and they can only act as far as their stories will back them.**

Implications for Your Practice

Reconfiguration requires growth in four ways, each of which relates well to one of the phases of the Narrative Coaching model:

- Their agency and accountability as the Author of their stories (*Situate*).

- Their role as an Actor in their stories of self in relation with significant others (*Search*).

- Their work as an Agent in reconfiguring elements in their stories and for what purpose (*Shift*).

- Their work as an Activist in upgrading the impact their stories have on themselves and others (*Sustain*).

To bring about change, work with people in terms of:

- Time (reconfiguring the relationship between the past, present, and future).

- Space (reconfiguring the relationship between outer/profane, inner/sacred, and in-between/liminal).

- Identity (reconfiguring relationship between the constructed, lived and imagined selves).

- Action (reconfiguring the relationships between characters in their stories and with the narratives in which they reside).

What are your key insights?
What will you experiment with first?

CHAPTER 8

HOW NARRATIVE COACHING IS DONE

*Those who can answer the essential question inside become more able to handle
the uncertainties around them.* | *Michael Meade*

Up until now we have focused on the foundations of the Narrative Coaching
model. This chapter offers an inside look at how it is used in practice, starting
with an overview of the whole flow. You will gain a deeper understanding
of each of the four phases and how they work together to support people's
growth. For each phase, you will learn valuable tips on what people
commonly need, questions for your own reflection, common problems that
are encountered, and contributions you can make to help people and the
process move forward. Lastly, an extensive case story is unpacked to show in
more detail how the work is done. It is important to remember here that the
four phases are best understood as points along a natural spiral rather than as
a linear sequence of steps. They are based in a circular view of development
and the belief that at any moment we can be born all over again. As people
reconfigure key elements in their stories as they tell them in coaching,

they are also moving through the transitions their stories both record and facilitate as well as addressing the developmental edges they encounter along the way. Ultimately, it is about inviting them to have the conversation they most need to have.

Narrative coaching is based in two key premises: (1) Being open and present to what is true is a prerequisite for bringing about change; and (2) everything you need is right in front of you. Your first order of business is to help your coachees be present to themselves and the stories they are telling. Be a clear witness and a loving mirror so they can see their own stories and behaviors with more honesty and less judgment. Help them see their narrative logic and its consequences before they try to change anything. This not only builds up their courage to do the real work, but also gives both of you more substantive narrative material to work with in the session. Otherwise, it is like trying to build a castle on quicksand. For example, listen for implicit or explicit "if–then" statements that bring their assumptions to light—e.g., if I work extra hard at pleasing my boss on this project, then I will get the promotion; if I have all the answers (or at least appear to), then people will respect me and need me (and never leave me).

Coachees have lived within these patterns and assumptions for so long that they often become just how things "are." By bringing them out into the open, people can see them for what they are—particularly where they no longer align with reality—and make new choices. It is important as a coach to work within their view of the world prior to exploring the possibilities for new narratives and perspectives. Allow yourself to see the world through their eyes, because it is *their* understanding, not yours, that matters most in coaching. You are there to be their witness, not to solve their problems. Let's turn now to the model and examine what the process looks like in action.

> See the world through their eyes, because it is their understanding, not yours, that matters most in coaching. You are there to be their witness, not to solve their problems.

Overview of the Narrative Coaching Process:

1. **Situate** | Be curious. What is going on?

   The first phase is focused on welcoming people and observing how they situate themselves with the coach, in the stories they tell, and in the conversation. **What is** true for them? What are their current **explanations**? *Situate* represents the beginning of the journey as the person acknowledges the reality of, and the desire for a departure from, the status quo. At this point, there is nowhere to go, no goals to set, no need for lots of questions. The focus is on deepening the human connection and the level of presence for both people so they can fully engage in the process. Until then, the person is not yet on board and is likely to say, "I won't" or "I can't" (Prochaska & Norcross, 2002).

2. **Search** | Be clear. What do they truly want?

   The second phase is focused on unpacking openings in their presenting stories. **What if** they told their story like this? What are they truly seeking? What **experiences** do they need to have? The focus here shifts from the person to her story. What does it need in order to feel complete? The emphasis is on one or two critical elements that will make a real difference. The focus is on gaining greater clarity about themselves and their situation to determine what is truly at stake and what will restore order and fulfill their desire. Until then, the person is likely to say, "I might."

3. **Shift** | Be courageous. What needs to change?

   The third phase is focused on working with the essential elements that emerged from the previous phase. **What matters** most to them in terms of what they want to bring forward? What **experiments** can they engage in to try out new identities, behaviors, and/or narratives? The focus shifts from the story to key characters who often represent what they most need to learn. The focus is on consolidating what they have learned in the process and preparing themselves for taking new action. They are developing a new sense of themselves as they move on from the old story and lay the groundwork for a new story. This phase is about getting the person to say, "I will."

4. **Sustain | Be complete.** What is success for them?

The **fourth phase** is focused on identifying the first steps to be taken to put the new narrative in motion. **What works** in terms of what they have done in the session? What **expressions** would be most meaningful and valuable to them? It is important in this phase to help them prepare for the narratives into which they will return and to create structures for their success. What do they need, internally and externally, to sustain their gain? The focus is on completing the cycle as they integrate the changes they have made. It is a time when new perspectives and habits are formed and new ways of being and communicating emerge. By this time, the person will say, "I am" and then, "I still am."

FIGURE 16: NARRATIVE COACHING MODEL (APPLIED)

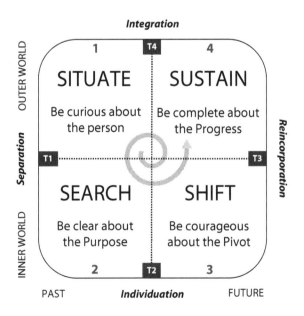

Guiding People through the Four Phases

1. Situate (Person)

It isn't that they can't see the solution.
It is that they can't see the problem. | *G.K. Chesterton*

The people who come to us for coaching tell us their stories with the hope that we can help them. They want to better understand their stories and themselves, why they do what they do, and how to bring about changes in their life and/or work. Our best gift to them in this first phase is to embody the adage to "be here now" and invite them to do the same. As Henri Nouwen (1998) once wrote, "Our most important question is not, 'What should I say or do?' but, 'How can I develop and offer enough inner space in myself and outer space between us where their story can be received?'" (p. 69). Coachees will be best served if you can (1) help them notice how they are situated in themselves, in their stories, and in the conversation; (2) stay within the frame, language, and experience of their stories as much as possible; and (3) and identify the turning point and the call to adventure that is before them. The irony of this phase is that the more you and your coachees can be *still* in the beginning, the faster they will discover what they are seeking and the more meaningful their results.

It sometimes takes a while for coachees to settle into this phase, especially if they are used to more goal-oriented, directive styles of coaching. One of your key roles in the beginning, particularly when coaching in high-paced environments, is to help coachees slow down so they can show up. The quality of your work in this phase is measured less by the clock and more by your presence, less by what you add and more by what you can do without, less by what you do and more by how you are. The guidance in this section is shorter than for the others because the sole focus is on situating the clients. It is about deeply welcoming the coachee and creating the field in which to work. That's it! There is nowhere to go; there is nowhere to be but here and now. You can often tell when a coachee is moving from *Situate* to *Search* because he starts to exhibit signs that he trusts himself and the process, and he has identified the turning point that surfaces the real purpose for the conversation. Make sure both of you are in his story and not yours before moving on.

Tips for Working in the Situate Phase

Aim

- To fully situate them in the conversation and the story.

Common needs for people
- A clear structure and frame for the process.

- Greater attention to their basic human needs.

- Greater awareness about themselves and their situation.

- Feeling seen and heard for who and where they are now.

Questions for the coach to reflect on
- How is this person doing?

- What support does she need in order to be here now?

- How is she defining the change?

- Why does she think the situation is the way it is?

- How would she describe what she has lost?

- What does she need to leave behind? Go in search of?

Common problems
- Gather too much information, most of which is not necessary.

- Rush to a premature solution, which only provides symptom relief.

Contributions from the coach
- Offer nonjudgmental compassion, deep empathy, genuine rapport.

- Foster honest assessment, full awareness, and existential acceptance.

- Encourage self-reflection (e.g., through keeping a log or journal).

- Build a platform of openness and trust for the work that is ahead.

- Provide important facts (*not* advice) about benefits of the journey.

2. Search (Purpose)

In order to come to the knowledge you have not, you must go by the way in which you know not. | *St. John of the Cross*

Once coachees have settled into the conversation, your next step is to help them to get clear on what they are searching for and, within that, how they can best use their time in the coaching session. You will often find your way to a suitable purpose for the conversation by noticing where the most vital energy is in motion. There is often tension in this phase between pursuing their aspiration *and* surrendering to what actually unfolds, and between exploring the depths of their issue *and* focusing on what can be done today. Once people are clear on the purpose for a session as part of a broader *Search*, they often realize that their aspiration and their surrender are two sides of the same coin. For example, I worked with a program participant around the difficulties he was experiencing with his business partner. He became most animated and engaged around his wish to make more space for *his* book in their business. He realized in the conversation that he needed to surrender a story *he* had been telling himself about their partnership if he wanted to fulfill *his* aspirations. He went on to identify what needed to change for this to happen and what it would look like if he did.

In this phase, coachees take on new perspectives from which to see their issues and alternatives and to release their initial constructions of their issue. With your help, they start to strip away false fronts and peel back the layers to get at what they really want from the session. As McKee (2004) observed, the root of most problems in our stories (as well as in our lives) is confusion about our desires. What is being asked of them by other people? By their own story? By their own soul? Narrative coaching helps people resolve this confusion so they are clearer about what they want and better prepared for what it will take to get it. In so doing, they become more open to exploring questions such as, "What am I trying to achieve with my story?" "How else might I tell it?" "How would that help me right now?" In the process, they start to surface their unspoken demands about how things "should be" and their values at risk because things are not that way. As McKee (2004) puts it, "What does the coachee want that, if she got it, would stop the story?"

233

Many coaching methodologies focus on asking lots of questions in the beginning because they are based on the belief that the *coach's* understanding is essential for success and *information* and *analysis* will lead to good solutions. In contrast, narrative coaching is based on the belief that the *coachee's* understanding is essential for success and *awareness* and *experience* will lead to good solutions. We surface the *essence* of the issue rather than gather lots of information. We are healers, not hunters. The purpose of our questions is to deepen the stillness and the experience so that the resolution emerges as if it was a rose ready to bloom. This is why we invite coachees to experientially enter their story and work with it from the inside out.

Everything you need is right in front of you.

By this I mean both inside themselves as they are telling the story and inside the story as it is being told. It is not about role-playing, acting, or reenacting as if from a distance. One of the techniques that works well here is freeze-framing the story at critical junctures. By pausing in those moments, you can draw coachees' attention to what is unfolding in more detail, help them feel into the truth of the experience and the narration, and discover openings for change that might otherwise be missed. You will also uncover tensions and dynamics in coachees' stories that have a direct correlation to the issue(s) they are seeking to address in coaching.

The *Search* is ultimately defined and refined through exploring these "complications." For example, a coachee who wanted to create a better work/life balance came to see that the real issue was ultimately not his over-commitment to work but his fears about going home. We got to this new awareness by freeze-framing his story about going home from work the day before—through which he realized that he was so stressed that he could not remember what he had for dinner, let alone if he even ate dinner. We now had an opening to explore his issue; it was accessible for him yet significant enough to get to the heart of his issue (what he was blocking out by compulsively staying at work). The *Search* phase is about helping coachees wake up to those aspects of themselves and their lives where they have been asleep, and to explore these with an open mind and heart to see what else is possible. You can often tell that a coachee is moving from *Search* to *Shift* when she starts talking about what she would like to do with her new insights and have identified a Pivot that incorporates a clear distinction between the old story and the new story. In the process, make sure that the coachee has the important pieces of the story out on the table so they can be reconfigured in the next phase.

Tips for Working in the Search Phase

Aim
- To clarify what they really want.

Common needs for people
- Opportunities and openness to face themselves and confront reality.
- Anchors, resources, and support from allies to move through the hard places.
- Encouragement to stay in the flow rather than seek a quick fix.
- Permission to let go so they can conserve energy to create what they want.

Questions for the coach to reflect on
- What does this person value? What will motivate him to change?
- What does he most need to learn in order to move forward?
- What about his narrative is most in need of change?
- What is he attracted to, avoiding, and/or anticipating?
- What does he desire? What is the critical choice to be made?

Common problems
- Analyzes too long, which leads to rumination and/or paralysis.
- Avoids real issue, which leads down rabbit holes or to superficial change.

Contributions from the coach

- Encourage candid self-reflection and whet his appetite for deeper learning.

- Help him explore his resistance and defenses as opportunities for growth.

- Work with him to identify the benefits of making changes in his language.

- Stay focused on his development and performance rather than fight his reactions.

- Invite him to prove to himself that the benefits of the change will pay off.

3. Shift (Pivot)

Before you embark on any path ask the question, " does this path have heart?"
If the answer is no, you will know it and then you must choose another path.
The trouble is that nobody asks the question. And when a man finally realizes
that he has taken a path without a heart the path is ready to kill him. | *Carlos*
Castaneda

In the *Shift* phase, people are preparing themselves to leave the liminal space and return to the world with a new narrative. They are putting together a resolution to the question that sent them on their quest in the first place. It is a time of sifting and sorting what they have learned thus far and experimenting with different configurations of their stories as they refine what they will bring to the world. As Poincaré (1952) observed, "If a new result is to have any value, it must unite elements long since known, but still scattered and seemingly foreign to each other, and suddenly introduce order where the appearance of disorder reigned" (p. 30). What we are looking for in this phase are the points of leverage where a shift would make a significant difference in the coachee's narrative and life. Ironically, these are often the very elements a coachees want to avoid at first. A lot of your work in this phase is helping coachees discover what matters to them most from the *Search* phase, what it would take to bring it to the world, and what they hope to gain in so doing.

Your patience (as measured by the quality of your presence, not the quantity of your time) is important in this phase too because people will be experimenting with new ways of being and acting. This is compounded by the fact that often at this point what they are working on is far from what they imagined in the beginning. This is one of the many reasons narrative coaches do not set goals with coachees before this point in the process (if at all). Few of us can see what it is we need to do differently from the vantage point of the *Situate* or *Search* phases. It is only through completing the purifying and clarifying descent into liminality that people can round the corner, so to speak, at T2 to get the necessary line of sight they need to see where to go from there. However, it is important to remember that this phase is still largely an inner one. The focus is on consolidating what they are learning, experimenting with what to bring back to their world, and preparing themselves for the return. While there is often an excitement as coachees imagine a new life with their new story, there may also be a sense of disconnection and disorientation as their identities and relationships shift in line with their new directions.

This is because they are still in a liminal space, even as they are increasingly orienting themselves toward their return to the world. To move through this phase, coachees need to practice the Pivots they have chosen and experiment with what the new story would feel, look, and sound like. You can support their success by helping them identify what may trigger the activation of the old story so they can strategize how to stay on track with and nurture the new story. This requires them to become increasingly able to notice when they are at the choice point, effectively self-regulate, and make the new choice. Jungian psychoanalyst James Hollis (2010) offers two questions coachees can use here: "Does this choice diminish me, or enlarge me?" (p. 13) "Does this path, this choice, make me larger or smaller?" (p. 71). I also ask questions such as: "Does this decision or action move you closer or further away from what you really want?" "What else would you need to address in order for this to work?"

While there is generally a cathartic release and a rising energy in this phase, it is important to temper that fire with the discipline coachees will need in preparing themselves for the realities of the return. This is because their first attempts at reincorporating themselves into their world with a new narrative may not go as planned. As such, they need to be willing to adapt it as needed (without diminishing its purpose), find external allies and resources (starting with those who will be most receptive), use their energy wisely, and create the structures they need in order to succeed. As always in this work, encourage coachees to use their own frames and language in setting intentions, using the reconfiguration tools, and making plans. Any knowledge that does not pass through their lived experience is seldom capable of bringing about deep and lasting changes (Carotenuto, 1985). As a coach, you can often tell that a coachee is moving from *Shift* to *Sustain* when he starts to put more of his attention on others, the future, and the world to which he will return.

Tips for Working in the Shift Phase

Aim

- To experiment with the new story.

Common needs for people

- Consolidation of learning and commitment in setting priorities.
- Opportunities to experiment, make mistakes (with feedback), have early wins.
- Support and reinforcement for the new ways of being and doing.
- Access to related experiences to strengthen and guide the new story.

Questions for the coach to reflect on

- What are the person's beliefs and assumptions about making this change?
- What will she gain from changing? Does she see it?
- What does she need to know in order to get started?
- What experiences might she need to have first?
- Who will be most affected by her changes?
- Can she address the key impediments to her progress?

Common problems
- Generating too many ideas, causing focus and energy to dissipate.
- Avoiding moving into the future, dealing with practicalities and realities.

Contributions from the coach
- Investigate and address with her any barriers to change.
- Invite her to formalize her pivots and write down her commitments.
- Help her develop substitutions for old patterns while new ones take hold.
- Ensure she has sufficient building blocks in place to get started.
- Find examples of the desired mindsets and behaviors in her past.
- Leave breathing room around her new stories so they can grow.
- Connect her with relevant positive role models and opportunities.

4. Sustain (Progress)

Here I stand; I can do no other. | *Karl Marx*

In true narrative fashion, this last phase is not about creating plans for the future as much as it is about identifying a plotline that connects the past, present, and future in a new way. In order for new stories or a new relation between stories to be integrated into a coachee's life, they must evolve from, yet contain, elements of the old, "familiar" stories (Sluzki, 1992). Any solutions she wants to take forward have to make enough sense to her within her *stories-as-is* and her *world-as-is*. The more coachees can bring about change using their own "laws" (Kaplan, 2002) and their own narrative material, the more likely they will be able to sustain their change.

As Vygotsky (1986) noted, new information will be heard and processed better by coachees when it is sensitively attuned to their current state. This phase is about helping people integrate what they have gained through a conscious use of cumulative nudges and the development of new habits. Invite them to practice in their current world as much as possible, especially as they start, rather than seek out too much that is new. For example, most coachees would more reliably be mindful as they brush their teeth than in trying to start a meditation practice for the first time.

Many of the steps coachees take in this phase involve their relationships to significant others in their life or workplace (e.g., renegotiating relational agreements, letting go of routines that no longer fit, making more space for new choices, and creating new structures of support). Their new narratives are more likely to survive if they can foster or find conditions in which they and their stories can naturally flourish. Otherwise, it becomes too hard to bridge between their old and new worlds. Therefore, ask yourself questions such as:

- Do they have what they need to bring the new story to life?

- Does the energy flow better now or are there places where it is still stuck?

- Do they have strong allies who can provide safe places to practice?

- Who will support and challenge them as they bring their new narrative into the world?

- Do they have old loyalties (to people or narratives) that hold them back?

One of the most striking features I notice when people have dropped into the *Sustain* phase is their profound and visceral sense of "coming home." For most of them, the telltale sign is the softening of their face as the tension and defenses drop away and they can be more authentic and transparent. Isn't that what we all really want in our heart of hearts?—"to return to some resting place inside ourselves, outside of all frantic activity, outside of time, that we sense is waiting for us, calling to us at every moment of our lives?" (Moody, 1997, p. 156). Take time in this phase to help coachees reflect on and celebrate how far they have come—both for its own sake and as the foundation for what is to come next. Create a point of stability and a sense of closure at the end of each session. It is not that it has to be complete (as in fully resolved), but more that they need to feel a sufficient sense of closure. You can often tell that a coachee is moving from *Sustain* back to

Situate when she starts to exhibit signs of increased intrinsic motivation and an internal locus of control; her identity, language, and behaviors are reorganizing to incorporate the change; others recognize a difference; and new results are appearing.

Tips for Working in the Sustain Phase

Aim of this phase
- To integrate changes and manifest the gift.

Common needs for people
- Discipline and recognition to practice consistently and deliberately.
- Provisions for lapses and external challenges in order to keep on track.
- Self-awareness, self-regulation, and simple practices as nudges.
- Ways to remember the new choices in the moment.
- Opportunities to hone and demonstrate mastery.
- Accountability for making decisions and taking action.

Questions for the coach to reflect on
- What has changed the most for him?
- What can he do now that he could not do as well before?
- How will this benefit him and others?
- What will help him sustain the change?
- Is his story rich enough to sustain his new future?

Common problems
- Making plans that are difficult to implement and/or not acted on.
- Failing to prepare for challenging responses from significant others.

Contributions from the coach
- Help him identify and connect with key supporters early on.
- Send reminders of his new stories with queries about his discoveries.

- Prepare him for the collective narratives into which he will return

- Identify likely obstacles and challenges and how to address them

- Craft further experiments to explore and experience his new narrative

- Invite him to make new connections in line with his new stories

- Develop the means for him to recognize lapses and respond effectively

- Establish new routines and support networks to reinforce the new behaviors

TAKING A CLOSER LOOK: A CASE STUDY

Wayne[10] was a man in his early forties who came to coaching to sort out some career issues. In particular, he was neither satisfied in his current role nor clear about what to do next. He had a vague sense of déjà vu in assessing his current dilemma and was curious how he could forge a new path for himself in his career. He had been seen as a top talent in his early corporate career but had migrated to smaller firms over time. Along the way, he had developed significant expertise, but he continued to struggle with finding suitable and satisfying employment. One of the key themes to emerge was the similarity between his interpersonal patterns within his family of origin and his choices of roles, leaders, and workplaces. Early in our sessions he identified what he saw as the crux of the matter: "I notice that whenever I go into really downward spirals in my career, it's been around injustice—in situations where healing and flow were being blocked by power and unfairness."

We co-created experiences in which he could experiment with other ways of being that would attract situations more likely to fulfill his deeper desires around work and self-expression. The key elements in Wayne's coaching journey across four ninety-minute sessions are organized using the four phases in the narrative coaching model as a reflection of the broader arc of his journey in coaching. The model was used as a frame for conducting the coaching sessions and for interpreting the data from the transcripts. I've included brief descriptions of what I did as the coach, representative excerpts from him, and some comments and reflections on the process (*in italics*).

Situate (*What is* true right now?)

We spent much of the first session reflecting on an initial dream about paddling his boat upstream to no avail and gathering stories about his family and career path. We were able to get beyond the feelings of anger and betrayal that emerged by remaining nonjudgmental about the characters in his stories and non-assumptive about what they meant. We explored related stories as the key themes started to emerge in order to develop a deeper understanding of his narrative patterns and dynamics. The primary focus in this first phase was situating him as the narrator and protagonist and on developing a rich field in which new experiences and stories could emerge. The following is one of the core themes that appeared early on in the comments from Wayne:

> I felt my family [of origin] life was unstable; I wanted to leave, but couldn't; I often felt stuck in the middle. I went on a number of long journeys in search of what I perceived I lost (or on behalf of what I perceived others lost), but I'm not sure where to go, often get blocked or lost along the way, and often feel like an exile.

In narrative coaching, all characters are welcome at first, because it is too early to tell which ones will end up being critical for discovering and/or implementing the resolution.

We explored key phrases such as "being stuck," "being lost," and "being an exile" so they came alive for him in a palpable way and could be used in creating subsequent experiences in our sessions. We worked with these narrative elements so that he had the full sense of those experiences, how he positioned himself in those stories, and the impact of doing so. We also explored his continual efforts to return "home" in the workplaces he chose in an attempt to redeem his unfulfilled quest on behalf of himself and others. He became aware early on in our work together of the price he had paid and the payoffs from staying stuck in this cycle as well as his strong desire to change this pattern. He had been here before, but this time he was looking for a new pattern and path.

We worked in depth with a story about being a kid in his front yard and feeling torn between home (his house) and the world (across the street)—and his subsequent sense of wanting to keep a foot in two worlds and thereby holding himself back. As he put it, rather than become the king (a man in his own right) and proclaiming his innate right to be here, he often abdicated his space or overspent his energy. He talked about these issues this way:

> Part of what keeps me stuck is a sense of the binary nature of my life—the sense that I have one foot in this camp and one foot in another—and a lack of faith that I can generate prosperity on my own. There is a sense of being trapped, a fear that if I turn one way I will be "sucked back into the evil empire" so need to keep it at arm's length, but if I go in the direction of my true values I can't be generative enough.
>
> If I could just find the right place, then my gifts could flourish. So everything is about the drama of finding the right place. And I go black-and-white over it. This is not the right place anymore. Now I've got to leave, but where do I go? It's almost like if I find the right place, then I'll know what my gift is or what my work is.

The last line foreshadowed what was to come soon in our conversation, a reflection of the recursive nature of narratives as temporal Mobius strips. By this point we had assembled a rich palette of narrative images and elements to work with.

It is important at this phase to get a few key stories on the table in a focused fashion, then circle back to the key theme(s) to better understand their dynamics and the developmental opportunities they may signal.

Search (*What if* I told my story like this?)

As we moved deeper into his issues, I asked Wayne to keep a journal of his dreams as they often shed light on what is at stake. *Dreams can be particularly useful in the* Search *phase in surfacing the Shadow and opening up new possibilities.* Wayne reported that:

> Images of leprosy, dissolution, letting go, unlocking doors behind which sits a sense of vitality (and danger) kept appearing in my dreams and stories—signaling to me that something important was happening.

There is often a quickening of the pace as coachees move through this phase—and new energy that had been locked up in old stories starts to become available.

We created an experiential activity to help him enact his perceived binary choice between: (1) staying in the family pattern (e.g., in the front yard), thereby losing himself but gaining rewards; or (2) leaving the family pattern (e.g., crossing the street), thereby gaining himself but losing rewards. The basic structure for the experience was drawn from the images and language in his actual stories, and it unfolded based on what we noticed as he stepped into the story in the coaching room. The aim was to give him a visceral sense of what it was like for him to live out these two stories, how it felt when he made these sensations conscious, how it sounded in hearing himself talk about them out loud, and what he would like to be and do differently. The latter emerged from his experience in the activity and the story itself, not by stepping outside the experience to analyze it or offer advice.

As was noted earlier, everything—including the new story—was right in front of us and already there.

We spent most of our time in this session working with the two primary obstacles that kept appearing in his stories and dreams: the "rock" to which he had been attached and the "fence/wall" he kept trying to break through. We set up an experience in which he tried to move away from the "rock"— which he discovered symbolized his parents and the stories surrounding them—and toward a new life. As he began to release the ties he felt from the rock, he sensed a chasm in front of him—not too dissimilar to the street in front of his house as a boy—that he would need to cross in order to more fully attend to his own family, life, and career. The persistent desire to break through the fence/wall was also captured in his urge to cross this chasm. In guiding him through the process, I moved between active guide and present witness positions as well as between facilitator and character roles, depending on what was called for. In the end, he gained a palpable sense of renewed energy by cutting the ties to the "rock" (with gratitude for them) and naming the chasm and then breaking free to cross it as a threshold. Once there, I helped him to solidify his new place so that he had enough of a foundation to begin embodying the new story.

He came to recognize in doing this exercise that the fight for him was not to change or redeem the others—to whom he often felt indentured for rescuing him from the pain of feeling trapped—but to acknowledge them and fight for what is important *to him*. We then could move on to explore what would have to change within himself and in his relationship with others in order to bring these new stories to life. Around this time, Wayne was having some initial conversations with another firm as part of his desire to move to a new job. At the next session, he shared:

> I noticed my old patterns appearing as I went through the interview process for a senior role with [this firm]. I began to connect the dots between that opportunity and my family pattern. I used what we have done in coaching to name the narrative drama I would have entered yet again and the all-to-familiar role I would have taken up as the peacemaker. I would have ended up playing small yet again, and I could see how it would all likely end for me. As a result, I turned down the offer.

It felt like a major victory for him to not take on that role and an honoring of the developmental journey he had been on. He was feeling empowered to open himself to discover new aspects of himself and new ways of being in the world.

This phase is about clarifying the deeper purpose for the coaching work, channeling the new insights and energy that have been liberated, and beginning to bring them to life. It requires patience and perseverance on the part of the coach and the coachee, as it is often tempting to want to skip this challenging work in an unfortunate rush to get to the end. However, skipping this vital step generally results in outcomes that are shallow and less sustainable. It is important in this phase to have a clear purpose for the conversation and yet not get overly attached to where it is headed or what it will mean in the end. As we noted earlier, it is quite often the case that neither the coach nor the coachee know what the latter's story or process is ultimately about until it resolves.

Shift (*What matters* most going forward)

As Wayne began to name what mattered to him most from the previous session, he shared:

> I was particularly struck by the return of energy, the thrumming, that came into my legs when I did the work with the "rock." Somehow the phrase "cut off at the knees" came to mind in thinking about my past. I now feel I can claim more of my right to stand on my own two feet, on my terms—and with this claim comes a new sense of energy.

I suggested that perhaps it was time for him to honor that "thrum" in his heart and body and explore what that would mean for him in making new choices about his work. I reminded him of what the rock had "said" in the powerful experience he had in the previous session, "You have our blessing to go embrace your own children and your life." We spent a fair bit of time letting that blessing sink in so he really felt it and owned it. He began to imagine a new place for himself in relation to others at work as he increasingly freed himself from old narratives and the roles he unconsciously felt obligated to take as a result.

As noted earlier, this accountability and anchoring was important here because new behaviors flow more easily from identities (and their stories) that support them.

We developed a profile for what kinds of work environments would bring out the best in him and support his efforts to live out a new story of himself at work. This became a template by which he gauged potential opportunities, particularly in terms of the relationships with key figures on any executive team with whom he would work. He was able to see the compensatory nature of many of his previous roles and was curious about how to do it differently. In doing this work he moved beyond the earlier fantasies about a place for him based on "if only." As a result, he was able to attain a significant breakthrough in how he was approaching his search for suitable work and his life as a whole. It came when he said:

> It seems like maybe what I'm being asked right now is the opposite of what I thought for a long time: I need to own my gifts and the right place will come to me [rather than the other way around].

As is often the case in narrative work, there was no need for goals at this phase. He was starting from a new sense of himself, and he had some key pivots, fresh experiences with trying new ways, a strong intrinsic motivation to chart a new path, and a template to use in making healthier choices about work. He ended this session by saying:

> There is a greater lightness and sense of freedom that is emerging. There were some wonderful moments near the end of our sessions when I felt much more in flow and could take an observer's stance on my own stories rather than being enmeshed in them.

Sustain (*What works* better as a result)

As we reached the final session, the focus was on consolidating his gains from our work together and identifying next steps for him. He decided to forego the job search for a while but quit his position, with a plan to do contract work while he sorted out the various aspects of his life that had been built up around the old story (e.g., some important conversations with his wife and kids). I referred him to a colleague who specializes in career strategies to get some tactical support in searching for a new job when he was ready. He also sought out opportunities at home and with colleagues where he could practice living from his new story. He concluded the final session with:

I feel such relief in beginning to put down all these burdens I have carried. I feel freer now to pursue a path that is healthier for me. I recognize that these are the first steps of a longer journey.

A postscript to this case story: I recently had the opportunity to work again with Wayne. He still wrestles with vestiges of the old narrative, but far less than before and with much more insight and resilience now. I noticed that, while the old language crept in a few times, he was starting from a much stronger place, and he pivoted much more quickly now. Wayne has set up his own practice and has developed a rubric based on our work that he uses to determine which clients would best suit him. It struck me how much more clarity and energy he has now that he is not tied up fighting old narrative battles. It is a great example of how this work continues to ripple through people's lives for weeks and months after their sessions. It is as if the changes takes place at a cellular level. What more could you ask for?

Putting It All Together

The velocity necessary for success exceeds the rate of reflection. The faster events move, the faster we move to try to keep up with them until we are overwhelmed by the escalating pace. | *Sam Keen*

Many coaching models are centered around (1) the imposition of a structure on the coaching conversation; (2) a linear progression toward goals; and (3) what the coach should do. In contrast, the narrative coaching model is centered around (1) the immersion in the story as it unfolds in the coaching conversation; (2) a circular progression toward new awareness and action; and (3) what the coachee is noticing and experiencing. Those who struggle at first to coach or be coached this way generally do so because they are stuck in their preconceptions about what coaching is "supposed to be." Therefore, imagine the Narrative Coaching model as a window through which you can look at a conversation rather than as a set of steps to which you must adhere. It works best when you can fundamentally trust the field as you coach rather than act as if you are responsible for driving the process. Otherwise, it is like trying to help a garden grow by constantly fertilizing and watering it rather than respecting its natural rhythms and needs.

> **As you incorporate the model into your work, remember that you are a guide in the boat, not the river.**

Coaching this way involves drawing from (1) *narrative psychologies* to understand people as narrators in supporting their development and performance; (2) *narrative structures* to use in listening to and reconfiguring the material that is narrated; and (3) *narrative practices* to use in guiding people across thresholds so they can re-enter the world with a new story. The Narrative Coaching model incorporates these three into a unified process of change that enables people to transform themselves, their stories and their lives at the same time. As you incorporate the model into your work, remember that you are a guide in the boat, not the river. Your role is to help people break free so they can engage more fully in reality as it *is*, develop more mature narrative strategies, and more consciously choose the stories they live by. Along the way, you can help coachees be more aware of where they are in their process, seek out what they need to move to the next phase, and determine what they will do once they are there. The more you have circled your own "trees" in your life and work, the more you can genuinely and effectively help others do the same.

It is important to note, however, that developing a higher consciousness does not inherently resolve your psychological issues or take away your anxiety, but it does enable you to find greater freedom for yourself and others. Find ways to raise your level of consciousness that work for you in your life, and practice them so you can hold more space for people and work with them at more levels. The more you can embody radical presence with coachees, the more they will relax, engage with the real work to be done, and resolve the questions that brought them to coaching. Your role is to provide a strong enough container and a robust enough process to meet them wherever they are and help them move forward. What my own journey has taught me is that the more courageously and fully I step into my own experiences and encounters, the stronger and more compassionate I am with the fellow human beings who entrust me with their stories. At its core, narrative coaching is about being willing to walk alongside people as they find their way to new stories about who and how they want to be in the world.

Here is a view of the model that incorporates key elements from each of the versions in the past two chapters. I would suggest using it as a reference as you study this work, and using one of the simpler versions as you practice and reflect on your coaching and your own journey.

FIGURE 17: NARRATIVE COACHING MODEL (COMPLETE)

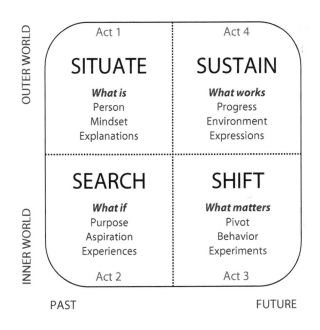

Implications for Your Practice

1. SITUATE   Be curious about the narrator.
    What is going on for her?
    What is true for her?
    Hold space for the human.
    Shift the Mindset.

2. SEARCH   Be clear about the story.
    What if it were told like this?
    What does she really want and why?
    Be a witness for the story.
    Identify the Aspiration.

3. SHIFT   Be courageous about the characters.
    What matters to her now?
    What needs to change?
    Give the characters a voice.
    Prototype the Behavior.

4. SUSTAIN   Be complete in the field.
    What works now?
    What is success for her?
    Prepare her to return home.
    Adapt the Environment.

What are your key insights?
What will you experiment with first?

CHAPTER 9

HOW TO BRING NEW STORIES TO LIFE

The harder we try, the more confused things become. More often than not, we do not need more instructions; we need more nonjudgmental awareness, more clarity about the desired result, more trust in ourselves, and more willingness to act. | *Tim Gallwey*

In this chapter, we will first look at goals as they are typically applied in coaching and talk about why they may be less useful than you think. This sets the stage for a look at the four core reconfiguration tools, how they are commonly used in narrative coaching, and what this means for your practice. They are effective in part because they are simple, down-to-earth resources that reflect the DIYT (Do-It-Yourself-Together) spirit of our times. The tools (Turning Points, Pivots, Vectors of Change, and Nudges) are designed to achieve the same outcomes as goals, but to do so in ways that are more in line with the narrative approach, the lives we lead now, and the way many people naturally operate. They support people's success by providing a flexible yet clear structure; tapping their intrinsic motivations; and keeping them in touch with themselves, their aspirations, and their environment as they change. As a result, people can move forward in ways they would never have imagined as possible had they stayed within the narrow confines of goals set in advance.

Coaching without Goals

People have used goals as a resource for achieving great things—from losing weight to meeting sales numbers to putting a man on the moon. There is a great deal of research suggesting that goal theory can be useful in understanding how people achieve their desired outcomes (see Grant, 2012). They are well suited for tracking readily measurable tasks (funds raised, time in a race, score on a test) and serving as markers for novices and benchmarks for experts. However, I have also observed over the past twenty years that goals are often counterproductive—in large part because of the way they are used. In both coaching and organizations, goals often end up increasing people's (1) over-emphasis on the end state, often at the expense of other considerations (e.g., ethics and unintended consequences); (2) orientation toward short-term pressures and measures; (3) fatigue with goalposts that keep moving, are not aligned, and interfere with healthy lives; (4) sense of overwhelm and feeling disconnected from themselves; and (5) tendency to foreclose on their search for what they really want (see Ordóñez, Schweitzer, Galinsky, & Bazerman, 2009). A narrative approach to coaching pays far less attention to goals, yet still provides internal and external structures people can use to achieve what matters to them.

Austin and Vancouver (1996) succinctly describe goals as "internal representations of desired states or outcomes" (p. 388). However, in real life, goals are almost exclusively discussed in terms of the external manifestations of desired states or outcomes, and there is often a disconnect between the two. Goals are often formed along the lines of "I am here and I want to be there." While this is useful as a focusing construct, it assumes that people (1) know where they are now, (2) are certain that "there" is where they want to be, and (3) know the path they need to take to get there. Unfortunately, this is often not the case. Working toward distant goals often leads people to act as if they can just jump the chasm between where they are now and their goal without acknowledging their current reality (inner or outer), doing the essential developmental work, or investing in what it takes to sustain the results. This seldom works because people often go into it with the same mindset and approach as they had in the past. To bring about change, coachees need to start from a new position that can only be found as they move into *Shift*. As they look "up" at *Sustain* with a fresh perspective, they will see themselves, their issue, and their resolution in new ways.

At a basic level, the challenge with goals is that people often set them for things they might not otherwise do and/or do not want to do (e.g., I will go to the gym three times a week regardless) or in terms of what they are not going to do (I will not have dessert this week). These are noble intentions, but people setting these types of goals often fail because willpower is seldom enough. Roy Baumeister's (Baumeister, Bratslavsky, Muraven & Tice, 1998) research on ego depletion makes that clear. His research and that of others suggest that people's discretionary energy and willpower would be far better spent building new habits one at a time than on striving toward a goal. I also find that when people set aside their initial goals (form)—even for a short period of time— there is more room for a deeper level of truth (function). This relates to what I call GET (Goal Evaporation Theory) in which many of the presenting problems people bring to coaching fall away as the real work to be done reveals itself in the process. This calls for coaches and coachees to stand still long enough to discern what is most true and what the latter are truly seeking. It is why we hold space for people's stories before any attempts are made to change them or their stories (Gallwey, 1981/2009).

EXAMPLE

I was doing a demonstration as a guest lecturer for a class of graduate coaching students. They had heard about my work and were quite curious to see how one could possibly coach without goals. The woman who offered to be coached had a classic goal: to lose five kilograms (about 11 pounds) after the birth of her second child. We stayed within this story—as it was true for her at that point—then spent eight to ten minutes exploring the story with her. At no point did we talk about how she was going to lose the weight or by when. We just held her idea lightly and nonjudgmentally. In the process, she came to realize that her "goal" was actually a familial and cultural construct about what she "should" weigh after having a child. She realized that she was happy and healthy as she was, and she released her internalized goal to lose more weight as a result.

In the end, the pursuit of goals is seldom as simple and linear as it is often portrayed. They are often depicted mechanistically as described in this critique by David Clutterbuck & Susan David (2013): "You decide what you want to achieve, gather the necessary resources and motivation, and take appropriate action. With apt, positive feedback you continue until the goal is achieved" (p. 31). However, having taught coaching skills to thousands of people inside and outside organizations over the past twenty years, I find that they quite often have the opposite experience. Here is what I have noticed:

TABLE 4: GETTING RESULTS THROUGH NARRATIVE COACHING

What gets in the way for people	How narrative coaching addresses the issue
• They seldom know what they truly want when they start (let alone why).	• We only explore what relates to what they truly want.
• They seldom have all the resources they need.	• We tap and adapt resources people already have.
• They waver in motivation since it is often extrinsic in nature at first.	• We identify intrinsic motivations that matter to them.
• They don't know what actions will lead to success.	• We give opportunities to experience and experiment to determine what works.
• They rarely get timely, relevant and constructive feedback.	• We give provide direct, clear and actionable feedback.
• They feel challenged by too many, often competing, goals (that keep changing).	• We invite the person to focus on one threshold at a time.
• They can't shake feeling that pursuing goals keeps them on the treadmill.	• We invite them into greater awareness of the bigger picture.

We have also been taught to believe that the best way to achieve our goals is to carefully reason about them and consciously strive to reach them. However, "many desirable states—happiness, attractiveness, spontaneity— are best pursued indirectly, and conscious thought and effortful striving can actually interfere with their attainment" (Slingerland, 2014, p. 18). When people focus too much on the external actions related to a goal, they often lose touch with themselves and what is true for them and about their situation (see Gallwey, 1981/2009; 2001, 2009). As such, they lose track of their higher-order, values-based goals that are linked to their desires and instead chase after lower-order goals that are often linked to other's demands. When people focus too much on the internal representation of a goal, they often become disconnected from their environment. Narrative coaching is designed to keep people connected with themselves, their environment, and their desired outcome as they move forward in coaching. In so doing, they can be more adaptive and attain better scaffolding to support their success.

This is particularly important when the truly desired outcome is uncertain in the beginning or their aspirations don't lend themselves well to a goal-oriented approach. As Kay (2010) noted, "Breaking down well-defined and prioritized objectives into specific states and actions that can be monitored and measured is not how people tend to find fulfillment in their lives, create great art, establish great societies, or build great businesses" (p. 71). In addition, the traditional view of goals does not account for the complexity and contingencies that are pervasive in modern life or help people authentically and effectively align their inner and outer worlds. As Ordóñez, Schweitzer, Galinsky & Bazerman (2009) argued:

> The simplest things to measure are not necessarily the most important factors in achieving the overall purpose, and focusing on short-term performance may impede learning and lasting personal growth. . . . Setting and pursuing specific goals may cause people to ignore important dimensions of performance that are not specified by the goal-setting system. . . . [N]arrow goals can promote myopic, short-term behavior that harms the organization [or the person] in the long run. (p. 8)

Narrative coaching starts with intentions as visualized, actionable internal representations because they provide a way for people to stay grounded in themselves as they are moving forward. This approach aligns with Timothy Gallwey's (1981/2009, 2001, 2009) great work on the "inner game" and newer versions of NLP in which you "set an intention" to do a particular behavior and let your unconscious mind figure out how and when to do it. Setting an intention is different than goal-setting in that "it is less focused on the outcome and more focused on the commitment. The theory is that if we are consciously congruent when we set the intention, the unconscious will do the rest" (Tompkins & Lawley, 2001, p. 6). Intentions involve setting a clear direction and the resolve to take an action or achieve an outcome—without the necessity of an ultimate goal or a defined path.

Results still matter and are what narrative coaches are measured by, particularly in organizations. It is just that we take a more mindfully emergent approach in terms of determining the true purpose of the conversation and how best to fulfill it. This shows up in narrative coaching in the fact that we focus more than most on enabling people to first be present in the conversation rather than gathering lots of information. This allows people to drop into a deeper truth and attain results that are more meaningful and sustainable. Intentions work well with the four reconfiguration tools because they encapsulate what the person needs as they move in the direction of their new narrative: a clarity about when and where to pivot, a vision for where they are headed, and a guide for course corrections along the way.

Setting a clear intention keeps coachees focused on trusting themselves, which allows them to be fully in the flow, engaged in the experience and aware of what is happening. Operating from goals often keeps people focused on the outcome, which means they are out of the flow because they are worried about making a mistake. Having a clear intent also creates "an integrated state of priming, a gearing up of our neural system to be in the mode of that specific intention: we can be readying to receive, to sense, to focus, to behave in a certain manner" (Siegel, 2007, p. 177). When your state is in sync with your intention, your actions are inspired and in flow because they are an extension of your being. When your identity and state are not in sync with your intention, your actions are often labored and less effective because it is all about your doing. This priming helps people notice when a pivot is called for, and it activates the resources necessary to move in the desired direction and act in line with their desired purpose.

EXAMPLE

> I used to play a lot of tennis. I had a memorable experience of the power of intention when I won a free lesson with a top coach. Unlike the others I had in the past, he talked very little and invited me to focus on being in the flow rather than on my techniques. I remember feeling my whole mind and body completely absorbed in what I was doing rather than worrying about if I was doing it right. There were no goals in sight. There was also no separation between my mind and my body, myself and my racket (or the ball). I soon was playing the best tennis of my life. How could this be when he was not teaching me anything? Or so I thought at the time. . . . My body already knew how to play good tennis; the secret was to let it do so.

His approach, which mirrors how we work in narrative coaching, challenged me to trust myself and act from that intention. Paradoxically, I was able to achieve my desired outcome (to play well) by releasing my attachment to how I was playing. This was certainly far more effective than setting a goal to improve my game by doing x, y, and z. I find that focusing on goals often takes coachees into their head and out of their felt experience and inherent trust—and, as a consequence, their performance drops. Instead, narrative coaches focus on pivoting in the present (in the direction of their aspiration) more than setting goals for the future. As we shall see later in the chapter, Pivots work well because they provide a simpler focus and allow for more adaptive responses. If you do use goals with a coachee because it works for them, they should be set near the end of the coaching process and in conjunction with the narrative reconfiguration tools you've used. The following chart lists some of the issues people often face when chasing after goals and what they can gain from choosing with clear intention instead.

TABLE 5: CHASING GOALS VERSUS CHOOSING WITH INTENTIONS

Chasing Goals	Choosing with Intention
• Multiple meanings	• Simpler focus
• Outside in	• Inside out
• Linear and direct	• Spiral and tangential
• Static and rational	• Dynamic and holistic
• Deconstructive	• Integrative
• Know destination	• Know direction
• Know optimum	• Know values
• Know path and steps	• Know pivot and signals
• Focus on future	• Focus on present
• Short-term gain	• Long-term growth
• Emphasis on execution	• Emphasis on experimentation

Using the Core Tools

Each of the core narrative coaching tools is most often used at one of the four thresholds in the change process. The tools were designed to reflect what people are naturally seeking at that point.

Four tools for reconfiguring narratives

Tool	Purpose
• Turning Point	Opening for change.
• Pivot	Choice between old and new story.
• Vector of Change	Nested pivots (BEAM[11]) to enact new story.
• Nudge	Simple ways to reinforce new story.

Each reconfiguration tool is particularly well-suited for one of the thresholds and the developmental step it represents (see figure 18 below). For example, the first one (Turning Points) is most often found as people *Separate* and begin their journey. The four reconfiguration tools are designed to be used when coachees are ready, willing, and able to do the work. Everything up to that point in coaching is about preparing them for this awakening and reckoning. It is also important to remember that the energy that emerges from the reconfiguration process must be equal to or greater than the perceived energy of the current narrative in order to bring about change. There has to be enough energy to make a difference, but not so much that it makes things overly complicated. The following is an outline of how to use the reconfiguration tools to guide people across their thresholds in coaching. The work that is done at each threshold in the process will come in handy at the next one, both as a source of material and as a resource for the new work to be done.

FIGURE 18: NARRATIVE COACHING MODEL (WITH CORE TOOLS)

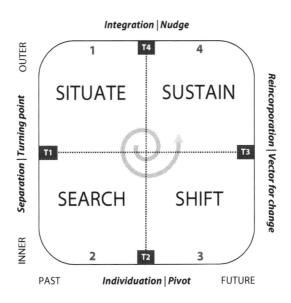

EXAMPLE

Using the four narrative reconfiguration tools

T1   Notice the Turning Point when the conversation shifts, signaling a potential change of direction that seems promising. Help the coachee to identify what she is leaving behind as she Separates and embarks on the Search so she can "empty the teacup" and ready herself to learn.

T2   Work with her to fashion a Pivot—her old story on one side (drawing on what she left behind and is in Shadow) and the new story on the other side (drawing on her desires and core values at stake). Invite her to articulate what she gains as she Individuates and embarks on the Shift.

T3   Create a Vector of Change by nesting three Pivots (Behavior, Environment, Mindset) that are aligned around a shared Aspiration. Invite her to articulate where she wants to Reincorporate first and who and what will help her as she embarks on Sustain.

T4   Identify a few meaningful Nudges that she can use whenever opportunities arise each day to move in the direction of her Vector of Change and her new story. Invite her to articulate how she will Integrate these changes into her life—which leads her to a new *Situate*.

Turning Point

In times of great change, the learners will inherit the Earth while those attached to old certainties will find themselves beautifully equipped to deal with a world that no longer exists. | *Eric Hoffer*

This tool is observed most often in coaching as people *Separate* and cross the T1 threshold from the *Situate* phase to the *Search* phase. Turning Points are often triggered by "inciting incidents" (see McKee, 2004) that reflect "breaches in the commonplace" (Bruner, 1986) where the status quo is disrupted. It is at these points where people turn away from or are turned away from their current trajectory and are seeking another way forward as a result. In those moments people realize, "I used to think or do that, but now

I want or need to think or do this instead." We saw this in Nancy's example as she turned off from the story, "I'm just one of the gang" when she realized that was not true anymore. When people recognize they are at a Turning Point—the proverbial fork in the road—help them begin to put into words the two choices that are before them and what they are seeking from the new path. Engage them with courageous and compassionate care as they grapple with the disruption that has occurred or is on the near horizon. Images and themes that will end up playing a major role in their journey are often foreshadowed here. In the end reconfiguration is only possible for those who have stepped onto the path and is only complete once they have finished the spiral.

> ## Reconfiguration is only possible for those who have stepped onto the path.

As you begin exploring a coachee's Turning Point with him, pay particular attention to what he perceives he has lost or is losing and is now seeking to (re-)gain. Most coachees will frame this in tangible and familiar external terms at first. Go with it to build rapport and then invite them to begin the inner journey as well. It is important to let the story unfold fully because the more open people are to the process, the more fruitful it will be as they move through it. The full significance of a Turning Point is not likely to be revealed until later in the process, but it serves a valuable purpose in signaling a turning away from the status quo.

You can think of a Turning Point as an entrance into the conversation a coachee most needs to have as he starts his journey. It is tempting to think that we know what their stories mean and, therefore, where people and their stories are headed (or should head). Instead, be patient so their true purpose can reveal itself. Manage your respective anxieties so neither of you prematurely forecloses on the process or the stories that are unfolding. Let them name the journey they are on as much as possible because they will be more committed to issues they have framed and solutions they have designed. At the same time, hold it loosely as it is a doorway not the destination.

Pivot

To have success in crunch time, you need to integrate certain healthy patterns into your day-to-day life so that they are completely natural to you when the pressure is on. | Josh Waitzkin

This tool is observed most often in coaching as people Individuate and cross the T2 threshold from the *Search* phase to the *Shift* phase. The basic distinction that began as a Turning Point is now coming into more focus as they shift their attention from the past to the future and from deliberation to implementation. A Pivot is a simple binary choice people can make in any moment between thinking and acting in line with an old story (the rut they are leaving behind) or in line with a new story (the aspiration they are moving toward). The new story in a Pivot is *not* defined as a fixed and specific end point as one would with a goal. Instead, it radiates from a choice point in two in the desired direction. Some of the differences between setting goals and making pivots are outlined in the table below.

TABLE 6: SETTING GOALS VERSUS MAKING PIVOTS

Setting Goals	Making Pivots
• Require a target to shoot for	• Offer a focus to be guided by
• Take people out of the present	• Keep the present and future connected
• Define destination beforehand	• Define direction to head
• Define optima by which to plan	• Define values by which to be guided
• Define path and steps to get there	• Define triggers and practice opportunities
• Focus on comparisons with the future	• Focus on performing in the present
• Focus on execution and explanation	• Focus on experimentation and adaptation

We saw an example of the value of Pivots in figure 5, which depicted the infusion of Shadow material to temper our strengths. Whenever the person finds herself in a situation in which she would otherwise default to the old story, she now has a simple, memorable, and actionable alternative she can choose in the moment. The more often she chooses the new narrative channel, the more its related neural pathways and habits are strengthened, the more her identity comes in line with the new story, and the more her environment can relate to her in that way. It is important that the taglines for the two stories neither exceed too dramatically nor stay too timidly within the range of their current narrative schemas (Russell & van Den Broek, 1992) so they are seen as applicable and doable in coachees' everyday life.

It is also critical for coachees to use words or key phrases from their own stories in defining a Pivot's two arrows so they fit within their normal discourse and have emotional and somatic anchors. These two stories can't be composed of simple platitudes; they work best when the distinction is crystal clear and viscerally experienced by the client. The following graphic defines a Pivot. The old story is depicted horizontally to indicate that the situation will likely remain the same if nothing is done. The new story emerges from the same decision point but rises up, indicating it is moving in the direction of the aspiration. The definition is followed by two examples and a depiction of how a Pivot functions in the narrative coaching process.

FIGURE 19: DEFINITION OF A PIVOT

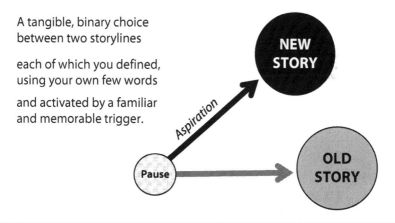

PIVOT

A tangible, binary choice between two storylines

each of which you defined, using your own few words

and activated by a familiar and memorable trigger.

Aspiration

NEW STORY

OLD STORY

Pause

Pivots are a simple binary choice people can make in the moment between an old story (what they are leaving behind) and a new story (what they are moving toward).

EXAMPLE

Using a pivot to change a team's mindset

Old story: We work from a medical model.

As a result: We deliver services to families as experts (irrespective of their experience).

New story: We work from a coaching model.

As a result: We empower families so they flourish (aided by our expertise).

Using a pivot to change a career search strategy

Old story: I am defined by what I have lost.

As a result: I am a victim who is stuck in transition and has to start over from scratch.

New story: I am liberated by what I have gained.

As a result: I am myself and will make the most of this transition to create what I want.

Pivots often crystallize as the coachee is moving between the *Search* phase and the *Shift* phase as a way to make a sharp distinction between the past and the future. It becomes possible at this point in coaching because people have articulated the old story and have begun to let it go, and the new story they want to take on is coming into focus. A Pivot that is formed at T2 presents a very clear choice for the coachee that they can use throughout their day to practice. If they act in line with the old story, it will take them back to *Situate* and the status quo they left behind. If they act into the new story (the purpose of the experiments in the *Shift* phase), it will take them toward *Sustain* and the aspiration they are seeking. This is one of the simplest yet most versatile and powerful tools used in narrative coaching. Part of why coachees like it so much is that it provides a clear line of sight on the consequences of the choice they make in the moment. Can you think of a Pivot you would like to make in your life or work?

FIGURE 20: PIVOTING BETWEEN OLD AND NEW STORY (T2)

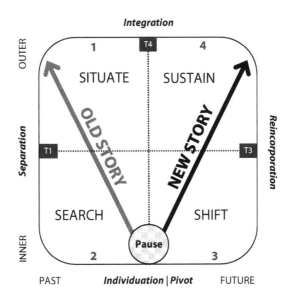

Work with your coachees to make a stark distinction between the two storylines in a Pivot, especially at first, so that there is no doubt. Later, people will need scaffolding to be able to do this on their own as the lines get farther apart—a reflection of the growing opportunities and challenges in living out the new story. You can see this in the figure above: As coachees set out in the direction of their aspiration, their intention, they are faced with a clear choice: Does what I am about to say or do send me back on my old trajectory (perpetuating my old story) or does it send me along my new trajectory (fostering my new story)? It is also crucial that they develop a greater awareness of their inner experience and signals from their environment so they notice opportunities to choose the new path. This is particularly important when they feel triggered because their initial reflex is often to return to their old and familiar ways. Therefore, encourage coachees as they start out to practice the Pivot whenever the choice presents itself, no matter how small the opportunity may seem.

Pivots are generally triggered by experiential cues (e.g., actions or words from others, shifts in their state, decision points), and provide us with an opportunity to avoid our habituated narratives and responses (Silsbee, 2008). They give people both the circuit breaker they need and a ready alternative that has been primed and practiced. Habit researchers have found that in order to develop new habits, it is more productive to focus on the cue than on the behavior (Verplanken & Melkevik, 2008). This is why we focus on noticing and pausing at the cue and having a Pivot to use in that moment rather than on setting goals for later. In many ways, it does not matter what the person chooses to Pivot around as long as it makes a meaningful contribution to what he is trying to achieve through coaching.

Pivoting is also an opportunity for coachees to learn a number of the meta-skills they will need, including being able to pause in the moment to reflect on their choices, observing reality and themselves without judgment, setting clear intentions, and learning through experimentation. The aim is for coachees to increase their capability to "become more present to themselves in their social context and able to act with more impact within that context and to experience more congruence" (Vogel, 2012, p. 7). In creating Pivots with coachees, invite them to:

- Identify actions they do frequently as points of practice.
- Notice the pivoting choice in the moment and make it.
- Remind themselves of the likely consequences of each arrow.
- Make the new choice even if it feels awkward at first.
- Remember that many small choices made often is best.

Sometimes when I'm working with a coachee, we will co-construct a visual diagram of the Pivot on a whiteboard so we can continue to refine the language and the significance of each of the two arrows as the session unfolds. I find that this is a powerful way of working because of the synergies between the insights, the drawing, and their development—and the fact that it is being co-created and documented in real time. I often take the lead at first given my role as the coach, but at some point—often when I've got something not quite right—the coachee takes over and sees the process through to the end. This swapping of roles reflects and reinforces the coachee's internal shift in taking more control of her own story and destiny. Every time coachees practice their Pivot, they reinforce a new pattern not only in addressing that issue but also others like it in their life and/or work.

Vector of Change

This tool is observed most often in coaching as people Reincorporate and cross the T3 threshold from the *Shift* phase to the *Sustain* phase. It involves using the integrative BEAM framework to break down the original Pivot into three Pivots, one for each of three of the elements—Mindset, Environment, and Behavior (Drake, cited in Drake & Pritchard 2016). This makes it easier for the person to stay on track to reach her Aspiration (fourth element). The three Pivots are aligned in a Vector of Change to increase the number of signals that will activate the new story and the number of anchors to sustain these changes in the person's life. Vectors provide a performance structure in which people are more likely to feel connected with others, gain immediate benefit, and enrich their sense of attachment security than with goals.

Vectors are a resource that people and teams can use to enrich their Environment (providing a sense of a safe haven), guide their Behavior (increasing their sense of a secure base), and shift their Mindset (creating a more resilient and mature working model) in order to fulfill their Aspiration (improving their abilities for empathy, exploration, engagement, and execution). Vectors generally work better in coaching than linear and fixed action plans because they are more agile and responsive to changing conditions, opportunities, and understandings of the new story. They help people stay oriented toward their Aspiration while giving them room to flex on the specifics as their grasp of the situation, their progress, what matters to them, and what is required become clearer.

Vectors of Change also have an advantage over goals in organizations because members of a team can all use the same Vector to guide their choices and actions regardless of their ability to deliver on it, their level of contribution to it, or their degree of accountability for it. In addition, they enable teams to work on their collective narratives in order to support individuals as they make shifts in their personal narratives. In working with teams, I get them to imagine these shifts moving out across the Vector as a wave, with more clarity and specificity close in and less so as it gets further out in time. This gives people on the team the opportunity to ask the same two questions as for individuals: Does the choice we are about to make move us closer to our new story or our old story? Where should we focus our attention in terms of the BEAM elements in order to be more in line with our new story more often? Vectors of Change provide a simple yet powerful way for people to individually or collectively bring forward what has emerged from the coaching process as they move back into the world.

Vectors of Change are very effective because they offer a systemic yet agile source of support for what coachees are seeking to achieve. As a coach, you can work with people to strengthen and use each of the three Pivots to achieve their aspiration. Mindset is the first Pivot because it reflects how people see their situation, make sense and meaning of it, and decide to take action. Without a new mindset as a starting point, most of us will remain fixed on old aspirations, revert to old behaviors and keep replicating old environments. Shifting the mindset is key to the formulation of a new narrative. Next comes the articulation of peoples' Aspiration. Based on how they now see themselves, their opportunity and their world—what do they want to change and/or achieve?

Once they have their proverbial North Star, you can begin to explore with them what they need to do differently to fulfill it and in ways that are meaningful for them. The second Pivot is thus around Behavior, and can be practiced quite easily in the course of coaching sessions. This Pivot is often the easiest to shift because people have opportunities at every turn to experiment with new ways of expressing themselves. The Environment comes last, yet is crucial for creating the conditions in which change becomes more possible. By shaping their environment, people will create a more receptive and fertile space in which they can naturally embody the new mindset and try out new behaviors. Collective and structural narratives have a profound influence, for better or worse, on people's ability to sustain change. Here is the tool, followed by two examples—one in graphic form and one in narrative form:

FIGURE 21: DEFINITION OF A VECTOR OF CHANGE

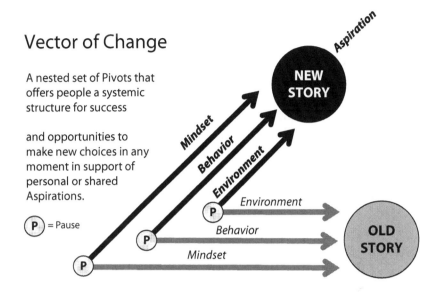

FIGURE 22: EXAMPLE OF A VECTOR OF CHANGE

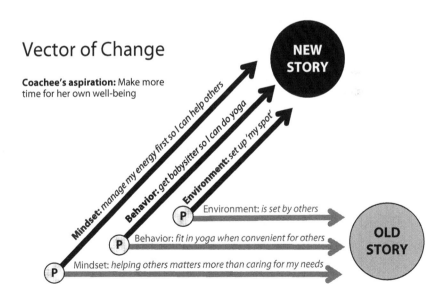

EXAMPLE

The person's old story: *I must respond* to what people ask of me (mindset). Because I feel uncomfortable in those moments, I rush my response to avoid what I feel and want (behavior). My workplace (environment) around me then feels very pressured because I avoid making my own choices.

The person's new story: *I choose to respond* when people ask something of me (mindset). Because I feel comfortable in those moments, I pause to consider what I want before I speak (behavior). My workplace (environment) around me now feels more neutral because I make my own choices.

Nudge

Pick battles small enough to win and big enough to matter. | *Jonathan Kozol*

This tool is observed most often in coaching as people Integrate and cross the T4 threshold from the *Sustain* phase back to the *Situate* phase. It is the final step in the process as coachees embed their reconfigured narratives in their identities, stories, and lives. Nudges are the small steps they can regularly take to make progress within the Vector of Change. They are important because as Silsbee (2008) notes, "We are creatures of habit. . . . In order to replace what we've done for decades with something better, we have to practice new ways of doing until they are sufficiently stabilized in us to be available even when the worn grooves of old habits still call us" (p. 152). I think of Nudges as tugboats with their deep, low motor and driven by captains with a keen sense of tides and winds, the experience to know where to push on a ship many times its size to get it to move in the right direction; and the patience to just keep nudging the boat to its destination—either to the right dock or out the right channel to the sea. Thinking like a tugboat, invite your coachees to:

- Recognize and take every opportunity (planned or unplanned) for practicing a pivot.

- Take steps, no matter how small, which will move them forward along their Vector.

- Appreciate what already works for them and use these to nudge and build momentum.

A Nudge is an opportunity, planned or unplanned, in which people can readily align with their desired behavior. It enables them to do so through resetting the default, offering immediate feedback, and reducing cognitive processing (see Thaler and Sustein, 2009). An example I regularly use to be more mindful: I use the start of the two-minute timer on my electric toothbrush as a cue to meditate for that period, twice a day. Examples of other nudges I've developed: (1) using a modified GTD system to keep my office surfaces largely clear to remove the distraction of unfinished business; (2) de-cluttering my file cabinets so I am free of "someday" files and can more easily focus on important work today; and (3) eating breakfast without multitasking to prime my system for simplicity as the new neural norm. For each of these, I am working to embed the three requirements for the formation of new habits (Duhigg, 2013): an environmental cue, a behavioral response, and a reward. It is important to start small, as early wins done consistently are more likely to contribute to long-term success.

Thaler and Sunstein's (2008) research on Nudges has led to the introduction of hundreds of applications that limit people's choices so as to guide them to the desired outcome with minimal effort. Well-known examples include placing "rumble strips" on highways that vibrate loudly to warn drivers they have drifted off the main pavement and switching the choice on forms regarding organ donation from *opt-in* to *opt-out*. Narrative coaching builds on this by helping people identify simple Nudges they can regularly use to reinforce their new narrative using all four BEAM elements (Behavior, Environment, Aspiration, and Mindset). In a sense, we are helping people become their own "choice architects" (Thaler & Sunstein, 2008).

People can deconstruct their current and desired behaviors in coaching sessions to determine the internal triggers and/or external signals they can use to define their nudges. For example, a coach in one of our programs became aware that she often over-extended herself by trying to be too helpful (based in old story). As she explored ways to remind herself of her new story, she found that paying attention to her upper back offered the best cue. If she noticed herself feeling tense in her neck and shoulders, it was a signal she may be taking on too much responsibility. This was enough to bring back to center each time such that the new story became her new norm. Nudges are an important part of the change process for people because they provide regular opportunities to practice in their everyday life.

They are closely tied to the Narrative Rewind process and its focus on triggers as cues for new choices. This is quite handy for our busy lives where things don't always go according to plan. Tompkins and Lawley (2011) similarly observed, "Practice regularly and put yourself in contexts where the desired behavior is likely to be required and notice what happens" (p. 10). Brief therapist Bill O'Hanlon (2000) talks about it in terms of the question, "What is one thing you can do differently?" Management scholar Karl Weick (1984) calls them "small wins" and writes that they "do not combine in a neat, linear, serial form, with each step being a demonstrable step closer to some predetermined goal. More common is the circumstance where small wins are scattered and cohere only in the sense that they move in the same general direction" (p. 43). Amabile & Kramer's (2012) research suggests that a sense of small wins and incremental progress is more important than big incentives in helping motivate people to engage and perform.

This has been consistently demonstrated by experts such as K. Anders Ericsson and his colleagues (Ericsson & Charness, 1994; Ericsson, Krampe, & Tesch-Römer, 1993), George Leonard (1992) and Jim Loehr (2007) in their work on mastery and the use of tools such as deliberate practice. It can also be seen in the ground-breaking work by Australian psychologist Daphne Hewson who makes an important distinction that can be used to help people sustain their fledgling new story. She (1991) writes:

> The new story is not a turn-off from the old road, but the continuation of a different, old road—one on which the person had been traveling without previously recognising they were doing so. I started to realize the importance of reconstructing a

past history of the new story, rather than creating a new story that is simply a deviation from the old one. But, even then, it was easy for the new story to be mainly present and future based, with only the old, problem-saturated story having a recognized past history. (p. 5)

Coaches are like midwives who assist people in bringing their new stories to life. Our success is often a result of blended strategies formed around motivations and structures that are both mythological and mechanical in nature. Goals can be part of the formula if used well as markers, but outcomes are often best approached through clearly set intentions and a more iterative and integrative approach to change and development. In using the Narrative Coaching model, invite coachees to move (1) between externalization and internalization; (2) between soaring above the tree with clarity and descending down to it with conviction; and (3) beyond the dyad into the third spaces so they can reconfigure their narratives and fulfill more of their aspirations.

The aim is to build up their self-awareness, self-regulation, and self-efficacy so they can shift in the moment again and again. The narrative reconfiguration tools—Turning Points, Pivots, Vectors of Change, and Nudges—are helpful here in that they support people in developing themselves and fulfilling their aspirations at the same time. Taken together they provide a solid structure to guide people toward their success and do so in a way that keeps people vitally engaged in their own change process. In the end, as author Mark Manson notes, "Instead of asking yourself what goal you would like to reach, go one step further and ask which habits you'd have to implement in order for that goal to be achievable."

EXAMPLE

Turning Point: After an initial conversation about her perceived lack of self-confidence after some time out of the job market, Rachel realizes that she is at a Turning Point because her two young children are now old enough for her to return to work part-time.

Pivot: After doing some archetype work, Rachel defined her Pivot as "I am not visible in the market anymore" *(old story)* versus "I choose work that fits my life now" *(new story)*. The old story had kept her from reaching out to others because she was sure that she would not make it compared to what she had before. As she began to rehearse the new story with her group, she started to build confidence in herself and, as a bonus, get contacts to help her get started.

Vector of change: Rachel realized that her first Pivot was related to her Mindset, which she used to look at her situation in a new light. She then worked with a peer to clarify her Aspiration: to find meaningful work with a healthy group of people that fit her other role as a mother. She drew on the archetype of the "Queen" to identify her Behavior Pivot that distinguished between "I will keep to myself since I am new to this" and "I will speak up as someone with a lot to offer." Finally, she developed an *Environment* Pivot that distinguished between "I have to do this all by myself" *(old story)* and "I will create the community I need" *(new story)*.

Nudge: Rachel identified two Nudges that would help her: (1) moving into her new *Mindset* just prior to calling a prospective client; and (2) talking with one person on every train trip about what she did for a living.

A third serendipitously appeared when another narrative coaching student happened to see her on the station platform, waiting for the same train into town for a follow-up workshop. She had shared at the previous program that normally she allowed herself to be "crowded-in."

However, he quickly noticed that she was standing there as if she was a queen . . . and people were walking around her as if they could sense her regal energy. This was her first piece of evidence that the inner changes she was making were slowly yet positively changing her outer environment as well. She decided to add a third Nudge, which was to stand like a queen whenever she was waiting for her train to work.

With each nudge, the reconfiguration of her stories solidified and blossomed—and she did the same as a result. *As a postscript: She secured a half-time coaching position a few months after the second workshop.*

Hopefully these examples give you a tangible sense of how you can think about and use these four tools in your coaching. You can use them with or without goals to help your coachees achieve what they are seeking from working with you. While each one tends to be particularly useful at a certain phase in the process, use them whenever and however they seem useful for a coachee. They are designed to support coachees in creating their structures of success, not to impose our structure on the coaching conversation. You will find that working this way feels refreshing and liberating—for you and your coachees—even as it increases your abilities to empower them to bring new stories to life. Join us for one of our retreats or training programs if you would like to know more about how to integrate this work into your practice.

Implications for Your Practice

Whether you use intentions and/or goals, ensure they are:

- Based in true conviction and commitment (Locke, 1996).

- Stated positively rather than negatively and in results or outcome language.

- Stated in sensory-based terms and specific enough to guide behavior.

- Co-developed in such a way that they will be recognized when accomplished.

- Initiated by the person and sustained until they are completed.

- Applicable in all relevant situations and able to readily applied.

- Strong enough to generate the highest impact within reach of person's current repertoire.

What are your key insights?
What will you experiment with first?

PART IV
narrative
PRACTITIONERS

CHAPTER 10

HOW TO HOLD SPACE

We have a choice . . . to be technicians or artists, or strive to be both. Each will
reveal some aspects of change and deny others. But if the whole is to be held
and respected as living process then some form of artistry is requisite.
We will not understand until we trust ourselves enough,
and quieten ourselves enough, to hear the silent melodies of
spirit playing on the instruments of matter. | *Allan Kaplan*

This final section of the book is about enriching your capabilities as a
practitioner. Even though we will cover many of the core skills you will
need, the emphasis is ultimately on you. It is about coaching using essential
principles, not using elaborate methods. As such, it is about your *being* more
than your *doing*. This first chapter is on holding space for people and their
stories; it is the lifeblood of narrative coaching around which everything
else is built. We will look at how you can tap the power of radical presence,
create a crucible for change, work in the field, and hold space in a generative
manner. In so doing, I stand on the shoulders of giants such as Carl Rogers
(1961), who wrote about his work as follows:

It is my purpose to understand the way he feels about in his own inner world, to accept him as he is, to create an atmosphere of freedom in which he can move in his thinking and feeling and being, in any direction he desires. How does he use this freedom? It is my experience that he uses it to become more and more himself. He begins to drop the false fronts, or the masks, or the roles, with which he has faced life. He appears to be trying to discover something more basic, something more truly himself. (pp. 108–109)

Rogers (1961) believed that a therapist's presence and empathetic listening constituted the most powerful sources of help and support one human being can provide for another. He was instrumental in developing our understanding of how to work this way. In particular, his awareness of the paradox that "people only change when they first accept themselves just as they are" became a cornerstone of narrative coaching. For example, he (1961) demonstrated the importance of practitioners' *authenticity* ("It does not help, in the long run, to act as though I were something I am not"); *accountability* ("Am I secure enough within myself to permit him his separateness?"); and *acuity* ("Can I let myself enter fully into the world of his feelings and personal meanings and see these as he does?"). Linda Graham (2013) put it this way: "All this talk . . . is just an excuse to hang out long enough for the relationship to do the healing" (p. 132). This same commitment lives on in narrative coaching in the way we hold space for coachees and their stories as well as in one of our core questions, "What does this person need most from me right now?"

> ### "What does this person need most from me right now?"

Heather Plett (2015) described holding space as being "willing to walk alongside another person in whatever journey they're on without judging them, making them feel inadequate, trying to fix them, or trying to impact the outcome." It is about using your body, voice, presence, and energy to create a sense of safe haven and secure base that is at the same time alive with potential. Holding space is a sacramental act that supports people in coming home to themselves and to what is calling them. It is a phenomenological activity (Ihde, 1977) in which there is heightened attention to the experience in the "field" that has been created and the energies that are in play. The more we can be with people this way in coaching, the more powerful their experience and outcomes will be. I see this in my workshops when participants drop their anxiety about "doing it right" and allow themselves to relax, pay attention, and support what emerges.

This attention to the here-and-now of a situation can be seen in the phenomenological practice of epoché, in which judgment is suspended and one's immediate judgment and interpretation of a situation is bracketed. Depraz, Varela, and Vermersch (2000) describe the three phases of this process as: (1) suspending our habitual thoughts; (2) converting or reorienting our attention from the external to the internal; and (3) letting go in order to respond to the immediate experience and the knowledge found there. Carnabucci and Anderson's (2012) offer this advice:

> The [coach] must maintain a state of relaxed inner stillness throughout the complex process which requires a great deal of skill. There should be an open awareness of all sorts of things— and not only the energies in the field but also thoughts and images that appear—while toggling back and forth between pre-existing . . . theory, personal experiences and the information of the present moment while bracketing preconceptions, beliefs and assumptions. Just like the meditator returns to the present with each breath, the [coach] stays alert to distractions and refocuses attention. (p. 38)

When we hold space well, people can dive into their own "lifeworld" (Husserl, 1931; Merleau-Ponty, 1945/2013), its existential nature (see Spinelli, 2010), and their phenomenological experience of it. This focus is served well by a narrative approach since that is what stories are designed to communicate. It is also why we place more emphasis on creating experiences than on seeking explanations. In narrative coaching we stay as much as possible within what I call *storytime* and *storyspace* (the felt experience of the story as if it is happening right now). Otherwise, it is too easy for both coaches and coachees to rush toward premature coherence as a defense against their "anxiety of sitting with undigested elements of experience until they take meaningful shape, however transitory or provisional that shape may be" (Josselson, 2004, p. 125). The more that you can do this when you coach, the sooner people will get to the crux of their issue and identify the scaffolding they will need for its resolution. It may sound simple, but it represents a fundamentally different way of thinking about how to bring about change in coaching.

Your role as a coach is to hold up a clean, clear, and loving mirror for coachees so they can more openly share of themselves and their stories in order to discover the resolution they are seeking. This here-and-now focus in holding the space for people has many advantages. It provides a safe laboratory in which coachees can experiment with new behaviors, experience new voices before trying them in the world (Anderson, 2004; Yalom, 2000), and embed any shifts in awareness or capacity in their life as an anchor for change (Drake, 2007). When you hold space for people, it creates more spaciousness in you, in them, and in the conversation—which creates more breathing room for new stories. As a result, they discover there is much more in their stories than they realized and more options for stories to be told. For example, in telling the story of what happened, they are often struck by some new element or aspect of the narrative of which they had not been previously aware (Grafaniki & McLeod, 1999). In the end, it is about having the confident humility to trust that the space you create with coachees is a primary contributor to change.

EXAMPLE

I was asked to coach a key contributor in a manufacturing company to help her address some difficult relational and performance issues. Her initial stories were of anger at her employer and her colleagues. However, through exploring her story more fully, she was able to reframe the issue as one in which she felt her professional passion and expertise had been compromised as the company had grown significantly. Her willingness to engage in these deeper truths emerged from a conversation about a pet and, with that, what "home" meant for her. We held that space for quite some time until she allowed herself to feel into her truths—one of which was that work no longer felt like "home" as it had in the beginning.

In the end, what she wanted was the chance to leave with dignity and the courage to return to her craft. To do so, she needed to shift from what she came to call her "they don't appreciate or respect me" story to her "I want to do what I love" story. In the end, she left the organization, moved to a new city, and found a new job where she could thrive again in doing want she loved. I helped the VP of HR reflect on how much the culture had changed over the years and what they could do to better retain and leverage their legacy talent.

Tapping the Power of Radical Presence

Be so still inside [yet vibrant] that you can listen at every moment to what life is offering you. | David Steindl-Rast

A few years ago I was asked to present again on my narrative work at a coaching psychology conference. I used the occasion to reflect on how I was using this work in moving through a time of great transition in my own life. One of the advantages of being in a liminal space at the time was that it gave me more direct access to and new insights on the deeper dimensions of change. I was using my life as a laboratory in which I could explore how to distill coaching to its essence and develop more advanced practices. I was also drawing from my observations of the profound shifts that were happening for people in the new workshops I had started to run. What emerged was a provocative proposition about coaching: "Radical presence contributes far more to growth and the desired outcomes than we realize." This became the core around which the six principles of narrative coaching solidified, and it has had a profound effect on how I teach and coach using this work. I saw *radical presence* as the embodiment of a fundamental trust in one's Awareness, Being, and Connectedness in the field to foster change. It enables us to drop into the experience and bring attention to what is essential in sessions while serving as its most fiercely curious and compassionate advocate. It is both the foundation and the means by which you can bring your full attention to what seems essential in your coaching sessions.

We can see parallels in engaged Buddhism (see Kramer, 2007), "relational flow" (M. Moore, Drake, Tschannen-Moran, Campone, & Kauffman, 2005), the pursuit of mastery (see Leonard, 1992; Sennett, 2008), and Silsbee's (2008) work on mindfulness in coaching, in which "presence evokes changes in others" (p. 5). It comes from a disciplined wisdom and a deep connection with oneself and the energy and flow of what is happening. It is analogous to what Josh Waitzkin (2007) writes about chess Grandmasters: "[M]uch of what separates the great from the good is deep presence, relaxation of the conscious mind, which allows the unconscious to flow unhindered. . . . The Grandmaster looks at less and sees more, because his unconscious skill set is much more highly evolved" (pp. 142, 143). Kohut (1971) talks about masterful psychologists in the same way:

> Her oscillating attentiveness is focused on barely perceptible cues that signal a change in state, in both patient and therapist, and on nonverbal behaviors and shifts in affects. The attuned, intuitive clinician, from the first point of contact, is learning the nonverbal moment-to-moment rhythmic structures of the patient's internal states, and is relatively flexibly and fluidly modifying her own behavior to *synchronize* with that structure, thereby creating a context for the organization of the therapeutic alliance. (p. 317)

The invitation for you, then, is to let go of your preconceptions about what ought to occur in coaching so you can be fully engaged with *yet* completely non-attached to what is occurring. This not only creates a stronger crucible for change, but it also provides important modeling for coachees. Working for a particular outcome provides structure for a coaching session, but it also often subverts other processes and outcomes (Brown, 2004) that may be more appropriate and effective. As a result, we teach coaches to not try so hard, but instead to notice and focus their energy on what is unfolding in the moment with another human. The more you can hold space for coachees—no matter what energies have been stirred up in the process—the more they will be able to do the same for themselves. The coaching relationship becomes a practice ground to develop their attachment-related capabilities such as self-regulation, trust, and authentic communication. By providing these experiences and responding differently than may have been the case with others in their life, you are demonstrating to people how to change their patterns of narration and behavior (Wachtel, 2008) and attain greater mastery in their life.

> Radical presence enables us to drop into the experience and bring attention to what is essential in sessions while serving as its most fiercely curious and compassionate advocate.

With greater presence, you can more fully immerse yourself in coaching conversations without losing yourself or the coachee *and* you can stand back to see the gestalt of what is occurring. This ability for multi-dimensional apprehension has been described as "evenly suspended attention" (Freud, 1912/1961) and as "free-floating" and "poised attention" (Reik, 1948). It is characterized by a temporary suspension of expectations about what people should or might experience or communicate as well as assumptions about the relevance and meaning of whatever thoughts and feelings may arise for either party during the session. This state of attentiveness can be thought of as *generative uncertainty*. It requires relinquishing your needs for control and understanding as the basis for moving forward in coaching and, instead, leaning into the uncertainty with both rigor and vigor. It is about listening for the authentic voice wherever it is found and letting go of any preconceptions of the "right answer" or the "good outcome." Paradoxically, the latter are far more likely to emerge when you stop trying to make them happen. This is based in a central premise of this work:

Resolutions are already present and, as such, are revealed rather than engineered. Therefore, listen as an "instrument of the speaker" (Charon, 2006).

> ## This state of attentiveness can be thought of as generative uncertainty.

Working from a place of radical presence enables you to circle up and down the proverbial tree as you coach—all the while staying present to yourself, the other person, the moment, and the arc of the narrative and the conversation. To be engaged means "to be present, available, and not to turn away. . . . [It] implies a nonjudgmental openness, a trust in the ultimate workability of *all* experience" (Morgan, 2005, pp. 140–141). "It is not about achieving a different state of mind; it is about settling into our current experience in a relaxed, alert, and openhearted way" (Germer, 2005, p. 16). It is about releasing the tension between what is and what "should be" (Siegel, 2007); letting go of trying to fix things long enough to see reality for what it is (Fulton, 2005); and viewing situations from multiple and novel perspectives (Langer, 1997). Each of these uses of mindfulness plays an important role in narrative coaching and aligns with the earlier section on attachment theory and the power of mutual regulation. If you can self-regulate well as you coach, especially when you are challenged, it enables the coachee to do the same. As a result, you can more candidly and courageously be present to and engage with whatever emerges as important.

Inviting coachees to approach their issues with greater mindfulness helps them in a number of ways. A more mindful awareness "allows [them] to step back from the experience of the moment and observe it from a larger field of awareness that is not any of those experiences, that is larger than any of those patterns. With that awareness, [they] can begin to see different possibilities for responding" (Graham, 2013, p. 52). When people are mindfully present to their stories, they can more readily notice where they are now, how they got there (in part as a function of their stories) and the door(s) they can open to begin a new narrative and a new way forward. Your radical presence has an impact on the coaching conversation and on coachees themselves in modeling another way of being in the world. As a result, they can more fully tune into themselves and the conversation, access more insight and energy, and take more conscious and focused action. Radical presence is one of the manifestations of the applied mindfulness work introduced earlier. It is based in a set of beliefs and actions that are summarized below and are essential in creating a fertile container for change in coaching.

Applied mindfulness invites us to be more:

- *Aware:* We are not separate, so we can be accepting of all experience. This helps *Situate* coachees in themselves, their stories, and the conversation.
- *Awake:* We are not asleep, so we can remain present with sensations and feelings. This helps coachees *Search* inside themselves and their stories.
- *Alive:* We are not on automatic pilot, so we can harness and focus our energies. This helps coachees release old stories and reconfigure new ones in order to *Shift*.
- *Agile:* We are not reactive, so we can act from a conscious, accountable state. This helps coachees learn how to *Sustain* their new stories in the world.

Creating a Crucible for Change

In the degree that I am governed by fear I become breathless and rush everything. I think about the next move rather than remaining in the experience of the moment—which is sufficient unto itself. | Sam Keen

The greater our presence as coaches and the more mindfulness we can bring to our coaching, the stronger the container will be in which coachees can do their work. It is what Christina Baldwin calls "holding the rim." It involves positioning yourself as a "good enough" caregiver (Winnicott, 1965) so that the people you coach can experience a secure attachment orientation and relax into themselves and the moment as a result. This is analogous to the ways in which good-enough parenting supports children so they can go "inside" and rest in imagination and the experience of self (Stern, 1985). The notion of a "container" is useful here as a safe yet vibrant space (think ecosystem not box) where people are free to be themselves and work on their issues. Crucible and crux are two etymologically-related words that capture the essence of a "container." A crucible is a vessel used to contain high-temperature chemical reactions. The coaching relationship, "field" and coach must be strong enough to process whatever emotional and developmental experiences emerge. Narrative coaching offers a crucible in which people can bear the opposites at the core of their issue long enough to find a third way, a path with heart (Meade, 2006), which enables them to get to the crux of the matter and resolve it for themselves.

Holding space well for coachees increases their attachment security (see Chapter 1) and enriches their sense of safe haven, secure base, working model and ability to contribute to better "family" systems. In creating a crucible, we are first offering coachees a *safe haven*, a "holding environment" (Winnicott, 1971) in which it is "safe to be nobody and thus to begin to find the self . . . and to be, instead of always having to do" (Stevenson, 2005, p. 39). Holding space in this way helps people to feel accepted and cared about, heard and validated, and understood and connected (Howe, 1996; Mikulincer & Shaver, 2007). People particularly need this as they start the coaching process and whenever they surface difficult aspects of their stories or lives. Our role is primarily to support the person's system to recalibrate itself and evolve.

> It is based in a trust that the resolution is already present and the subsequent belief that our role is primarily to support the person's system to recalibrate itself and evolve.

Second, we can see the crucible as providing a *secure base* from which people can explore and grow. This calls for a coaching relationship in which you can hold space for difficult affects (Levine, 2010) and painful mental states (e.g., anxiety, frustration, anger) (Bion, 1967) the coachee is not yet able to tolerate or understand until such time as the coachee is able to do so. Please be clear, this does not imply that we take them on ourselves, as that leads to burn out among other issues. It means we can allow them to be in the room and the process, trusting that they will be resolved when the time is right. Your ability to stay with, process, and communicate difficult emotions and uncomfortable experiences helps coachees to engage them more fully and in new ways (Stadter & Scharff, 2000). Therefore, be willing to move between confrontation and affirmation (Cozolino, 2002; Wiener, 1994) so that coachees feel safe enough to stay present and consolidate what is happening, but not so safe as to lose momentum, the developmental edge, or the motivation to change. It is about communicating to coachees, "I see you as you are right now, and I see who you want to be."

Third, we can see the crucible as a space where people can upgrade their working models. This often involves them developing new narratives as a result of what Fritz Perls (Perls, Hefferline, & Goodman, 1951) called "safe emergencies". These events, whether provoked in coaching or occurring in their life, can be used to upgrade their secure base and their larger working model. This entails holding space for them to be with their unintegrated and deregulating thoughts and feelings as well as gain tools and support with which to integrate these experiences. The fiery nature of a crucible is reflected in the fact that our role is, in part, to frustrate the person in such a way that he is forced to "find his own way, discover his own possibilities, his own potential—and to discover that what he expects from the [coach], he can do just as well himself " (Perls, 1992/1969, pp. 56–57). Invite coachees to notice what frustrates them and how much of their energy goes into manipulating the world in response instead of using it to grow. You can then accompany them in expanding their windows of tolerance and maturing their working models so they can function at higher levels across more situations.

Fourth, as coaches we have a strong interest in our clients being able to enact the changes that begin in sessions out in their lives. In so doing, they can not only improve themselves but also contribute to the well-being and success of the "family" systems in which they live and work. In this way, narrative coaching can be seen as a maieutic process because "everything new needs to be held, a place into which it can be born" (Tarrant, 1998, p. 175). Maieutics is the science and art of midwifery, of attending to the process of giving birth. "Psychological maieutics, then, is the science and art of facilitating the psyche's transformation and the emergence of new psychological structures" (Stein & Stein, 1987, p. 298) through which new stories can be born. People "have periods when they need a cradle in which to experience rebirth; they also have periods when they need a grave in which to experience the warrior" (Paris, 2007, pp. 154, 155). When we are good stewards of the containers in which we coach we can foster a more productive "field" and our coachees can generate more transformative results for themselves and others.

Working in the "Field"

Real human freedom is our willingness to pause between the events in our lives and the response we choose. | *Rollo May*

Within the broader notion of holding space, we have looked at your presence as a coach and at the container in coaching conversations. We now turn our attention to the "field" that emerges when it all comes together. A "field" in this context is seen as a defined space with a felt sense of heightened energy related to what has transpired (or is transpiring) there and which influences those who enter. It is the multi-dimensional sense of time and space that is ever-present, but is more palpable in charged moments such as the awkward silence after a social gaffe or in critical points in coaching. Learning narrative coaching will enable you to become more astute to the dynamics in the "field" while you work, which will enable you to pick up clues others miss. The following describes the palpable sense of a field:

> While in Vienna several years ago to run a narrative coaching workshop, I went for a long walk to explore the city as I do whenever I arrive in a new place. One of the destinations was the museum that is housed at Sigmund Freud's former apartment. The museum had retrieved many of the original furniture items that had been scattered around the world in the years following his death in 1939. After exploring the first few rooms, I came around a corner . . . and there in front of me was the famous living room, re-assembled as it once had been. Many of the pioneers of psychology had once sat on *these* couches and in *these* chairs. It felt so palpably real, as if their conversations were happening right in front of me at that moment. The energy was electric, and I was very moved by the experience. I noticed a distinct shift in myself, as if I was both elevated and grounded as a professional.

I want people in my coaching sessions and workshops to have a similar experience. I believe that the field is the conduit for much of the work in coaching. I see our role as learning how to attune ourselves to it and notice what is present in it—without worrying about how it got there or what it means yet. In a field, "our intention, body, and mind become integrated together. You start to be aware of perception happening from the whole field, not just from within a separate perceiver" (Scharmer, 2007, p. 149). He goes on to write that to access this deeper level of knowing, one needs to observe deeply, connect to what wants to emerge, and then act on it instantly. It requires that we move beyond an atomistic view of coaching and human interaction to take a more systemic view. For example, "Can we recognize when there is enough trust in the field to ask a more daring question? Can we trust the field to hold the energy that it stirs up? Can we trust that the resolution is already present in the field?" Once I shifted my attention from worrying about what I would do next to observing what was already there, my effectiveness and my coachees' growth increased dramatically. Support for the notion of a "field" and its importance as a transformative resource can be found in other disciplines as well.

Kurt Lewin (1951) saw a "field" as a topological construct. He viewed situations as maintained by a set of forces that interacted to create a field in which groups and individuals operate. He defined a field as, "the totality of coexisting facts which are conceived of as mutually interdependent" (p. 240). He believed that changes in people's behavior stem from changes in the forces within the field. Narrative coaching builds on this notion of fields by accentuating their sensory, emotional, and nonconscious dimensions and by leveraging the integrative nature of these forces. We help people reconfigure the relationships between their stories about themselves and their experience in their environment, the characters in their stories and their life, and the larger narratives through which they are defined and by which they act. Lawley and Tompkin's (2000) work on *Clean Language* offers a similar view on fields: "After a time the Landscape becomes a four-dimensional, multi-layered, systemic, symbolic world which with uncanny accuracy represents and reflects how the coachee experiences, behaves and responds in 'real life'" (pp. 17–18).

> Once I shifted my attention from worrying about what I would do next to observing what was already there, my effectiveness and my coachees' growth increased dramatically.

Margaret Wheatley (1994) believed that "fields encourage us to think of a universe that more closely resembles an ocean, filled with interpenetrating influences and invisible structures that connect" (p. 52). Edmund Husserl (1931) wrote about fields as phenomenological experiences, and Rupert Sheldrake (2009) described them as unseen structures, occupying space and becoming known to us through their effects. Psychologist Nathan Schwartz-Salant (1998) noted that the field "contains all of the past individual and collective stories, and it is affected by the inner life of each person. I learned a lot about "fields" from traveling with a shaman in the mountains of Peru, who taught me about the indigenous Peruvian beliefs in what we would call "filaments" in English. They saw them as the lines of energy that connect all of life and are the true source of power—a sense I often have when I am working. Harriet Rubin (2000) offers some good advice on how to work in fields: "It's a matter of intentionally letting go of your focus, of your sharp focus, and of letting yourself see with your imagination" (p. 340). All of these point to the importance of preparing for and attending to the field that is constellated in coaching and the value of holding space well so its energy can be experienced and leveraged.

Understanding the nature and power of fields is important because, as noted earlier, all problems are problems of the present. Therefore, I think of the space in which I am coaching as a stage and use it in whatever way would support the transformative process. I make use of whatever props are available and slowly turn the profane space into a sacred space—and then back into profane space as coachees prepare to "go home." In Greek, the word is *temenos*, the ancient idea of a "sacred space within which special rules apply and in which extraordinary events are free to occur" (Nachmanovitch, 1990, p. 75). It refers to a "psychic and physical area that has been ritually set aside, 'cut off,' so to speak, from the mundane, so that one may focus on the unsaid" (Kailo, 1997, pp. 195–196). It is much easier to foster a strong field in which to work if you treat the space around you, *wherever you are*, this way. For example, the power of the field in Freud's apartment came not from his furniture as separate objects, but from the particular constellation and history that was re-created in that space—and was experienced by someone who appreciated its significance.

You can access more of the power in the field by diving *into* coachees' experience as opposed to diving *under* their experience in search of an explanation. For example, be alert for moments in their stories in which new dimensions of experience can be accessed, as they often serve as a gateway to another world (Milton & Corrie, 2002). These opportunities often emerge at unexpected moments and in unexpected ways for coachees as they are telling their stories. They can be discerned through sensing ripples in the field. For example, you notice there suddenly is a sense of sadness in the session. It is like the feeling you have when you walk into a room and can feel tension or excitement in the air. A heightened ease and vitality in your body and the sense that the characters in the story feel alive in the room (Badenoch, 2008) often indicate you are at such a point. Sometimes you have to pause when you are coaching and rewind to when you first sensed a shift in the field. Holding space, especially in moments like these, is vital because, it enables both people to trust and engage in the process that is underway. Along the same lines, I offer coaches and coachees the same advice to help them stay present to their experience in the field: "Relax and have faith; you don't have to push. The current will carry you, even if it feels like you are in the dark" (Tarrant, 1998).

A story-based approach to coaching is well suited for working in the field because the two-way traffic between implicit and explicit dimensions, between signs and the signified, is inherent in the very nature of narratives. When coachees immerse themselves in the experience of their current or potential story, they have a rare (and often cathartic) opportunity to experience the emotions of an event and its meaning in the same moment (McKee, 2004). This is possible, in part, because stories draw from and make new connections between the parts of our memory system that store consciously processed information about events and the parts that store the actual emotional experience of the event (Greenberg, 2002). This means coachees can directly experience and process what is emerging from their narration at the same time, which makes it possible for them to experiment with new possibilities *in the session*. In addition, as Mishler (1999) pointed out, "Given the interconnectedness of its parts . . . a change in one part of the field is consequential for all other parts" (pp. 121–122).

The here-and-now focus inherent in a field-based approach imparts a sense of immediacy to coaching sessions and provides more accurate data than "relying on patients' imperfect and ever-shifting views of the past. . . . Moreover, the here-and-now provides a laboratory, a safe arena, in which a [person] can experiment with new behaviors before trying them in the world outside" (Yalom, 2000, p. 149). Again, we can see the connections to drama, in that it affords a bit of distance from real life—enabling people to gain more perspective on their roles, patterns, and actions; and experiment actively with alternatives. "Drama liberates us from confinement, be it socially or psychologically induced. The dramatic moment is one of emancipation" (Emunah, 1994, p. xiii). In holding space for people, we can invite them into these moments to cross the threshold that will free them *from* what has held them back and free them *to* what is calling them forward.

EXAMPLE

I remember the time when an old friend who was in my workshop shared with the group what she had written as part of one of the practices. The first time through she seemed unconvincing, so I invited her to speak to her discovery again. I did so because the situation felt flat; the "good girl" in her had performed nobly but there was barely a ripple in the "field" as a result of doing so. What came next was much closer to the ground truth she had been avoiding. When she was done, she said with a warm smile and a tear in her eye, "I hate you, David." As she shared during the debrief, it was actually an expression of endearment and gratitude for "seeing" her and what was really true for her. While it was tempting to invite her into another round, my sense was that we had done enough for now.

> Hold space for people with a fierce tenderness and a warm tenacity. Remember that it is their journey, not yours.

My invitation for you is to hold space for people you coach with a fierce tenderness and a warm tenacity. Remember that it is their journey, not yours. Sometimes this means believing in them in ways they can't yet for themselves; sometimes it means walking alongside them as they move through big experiences; and sometimes it means standing behind them and watching them venture out on their own. What makes all this possible is a willingness to be radically present to your coachees, to build a sufficient container as a crucible for their transformation, to meet them in the field to discover what else is possible, and to offer them what they and their stories most need in the moment. This is why in our narrative coaching training programs we focus on developing the practitioner first before everything else. You are your own greatest instrument as a coach. When in doubt, keep pausing, returning to holding the space and noticing what is happening in the field.

Implications for Your Practice

Be radically present:

- Be open so that you can move into whatever role would be most advantageous in the process.

- Let your perceptions and the process itself unfold and ripen according to their own rhythms.

- Remain open to the unknown so there is more spaciousness for both coachees and their stories to reveal themselves.

Build a strong yet fluid container:

- Remember that people will only recognize the truth when they are ready and will benefit most if they can use their own terms.

- Make room in yourself for thoughts feelings coachees find unpleasant, frightening, or shameful so they can do the same.

- If you are tired after coaching, you may be working too hard. Remember, everything you need is right in front of you.

Sense and engage with the field:

- See coaching as improvisation in which the rule is "yes, and", and the aim is advancing the story (Johnstone, 1981, 1999; Spolin, 1999).

- Honor the "white space," the "empty space." Focus on "objects" in the space and the space itself, each of which is important.

- Let go of the compulsion to solve a problem, be clever, be powerful, or be omniscient.

CHAPTER 11

HOW TO LISTEN TO STORIES

Do you have the patience to wait until your mud settles and the water is clear?
Can you remain unmoving until the right action arises by itself?
Masters don't seek fulfillment. Not seeking, not expecting,
they are present, and can welcome all things. | Lao-Tzu

In the last chapter we looked at three skills involved in holding space as coaches: being radically present, building the container, and working in the field. While a narrative approach may seem passive to coaches who are used to more directive and verbal methods, it is actually a very active and dynamic process. What makes it distinct is that a narrative coach's energy is primarily invested in sensing into the conversation as opposed to steering the conversation. Our role is observing, listening and inquiring into an unfolding narrative as it reveals itself, not talking to make things happen. This requires a light yet disciplined touch, a commitment to slow development and deep attention, and a fundamental trust that everything is already present and right in front of you. As Rachel Naomi Remen writes, "The most basic and powerful way to connect to another person is to listen. Just listen. Perhaps the most important thing we can ever give each other is our attention. A loving silence often has far more power to heal and connect than the most well-intentioned words."

> Our role is observing and listening to an unfolding narrative as it reveals itself, not talking to make things happen.

This chapter will focus on engaging with silence (both for itself and for what it can offer), seeing coaching as relational process of inquiry, and understanding what it means to listen narratively using the *Narrative Diamond*. As you read, imagine what it would be like to use silence more often in your practice such that what you hear becomes *the* organizing principle for your coaching, not just something you do after you are done talking. I found the following image from John Freeman's (1964) description of Carl Jung's writing helpful as a reminder in listening this way:

> Jung's arguments spiral upward over his subject like a bird circling a tree. At first, near the ground, it sees only a confusion of leaves and branches. Gradually, as it circles higher and higher, the recurring aspects of the tree form a wholeness and relate to their surroundings—a persuasive and profoundly absorbing journey. (p. 10)

I was taken by this image of a bird circling a tree and came to realize it was a fitting analogy for what narrative coaches do as they listen and inquire. Sometimes we help coachees find the "thermals" and rise above the confusion to see the bigger picture, recognize patterns, and/or get a new perspective. It opens up more space in their stories (and identities) and increases their awareness and alternatives. Sometimes we help coachees descend to find a new branch on which to land, consolidate their gains, and make decisions. It focuses their stories (and identities) and increases their clarity and ability to take new action. When you can mindfully "circle the tree" with your coachees, they can get closer to the core dynamics of their issue and make more powerful changes in the end. The circling shows up in the model as the spiral and reminds us that people may need to circle several times before the most potent opening for change becomes apparent. In the end, follow the coachee's lead in terms of what depth is required for the situation at hand.

In my experience, it does not matter which stories people choose to share first. They will begin at the level at which they are ready, and the critical themes will be forthcoming regardless of where they begin. Any story or set of stories can be a portal into the larger issues at play and the path for people to reach their resolution or aspiration. There is no need to search for a "bigger" story as you coach; start with whatever you get from your coachee and deepen their presence as they tell it. For example, one of my most touching coaching conversations ever was a brief demonstration that began with "I've moved house," stayed focused on the moving boxes in the story, and ended ten minutes later with a powerful revelation by the coachee about why the kitchen was still unpacked. There are many roads to the top of the mountain. What matters more than where you begin is how well you walk alongside people as they discover where their stories are leading them. Contrary to some people's fears that focusing on listening to stories takes too long, I find that the more attuned we can be as a listener, the sooner people get to the crux of their issue.

In listening to coachees this way, attuning yourself to them, and staying with them in their stories and their world, you are "hearing them into speech" (Morton, 1985). You are providing "a pure, objective, loving witness to what is happening within and without" (Brown, 2004, p. 14). I think of it as *360° listening*. It encompasses the whole space in which the conversation is being held, not just the exchange of content between two people. It is about listening to yourself, the other person, the stories, and the field *all at the same time*. Your ability to truly hear the other person is diminished when you overly focus on one dimension because it limits both your awareness and the narrative material that is available. Therefore, worry less about what to ask next and focus more on astutely listening to people's stories in multiple dimensions as follows.

Four dimensions of listening:

- What is happening between the two of you.
- What is happening in the room.
- What is happening in the narration.
- What is happening in time.

While this might seem like it would require extra effort and prompt us to try harder, it is actually an invitation to listen with what I call "soft eyes" and "soft ears." It is analogous to how much more you can often see at night when you are out in nature by turning off the flashlight and allowing your eyes to adjust. Taking a "softer" approach enables you to more keenly perceive the invisible wholeness that lies beyond the parts, the narrative red threads that are often subtle and gradual, and the underlying movements. As a result, you are more able to stay open and attentive as the story reveals its inner secrets to you and the storyteller (Kaplan, 2002). Even more, you will be able to get to the crux of the issue in less time and in more depth—enabling coachees to achieve more significant "hard" results.

You will be more able to do so if you can access all of your senses as a listener, create a greater sense of spaciousness in your sessions, and avoid the temptation to grasp for interpretation. This spaciousness relates to your inner experience, the coachee's inner experience and the shared experience as it unfolds in coaching. This often creates a significant shift in the person being coached before they can fully articulate or manifest it. A recent coachee described the experience as "the effects reverberated subtly, within me and my life, for weeks." This is why we teach the four levels of regulation through *Mindfulness in Motion* and the four levels of somatic knowing through the *Four Gateways*. As narrative coaching tools, they will expand your capacity to listen and enrich what you hear. Let us turn now to silence and the *Narrative Diamond* as two of the key elements in a narrative approach to listening.

Engaging with Silence

Do not speak unless you can improve upon the silence. | *Ram Dass*

An ability to embrace silence—and the stillness and clarity it brings—is essential as a coach. However, it is important to state up front that being silent is more than just "not talking." As Max Picard (2002) writes beautifully, "When language ceases, silence begins. But it does not begin because language ceases. The absence of language simply makes the presence of Silence more apparent" (p. 15). Silence is not merely empty space, a place of nothingness; it is an open space you can move into, a place of discovery and full of potential (Baker, 2002).

Silence is a place in which your restless minds, internal chatter, and fragmented attention can find the stillness you need to listen well. It is from this stillness that you can observe and hear the coachee at multiple levels at the same time. When you are still, the nonessential drops away and underlying truths surface—pointing you toward right action (Scott, 2002). We can learn a lesson here from research on blind adults, which suggests that "their auditory superiority occurs not at the level of detecting when a sound has arrived but in higher-order processing of language, sorting out a conversation they're paying attention to from background chatter" (Begley, 2007, p. 97). Silence is not what you do *after* you stop talking, but the very ground from which to speak.

As Joan Chittister (2010) observes: "Silence is the lost art in a society made of noise. . . . But until we are quiet and listen, we can never, ever know what is really going on—even in ourselves" (p. 106). Silence is one of life's greatest teachers. It often brings people face-to-face with the deeper truth and, in so doing, reveals and amplifies what they have not yet resolved within themselves or manifested in their lives. To make fuller use of silence in your coaching, think of listening as receiving and noticing what is already present, rather than as something you do to make things happen. Be willing to engage coachees with silence, and engage the silence itself. Listen for what is in the silence (e.g., unspoken words, missing details, omitted events, unmentioned characters). Be alert to the significance of such omissions, for they often indicate hidden narrative treasures. Silence is like a down pillow on which you can lay your head. Sink into it and all that it has to offer.

> To make fuller use of silence in coaching, think of listening as receiving and noticing what is already present, rather than as something you do to make things happen.

A question I am often asked is, "How does my silence help people get the outcomes they want?" In my experience, effectively using silence benefits both the coach and coachee by:

- Fostering a stronger trust in themselves and each other so they can show up in the conversation with more consciousness, compassion and candor.

- Enabling them to better self-regulate and mutually regulate in the midst of challenging emotions and create a stronger platform for what the coachee wants to achieve.

- Supporting a greater sense of safety so there is more somatic awareness, attunement to natural rhythms, willingness to experiment, certainty of what needs to be done, and honesty about progress.

- Equipping them to "sit" with issues long enough to gain a truer awareness and a better understanding of what is happening rather than rushing to action.

Again, it is important to remember that silence is not the absence of talking, but an active and generative practice in its own right. Your use of silence signals your trust in the process and your willingness to remain radically present so coachees and their stories can do what they need to do. In this sense silence is both an inner state and an outer stance. It is what makes it possible to listen narratively to people in ways that will be transformative for them. The evidence for this can be seen in our own lives in that, while we may forgot the words spoken in life-changing conversations, we never forget how we felt.

Listening Narratively

If you want to understand what other people are saying, you have to assume that what they are saying is true. So then you have to figure out what's going on within their view of the world that makes it true. | *George Miller*

Listening to people's history is less about gathering all the facts and more about surfacing the essence of the fictions by which they live. This distinction is important because people can do no other than to begin in their own world—and so you might as well meet them there. They will only be able and willing to travel with you to new places—and consider new stories—*if* you can be with them just as they are right now and without judgment. Any judgment from you or them excludes aspects of the present moment and thereby makes them unavailable for the work at hand. Ultimately, as coaches, we have a professional responsibility to listen to coachees with our expertise and experience *and* to stand in their shoes and engage them with compassion and acceptance at the same time. Kaplan (2002) describes it as follows: "To apprehend [what is going on], we have to move into a different state of being—one which is simultaneously inside and outside, participant and observer, analyst and artist" (p. xvii).

Many of the breakthroughs people achieve in coaching are made when we work with them and their narrative material at the edge of their awareness. This is because people's stories have their own internal logic and coherency that often makes changing them hard, particularly if we try to approach them straight on (Bridges, 1980). I find that in my own practice it involves intently listening to what is being said, while at the same time being peripherally aware of ripples in the field that warrant closer attention. To do this, you need to be simultaneously attentive to both the explicit verbal content and the implicit experience (Stern, 2004) in the narration. This involves using both de-focused attention and focused attention—operating like a camera with a wide depth of field in which the foreground and background are both in focus. Bateson (1982) used the related analogy of binocular vision to refer to the convergence of two perspectives that vary slightly different from each other. Listening narratively gives you a sense of depth perception that is otherwise easy to miss.

Theodore Reik (1948) described it as listening beyond the spoken word with what he called "the third ear." By this he meant not only to listen to what the other person is saying (and not saying, but thinking and feeling), but also to our own inner voices. It requires thinking of yourself as a sensor to pick up clues about what is happening in the field, not so much as an interpreter who is planning what to do next. Listening with a "third ear" enables you to hear more of what is happening at symbolic, somatic, and unconscious levels. Fulton & Siegel (2005) described it as listening to "the unspoken, the avoided, and the accidental—to find the reality that lies imperfectly revealed and imperfectly disguised in thought" (p. 36). To be able to listen this way, it helps to think about what is happening in coaching as happening at a number of levels beyond just the dyadic exchange. The search to understand why this is so led me in my doctoral research to develop the notion of stories as projective devices and the initial modeling to be able to work in the resulting third spaces.

Working in Third Spaces

For he that is freed from the pairs is easily freed from conflict. | *Bhagavad Gita*

In developing narrative coaching I came to realize that in the public domain, storytelling is often seen as a monologic process that focuses on the oratory, dramatic, and/or persuasive skills of the storyteller. In fields such as communication studies, and narrative analysis, storytelling is often described as a dialogic process that focuses on the exchange between a teller and a listener(s). However, through my research I came to see that tapping the full hermeneutic potential of narrative work requires a trialogic approach, a "third space" beyond the narrator and her story (the first and second spaces respectively). I identified the three spaces in this trialogue as the *declarative space* of the narrator, the *narrative space* of the story itself, and the *projective space* of the narrative elements. I later described the three spaces in terms of "once, twice, and thrice upon a time" (Drake, 2008b) to extend the classic opening frame for fairy tales and highlight the need for multiple perspectives on the same story. Using a trialogic approach enables us to move between these three spaces as we work with people's stories.

The use of third spaces is based in the recognition that two terms are seldom sufficient to describe the situations people bring to coaching, and therefore it is often necessary to introduce a third term to find a resolution (Evanoff, 2000; Lefebvre, 1980; Schwartz-Salant, 1998). Many of the stories that people bring to coaching reflect an unconscious search to resolve an inner conflict resulting from what they perceive is a pair of opposites. Their stories often reflect their attempts to get unstuck from an oscillation between two poles or a fixation on one. Their attempts to resolve the conflict by choosing one of the two opposing positions may temporarily relieve their internal unrest, but won't reveal the deeper truth or provide a strong enough platform for real change.

Narrative coaching provides a way out through its non-dualist orientation. It reflects a shift in thinking about stories as commodities transmitted from one person to another to thinking about stories as co-creations in a narrative field that lies between, yet beyond, the participants. As a coach, you can shift move back and forth between nurturing this field and attending to what emerges there, depending on the needs of the coachee in their process. This parallels what coachees are doing in the course of telling their stories. Each story serves as a new stage in which the coachee as narrator "repositions the characters in his life within a constantly moving interpersonal field in which they are continuously moving toward and away from each other" (Anderson, 2004, p. 317).

This is consistent with narrative researchers such as Riessman (2002) who wanted to know, "How does she place herself in relation to the audience, and vice versa? How does she locate characters in relation to one another and in relation to herself?" (p. 701). By addressing the characters in the field, you exponentially increase the places from which transformation can emerge. For example, an opening for awakening or change could emerge from a deep exploration of a single element (e.g., a metaphor) used to describe the situation, a change in the relationship between two elements (e.g., when the person saw her situation from the other person's perspective), or from a third space beyond the two elements (e.g., when a new option or a better solution unexpectedly arises from the gestalt).

> By addressing the characters in the field, you exponentially increase the places from which transformation can emerge.

Jung repeatedly argued that the tension of opposites must be held until their meaning, the unknown "third," appears. However, it is difficult to do that through direct introspection, so we project this conflict onto other people in our life and in our stories. As a result, the characters in people's stories are often made to carry certain emotions, positions, characteristics, etc. on their behalf. Projection provides a temporary outlet valve for our psyche but, in the end, development only occurs when we take back the projection and own it as a part of ourselves. We would be forever stuck in our current state of consciousness if what Jung called our transcendent function did not continually create symbols, such as the characters in our stories, to help us grow beyond our either/or thinking to the next level. These symbols are valuable as surrogates for the same reason that coachees learn new things about themselves through looking at their stories as the protagonist instead of as the narrator. We can even go so far as to say that projection is an integral and indispensable step in all learning and development.

By "allowing each opposite in a pair to exist in equal dignity and worth" (Jung, 1970, p. 304) in coaching, the contents of the unconscious can join with the ego to create a third position and a new state of consciousness can come into being (Raff, 2000). It is about alchemically bringing one and one together to equal three, as we saw with Shadows and strengths. For example, I can be passionate *and* decisive in stepping up as a *compelling* change leader. You can help coachees to better understand the nature of their issues if you see them as projective spaces in which they can explore the characters (including themselves) and how they inform and relate to each other. These third spaces are projective because they capture elements outside of the conscious awareness of the person telling his story and the usual frame for how the story is told. The aim is to help people identify, reclaim, and integrate the projected material—and the potential it represents—so they can resolve the issue within themselves.

Development occurs in third spaces through integrating the split-off energies of these potential stories and the imagined selves that go with them. Narrative coaching focuses on individuation and maturation because, in the end, people come to realize that their issues—which they often initially attribute to forces and characters *outside* themselves—need to be first addressed as issues *inside* themselves. For example, a coachee's story about an angry boss eventually yields insights related to his drive to embody more of his own power in asking for what he needs. This often requires confronting an imagined self he has avoided for fear that he would become like his boss (with perhaps memories of his raging father blended in as well). By de-stigmatizing and de-polarizing the issue, more space opens up for a third way through which he can change, his relationship with his boss can change, and his underlying narrative can change.

This enables people to escape the usual drama triangle (perpetrator, victim, rescuer), recognize each of the elements in themselves and begin to integrate them at a higher level (like with maturing your strength in figure 8). Working in this projective third space allows people to stay in relationship with the other characters in their stories while they access their inner experience. This is important not only to help them deepen their inquiry in the coaching session, but also to start building the scaffolding they will need to put their new insights into action. People will be more able to sustain the changes they begin in coaching if they can experience these changes first through working with the characters in their stories as a practice ground.

You do not need to dig into their past or gather numerous details since their unconscious tends to bring enough of what is needed into their stories—which you can then bring into the conversation. The secret is to notice which elements of people's stories are being re-experienced in the session and why (Casement, 1991) and to see where they take you. By temporarily distancing themselves from the issues through projective activities, people are often more open and able to identify and address their issues. As the fuller truth becomes more apparent, you can start to bring the mirror closer to them so they can see that, in the end, the issue is ultimately theirs.

> Working in this projective third space allows people to stay in relationship with the other characters in their stories while they access their inner experience.

Whenever possible, I use the entire area where I am coaching or facilitating to give people all the space they need to experience the differences between the first, second, and third spaces. I do so because I want people to live and breathe their stories rather than try to hold it all in their head. I want them to work with a deep sense of serious play so they can move between exploration and experimentation in any given moment. I frequently invite people to imagine the narrative landscape spread out in front of them such that we both can see the three spaces (narrator, story, and characters). The aim is to bring the elements in their stories alive and out in the open so they can be observed and experienced. This allows people to be *in* but not *of* their stories. They can then see them with fresh eyes, explore their elements with more courage, and discover new ways of moving forward. It is the fastest way I know to get people in touch with the deeper change that is being called for. You can always re-establish the relationship with a coachee in her first space (narrator) whenever it is needed—e.g., to reassure her, draw her attention to a truth in the moment, or invite her to step into it.

Using the Narrative Diamond

Almost every encounter in life presents possibilities for growth. But these transformations require that a person be prepared to perceive unexpected opportunities. Most of us become so rigidly fixed in the ruts carved out by our conditioning that we ignore the options of choosing any other course of action. | *Mihaly Csikszentmihalyi*

I share Ricoeur's (1988) interest in the fact that the *space of experience* (the narrator) and the *horizon of expectation* (the story) condition each other. This is important because events that are included in (and excluded from) our narratives, the main themes around which we organize them, the characters we regard as significant or non-significant, and the voices we privilege or silence all shape both our identities and our stories (Botella & Herrero, 2000). The *Narrative Diamond* was developed to teach people how to coach with these elements in mind, with a unique focus on the role that characters and third spaces play in people's stories. We can think of stories as people's implicit and explicit conversations with other characters, and we can assume that if a story mentions an event or character, this element is in some way relevant to what the protagonist is seeking (Mar, 2004). Many of the tensions in people's stories in coaching can be traced to disparities between the narrator's point of view and that of certain other characters. These disparities often literally or figuratively mirror tensions in their life (and vice versa). As such, the characters in people's stories often provide the key to transforming their stories and resolving their issues.

Any resolution attained between the characters in a coachee's story often sheds light on the steps to be taken to resolve the issue the coachee is facing in her life or work (and vice versa). This is important because people are more able to face important challenges, answer essential questions, and make hard choices (McKee, 2004) if they see the connections between their inner stories and their outer lives. In narrative coaching, we do that by listening to people's stories so as to bring their internal narrative processes into the room so they are more accessible to change. This allows the coachee to move between the author's stance and the protagonist's stance—as well as the stances of the story, other characters, and the field—in order to gain new perspectives on and new options for their stories. This also allows the coachee to separate his role as the narrator *of* his story from his role as the protagonist *in* his story (Linde, 1993) so he can appreciate the difference and make the necessary adjustments. I find that sometimes it is enough to help coachees even recognize there is a distinction and to make new connections as a result—e.g., "I see myself as a strong person, yet I seem to be acting like a victim in my story."

If people can create some distance from their story, they can often see it more truthfully and engage with it more viscerally. It is often easier for people to be more accountable for their narration and its impact if it first becomes more malleable and approachable. After working with their stories out in the open, coachees can take what they've experienced and learned in the session and put it "back in themselves" (albeit transformed) as a guide for moving forward in a new way. The more that coachees can picture their inner community, the easier it becomes for them to understand how they see themselves and others as well as act and communicate—and the more fully you can track and support their development (Badenoch, 2008). The very act of telling their story in a safe space like coaching enables people to "observe, correct, and comment on the self that is being portrayed in and shaped by their stories" (Josselson, 2004, p. 112). However, it is important to remember that it is not about where *you* think the story is going or should be going, but rather about where the story wants to go on behalf of the person. What is it seeking? What is it asking of the coachee? The session?

The Framework

The *Narrative Diamond* is based in the premise that the characters (e.g., people, objects, metaphors and analogies, events) that appear in coachees' stories are systematically related to each other and correspond with aspects of their lives in ways to be discovered. Each story serves as a stage in which the narrator locates and positions the characters relative to herself and the others within a fluid interpersonal field (Drake, 2003; Osatuke et al., 2004; Riessman, 2002). This is important because "two paces east or west and the whole picture is changed" (Durrell, 1988, p. 210). As a matter of fact, I have seen the meaning and outcome of a narrative coaching process hinge on mere inches (like with the Three Chairs process). This framework for listening provides a way for you to track the positions of and relationships between characters involved in the issue at hand as well as to guide explorations with coachees about what most needs to change. In saying this, it is important to remember that this is about increasing the coachee's understanding far more than yours as the coach. As with the broader narrative coaching model, the Narrative Diamond reflects the natural process of how stories are formed in conversation so you can listen to the flow that is already under way rather than try to (re-)direct the flow.

> The characters that appear in coachees' stories are systematically related to each other and correspond with aspects of their lives in ways to be discovered.

Listening this way is particularly important when coachees are wrestling with challenging issues and their true nature is more exposed as a result. We can generally tell if something is amiss in a coachee's story when something about a character doesn't seem quite right. It is similar to the reaction we have in a movie when one of the characters acts completely "out of character." While in a movie that might turn us off, in a coaching session it alerts us to the fact that there is an element of the story that is trying to get our attention. As Hillman (1983) observed, "The action is in the plot . . . and only the characters know what's going on" (p. 59). Find ways to join with coachees in exploring what these characters are doing in the story and how they might contribute to (or challenge) the resolution of their issue.

Working with the characters in coachees' stories is quite useful because they often arise from unconscious sources within the coachee and, as such, bypass her more habitual and defended patterns of narration. Richard Seel (2003) offers a number of questions you can use to help coachees get inside their own stories to explore key characters:

- Which character resonates with you most?

- What is the character feeling?

- What are the character's assumptions and agendas?

- What are their values and what do they care about?

I would add:
- Which character(s) trigger an adverse reaction in you?

- Which character has the most to teach you?

Each of the four phases in narrative coaching corresponds with one of the four elements of the *Narrative Diamond* framework: The focus in the *Situate* phase of coaching is on the Narrator; in the *Search* phase it is on the Story, in the *Shift* phase it is on the Characters; and in the *Sustain* phase it is on the Field—and the return to the Narrator to make choices. You can use this framework to bring the initial story further into the field, surface aspects of the story as seen in the characters but not previously recognized or allowed as part of the narrator, and support the emergence of a new narrative from within the field. In the diagram, the listener is depicted off to the side, not in the usual dyadic position across from the narrator. This is done deliberately in the diagram and in practice to demonstrate a more fruitful position from which you can engage the narrators as well the stories and the characters in the field. The flow of the framework follows the solid arrows in the diagram from the Narrator to the Story, to the Characters, and back to the Narrator. The dotted arrows radiating out from the coach and the characters represent the support you can offer throughout a coaching conversation to bring material into the field and work with it there.

FIGURE 23: NARRATIVE DIAMOND FRAMEWORK FOR LISTENING

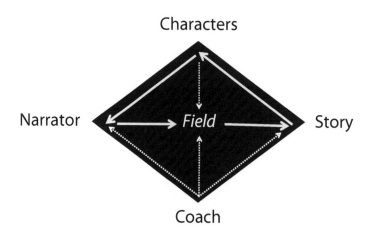

Each of the four elements is often best served by a mode of listening and a phase in the narrative coaching process. The connection between the flow of the narrative coaching process and the flow of what you can listen for can be seen in the following:

1. Welcome the *Narrator* and pay attention to what *is being said* as a way to build the rapport that is required for coaching. This is important in the *Situate* phase because the aim is to empathetically connect with a fellow human being and observe *what is*.

2. Advocate for the *Story* and pay attention to what *is not being said* as a way to discern what is missing or lost, what is truly at stake and desired. This is important in the *Search* phase because the aim is to identify the agenda for change through exploring *what if*.

3. Engage the *Characters* and pay attention to what *wants to be said* as a way to determine what the story is trying to communicate and what needs to change. This is important in the *Shift* phase because the aim is to experiment with new options related to *what matters*.

4. Work in the *Field* and use what is already shifting and being *said differently* as the basis for creating a supportive structure for the new story and bring it to life. This is important in the *Sustain* phase because the aim is to develop a new way forward based on *what works*.

FIGURE 24: NARRATIVE DIAMOND (EXPANDED)

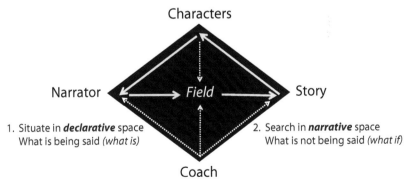

3. Shift in **projective** space
What wants to be said (*what matters*)

Characters

Narrator — Field — Story

1. Situate in **declarative** space
What is being said (*what is*)

2. Search in **narrative** space
What is not being said (*what if*)

Coach

4. Sustain in **generative** space
What is being said differently now (*what works*)

EXAMPLE

The following example is from a coaching client whose presenting issue was her frustration with and judgment about her boss. It summarizes the key insights she had in the session as framed by the four phases of the *Narrative Diamond* and the overall Narrative Coaching model. A breakthrough in the process was getting her to own and be accountable for the story *as hers*. At that point, the coaching could kick into a higher gear because she was fully present in it as the narrator rather than talking about it as if she were merely an actor (in someone else's drama). It also reflects one of the key maxims in this work: You can only coach the person in the room.

1. Narrator | *Situate* | Listening for what is being said

   I am feeling very frustrated. I'm upset because the leader in charge of this project regularly points out small mistakes in our team's reports, but he doesn't acknowledge what we are doing well or how hard we are working.

2. Story | *Search* | Listening for what is not being said

   When I hear myself talk about what it is like to put together these reports every two weeks, I realize that I am not putting in as much effort as I used to. On top of that, I frankly don't like working at this level of detail anymore or see the value in what we are doing.

3. Character | *Shift* | Listening for what wants to be said

   When I look at my situation from the perspective of the reports, they feel like a heavy burden. I was thinking I wanted coaching to help move on, but I see now that this was just a reactive response. What I really want is to figure out how to talk with my boss about communicating with us in a very different way, perhaps even modeling what we are looking for.

4. Coach | *Sustain* | Listening for what is being said differently

I am noticing a shift in myself from blaming and reacting to my leader to a deeper appreciation for the real issue and moving forward. This has helped me realize that I actually enjoy most of my current job. I'm excited to stretch myself by presenting this request to my boss and working on a solution with him.

> I imagine the Narrative Diamond being projected onto the space in front of us as a guide for where to position my chair relative to the four elements as the process unfolds.

More on Using the Framework

The *Narrative Diam*ond is useful for mapping coachees' stories and noticing where they place themselves in the room and in their stories. James Lawley and Penny Tompkins (2000) made the same observation: "[W]here coachees sit and where they want you to sit is often determined by their dominant lines of sight. . . . Coachees naturally place themselves where it is most appropriate for them to explore their symbolic world" (p. 93). I often find there are some interesting parallels, which makes sense given that we are working with stories in the room that are expressions of the stories coachees tell themselves.

I find that sometimes shifts in the room reflect shifts in coachees, and sometimes shifts in coachees lead them to make shifts in the room. This attention to physical arrangements can be found in the work of psychotherapists such as Harry Stack Sullivan, who would sometimes sit next to a patient so they could look out together at the problem troubling the person. It can also be found in some Native American traditions in which people would face each other to build sufficient relationship and agreements for the conversation, turn in the same direction to look out at the issues and develop a shared resolution in that space, and then turn back to face each other to make new agreements for moving forward.

Given the spatial nature of stories and narrative coaching sessions, it is no surprise that the notion of positioning is important in this work. Every position provides a particular point of view that shapes what we think we see, what we think it means, what experiences we have as a result, and the stories we tell about it. As such, be curious about the positions your coachees adopt relative to their issue and their stories—both in the telling and in the stories themselves. You can use the *Narrative Diamond* framework to help them explore their stories from multiple points of view in order to increase their awareness, understanding, and alternatives. For example: How would the *character* with whom you had the argument see the situation? What is missing from the *story*? How do *you* feel as you tell that story? Why are you telling *me* this story? What are you noticing in the *field* now? It is about helping people establish new relationships between existing elements in their stories and/or introduce new elements (Hermans, 2004) in order to better align their narratives with what they are trying to achieve.

It is a dance between responding to what is present and sensing what may be on the cusp of what's next. For example, I might start out facing the coachee to build sufficient rapport and trust, shift to be more at an angle as I explore the narrative material with him, and move in closer again if a stronger relational connection (e.g., due to increased vulnerability) or a new experience is needed. I often invite coachees to try out other positions in relation to me and/or the story as well in order to open up new ways of seeing themselves and their stories, others in their stories, and the coaching relationship. I usually take more of the lead in the conversation at the start of a session, but then support the coachee to take more of the lead as soon as he shows signs of wanting the "baton." The aim is to see where the coachee and the story want to go as they seek resolution and a return to greater wholeness. The insights gained in the process largely determine where the conversation goes.

When a coachee tells you his story, he is telling more than he can know at the time. Your role is to reflect back to him—sometimes frame by frame—what he said and did not say as well as how it affected you and may affect others. You can use the *Narrative Diamond* to work with the person's constructed self (how his past makes its way into the present), or the person's imagined self (how the future makes its way into the present). It is often the case that the resolution to people's issue is found in the projective spaces in their stories about the past, present or future. However, regardless of which time frame the story comes from or is about, it is important to bring it into the present moment in the session. This is because change only occurs in the present, even if it is about the past or future. This is why we keep bringing the person back to their current experience as we move through a session, and why one of our "go to" questions is "what are you noticing right now?"

In so doing, you can draw from Stern's (2004) insight that there are actually three present moments when people tell their story—each of which deserves our attention as we listen: "(1) the present moment of getting the original experience into verbal narrative form; (2) the present moment created in the teller during the telling of it to someone; and (3) the present moment evoked in the listener during the telling" (p. 192). The first informs how we listen to the narrator, the second informs how we listen to the story and its characters, and the third informs how we listen to ourselves and the field as we coach. In so doing, recognize that in narrative coaching we are not only dealing with the individual stories of the person we are coaching, but also the collective narratives in which they operate across time and space.

Narrative coaching is ultimately about the depth of your radical presence, the astuteness of your sensory observations, and the non-attached yet full engagement you bring to your listening. The more mindfully aware you can be, the more fluidly you can move between stepping back from the experience of the moment, being immersed in it, and observing it from a higher level of awareness (Graham, 2013). Consequently, narrative coaches make far greater use of silence, the field, and the narrative material than other approaches. This requires listening with a "third ear" so you can hear the subtle yet powerful clues about where the conversations and the stories want to go.

Implications for Your Practice

This means asking yourself:

1. *Situate:* Who is this person telling this story and what is that like for the narrator?

2. *Search:* What is the story trying to achieve and what is it asking of the narrator?

3. *Shift:* Which of the characters are important for the resolution of the story and why?

4. *Sustain:* What is already changing in this conversation and how can that be leveraged?

Here are some tips on listening this way as a coach:

- Pay careful attention to the circumstances that seem to trigger the telling of a particular story by a coachee (Edelson, 1993).

- Listen for different voices in her stories to elicit different aspects of herself, particularly silenced ones (Gilligan & Brown, 1991).

- Uncover patterns that are choking off her inner knowing so she can recover more of her existential sense (Bugental, 1990).

- Generate experiences and move toward the not known more than gathering information and moving toward the known.

What are your key insights?
What will you experiment with first?

CHAPTER 12

HOW TO INQUIRE INTO STORIES

The patient needs an experience,
not an explanation. | *Frieda Fromm-Reichmann*

One of coaching's greatest strengths is its use of powerful questions. One of the unique features of narrative coaching is that we inquire *into*, not *about*, people's stories to keep the conversation in the present moment as much as possible. This is because it is often more productive to ask questions that increase coachees' awareness of what is already present than to ask questions that introduce more information into the conversation. We are regularly asking ourselves and our coachees, "What is this story, this moment asking for?" You can often tell when a question really hits home for a coachee because of the pregnant pause that follows. In developing narrative coaching, I took it one step further and asked, "What if that profound pause was already present, and it is the pause that makes these questions possible and powerful—not the other way around?" Pausing is one of our most powerful tools as a coach and it is the soil in which the seeds from our questions can grow. It is based in a fundamental trust that most of what you need to work with in the session is in the person's stories, including the sources of their suffering *and* the sources of their liberation.

> Inquire *into*, not about, people's stories so you keep the conversation in the present moment as much as possible.

In this chapter we will look at deepening your capacity for inquiry through the *Four Gateways*, using a simple structure for inquiry, and working with metaphors and analogies. In narrative coaching, inquiry is seen as both a mindset (how we see our role) and an act of communication (what we say and do as a result). We ask questions which enable people to (1) notice their present phase (and state); (2) discover what they need to move to the next one; (3) find an opening to get across the threshold; and (4) map the coaching process to *their* change process. We are curious about the answers to questions such as:

- What essential question is the coachee trying to answer?

- Are these still the right questions?

- If not, what is the essential question now? Really?

- What would change if the coachee asked it?

- What is the conversation this person most needs to have?

The primary focus in narrative coaching is on using your questions to generate transformative experiences rather than gather information or probe for explanations. This is based in the premise that there are no "correct" explanations and, even if there were, there is little evidence to suggest a strong correspondence between having more information and making better choices (beyond a rudimentary level). This is a welcome respite for many coachees who, in addition to information overload, are awash in a sea of fads, acronyms, and labels. Another appeal of narrative coaching is its focus on the lived human experience and the available narrative material rather than on normative diagnostic measures and canonical professional discourse. In keeping with Erickson's "utilization principle," we use the coachee's own language as much as possible in our inquiry to minimize resistance and maximize impact. Doing so not only enhances rapport, but it also enables coaches and coachees to more readily stay in the present moment and have anchors for what emerges. As Alexander (1961) put it:

> The key lever of change is direct experience that contradicts long-held expectations rather than interpretations that explain them as rooted in the past. . . . The emphasis shifts from insight to experience, although the role of insight as a secondary but often powerful consolidating factor is by no means denied.

The key is to ask questions that keep coachees grounded in the experience of their own narration as opposed to detached through analysis or premature planning. For example, instead of asking, "What could you do differently next time?"—which takes people into an imaginary future—first ask, "What is happening for you right now as you talk about the future?" This supports people in developing themselves *at the same time* they are addressing their issue so they can resolve it (and others like it later). Narrative questions tend to be more vertical in nature—rising above or diving into the present situation—as opposed to the typical horizontal approach to questions in which each one leads to another like fence posts across the prairie. It is not about taking the person or the conversation somewhere with your questions, but rather using your questions to make the most of each and every moment. For example: Where does the coachee invest the most energy? Where does she turn for guidance? Where is the energy stuck or misplaced? What is truly calling for our attention right now in this conversation?

Deepening our Questions

Think of your questions as inviting coachees to develop a new relationship with their internal and external experiences (Carotenuto, 1985) in order to resolve their issues in the most elemental way. Otherwise, you both end up trying to solve the wrong problems, and as a result, the issues persist. Ask yourself, "What is the simplest and most direct path to a breakthrough?" In the process, it is important to remember that your understanding of what is happening is secondary and, ultimately, seldom necessary for coachees to achieve their purpose. The fundamental purpose of your inquiry is for *them* to become clearer. Beyond that, coaching is seldom about gathering more information anyway—much of which will not be relevant in the end and is often more for our own needs—but about using our inquiry to create new experiences for coachees that open new doors. As Moore (2000) describes it, "I've no intention of tracking down a culprit. I only want a fuller story" (p. 66). Therefore, think about coaching as accompanying people on a developmental process that is already under way rather than as imposing a structure on a conversation. It is less about asking ourselves, "What do I do next?" and more about "What does the story—and the change process it represents—want to be asked?" This approach works well because it mirrors the innately human process of growth.

> Your understanding of what is happening is secondary and, ultimately, seldom necessary for coachees to achieve their purpose in working with you.

Think of inquiry as a way of being *with* people, a deep and attuned curiosity, more than as a way of asking questions *of* people. It is about coming alongside coachees to inquire into their stories *with* them, rather than standing outside their stories and asking questions *to* them. This requires us to bring our questions into the profoundly here and now and to be more courageous in what we ask. Tompkins and Lawley (1997) offer a great example: "What's the next question the coachee would really like to be asked?" At the same time, recognize that he may be dreading it as well because he knows at some level that if he truthfully answers that question, it may serve as a threshold from which there would be no going back. *Ask anyway.* This is why it is important to provide enough time and space for coachees to first settle into the conversation and into themselves. Many people are slow to recognize what they are actually feeling or wanting, let alone able to put their feelings or experiences into words. If you rush them or they feel you are somehow interrogating them, most people will withhold aspects of their stories and themselves. Instead, align your rhythm and pace with what is happening in the session and what the person and the process are calling for.

A common way this is done in narrative coaching is to invite people to access aspects of their story that are hidden by their egoic and rational(izing) mind, but available through activities such as movement, meditation and mindfulness practices. I've increasingly incorporated somatic methods and questions in narrative coaching to help people be more present in and have more access to their body. I ask questions such as, "What do you notice in your body as you are telling this story? "Where do you notice it?" "What comes up for you there?" "What happens if you speak with your hand on your belly? While standing like a warrior?" I ask people where emotions and sensations are in their bodies to:

- Ground them in their lived experience and in the process.

- Increase their acuity of what is happening in and around them.

- Identify anchors to support the integration of what they have learned.

- Increase their sense of agency in developing themselves and resolving their issues.

- Keep the focus on their process not my work as the coach.

This is important because as Ginette Paris (2007) observes, "What the psyche refuses to acknowledge, the body always manifests. Whenever the body says 'no more,' it is sending a message that should get our attention" (p. xii). For example, a recent coachee claimed that he wasn't feeling any real stress around recent changes at work, yet in our session he acknowledged persistent tension in his shoulders, a shift in his eating patterns, and unexpressed emotions he was projecting onto others. These certainly sounded like stress responses to me. Through an inquiry into his current experience (in the moment but also in his daily life), he realized that he was in denial. It is a powerful and moving experience for coachees when they allow themselves to slow down long enough in a session to more fully experience a truth in their story and its telling.

Therefore, inquire from a place of trust that what your coachees are seeking is already present and walk with them on their journey to discover it. To deepen the inquiry, I will sometimes get them to move themselves into postures they associate with the story they are telling me, particularly if it relates to how the story was formed (Dijkstra, Kaschak, Zwaan, 2007). This activates the muscle memories and associations that we can then use to deepen their awareness of their current story and its impact on their lives. Then we can work with them using some of our latest practices to shift these postures or gestures to align with a healthier new story. The following is one of the simple processes I use to help people access more of their stories and more of their knowledge in order to better address their issue. It reflects the broader commitment in narrative coaching to do what we can to enable people to step into their issues as a whole person—so they can then tell the whole story and find a more whole solution.

Using the Four Gateways

I developed this process as a way to help coaches and coachees drop into their bodies (Drake, 2014c, 2017) as they work together. in order to discern what is going on in sessions and how to respond. It is based on the system of chakras found in a number of philosophical and spiritual traditions. These gateways represent access points to the flow of energy in the body, and each one can be seen as associated with a different type of knowledge. The use of energy as a construct finds support in the neuroscience of attachment patterns and mutual regulation, and it provides a way to ground intuition and increase self- and other-awareness. The aim is to notice where the energy (knowledge) is flowing and where it is blocked, where it is aligned and where it is not.

I focus on these four gateways since they are generally the most accessible for people; with more advanced students, I introduce four other gateways to deepen their capabilities. The gateways can also be used to develop your ability to hold space, "read" the situation, and support coachees in making more informed choices. It is analogous to what Susan Greenburg (2002) notes in her work, "People who do well in therapy move from talking about external events in the detached manner, through focusing on internal feelings in a richly descriptive and associative way, to readily accessing feelings to solve problems" (p. 8). This process mirrors that flow in getting people out of their heads, out of their stories and into their lived and felt experience. In the end, they can circle back to determine the desired course of action.

The Four Gateways:

Focus	Four Gateways	Purpose
Think	*Put hands on head*	Make sense
Feel	*Put hands on heart*	Make meaning
Be	*Put hands on hara (gut)*	Make decisions
Do	*Put hands on hips*	Make commitments

The body is an often overlooked but very important source of evidence about what is happening and how we are formulating as we coach. You can use the Four Gateways to help yourself and your coachees become more grounded in the truth of your respective stories and more aware of your somatic knowledge. The following is a brief description of why each of these gateways is valuable for coaches:

- The *Thinking* gateway (the head) connects us to our thoughts; it supports our ability to theorize about what is happening as we work and help coachees make sense of what is going on.

- The *Feeling* gateway (the heart) connects us to our values and emotions as sources of meaning; it supports our ability to humanize our work and help coachees connect with us and others.

- The *Being* gateway (the hara) connects us to our gut instincts and grounded knowing; it supports our ability to prioritize our work and help coachees get to the crux of the matter.

- The *Doing* gateway (the hips) connects us to the lower half of our body and what is in motion; it supports our ability to actualize what we know in a fluid and effective manner and help coachees take action.

A coachee's mind is consciously and unconsciously drawing from all four of these gateways anyway; we are just accessing that process so the person can become more aware of what is going on. When using this as a process of inquiry with coachees, start by drawing their attention to their hands as a way to get in touch with their body's knowledge. The act of focusing on their hands is in itself helpful because it gets coachees out of their heads. You can then guide them to place their hands at each of the four spots on their body, one at a time at first, while focused on their question or decision. With each of these gateways, the question is the same: "What does this part of me, this way of knowing, have to say about my question?"

You can guide them to move up and down these four gateways as needed to gain the knowledge they are seeking. What often transpires is an emerging awareness of energy (information) that is blocked at a gateway or between gateways. I then work with the person to explore what is happening at that gateway: "What do you notice?" "What is missing?" "What would it take to restore the flow here?" "What is it trying to tell you?" When they feel complete and there is a stronger sense of flow—or at least a sense of what is needed to restore flow—they are more informed to do the work at hand and make the changes they are seeking.

EXAMPLE

- Using the *head* gateway, the coachee notices that his story is jumbled as he tries to think about whether or not to stay in his current role.

- Using the *heart* gateway, he feels a sense of sadness and loss he had not been aware of before; he realizes it may be time to move on.

- Using the *hara* gateway, he first senses fear but then, as he breathes deeper into it, he discovers a sense of adventure he had been stifling.

- Using the *hips* gateway, he becomes aware of a new energy as he imagines himself exploring other options.

- Moving back through the gateways, he feels the clarity and alignment he needs to start looking for a new role.

Using the Four Gateways helps people to access additional sources of knowledge which they can then use to gain more clarity, make better decisions, and take new actions. The first step for many of them is getting them out of their heads. I find that in our fragmented and distracted world, they can access more of their truth and make more grounded decisions by using their head last rather than first. Otherwise, the executive function of their mind is often overwhelmed and not nearly as effective. However, I start the gateways process with the head because that is where most people begin as they tell their stories in coaching.

They generally assume that decisions are made in their head, yet they inevitably discover in this process that the energy and knowledge there is often confused or unclear (or clear but flat). They soon realize that vital information related to their story and its resolution are elsewhere in their system. Much of the time, the best overall decisions and actions come when we draw from our whole self. Otherwise, we make choices that make sense on paper (satisfying the mind), but result in a poor outcome because the impact on others (heart), what we truly wanted (hara) or what we actually can deliver (hips) are not considered.

You can use the Four Gateways to help people get a better sense of how they are truly doing and what they truly know by:

- Quieting the noise in their *head* so they can see how they are *Situated* in a new way.

- Noticing in their *heart* what values are at stake so they can clarify their *Search*.

- Breathing fully in their *hara* so they can *Shift* to a deeper sense of what is true for them.

- Adjusting their *hips* and overall stance so they can act with more confidence and *Sustain* their intention.

- Returning to their *head* so they can confirm their course of action and be more grounded and confident as they start out because the rest of their body is aligned.

You can use one or more of the gateways as needed: e.g., invite the coachee to put her hand on her heart as she names how she feels, put one hand on her heart and the other on her hara to ground her grief, or put one hand on her hara and the other on her hips to gather more strength to make a tough decision (and act on it). As you gain experience with this process you will start to get a feel for the aspects of themselves a coachee prefers to draw from and the ones he tends to avoid—which often become the avenues to explore in order for him to grow. The same can be said for you as a coach in terms of maturing how you work in sessions and how you live your own life.

You can use the Four Gateways to enhance the quality of your inquiry in many ways. For example, a coach notices a tightness in her belly *(hara)*; pauses and realizes that she feels disconnected from the coachee *(heart)* even though the content of the conversation is making sense *(head)*; she acknowledges that she is avoiding the harder issue which is the action to be taken *(hips)*. The more fully you can access your body as you formulate, the more it opens up possibilities for coachees to do the same through your mutual regulation. This is important because narrative formulation is less about figuring things out and more about paying attention to what is already present. The spiral from the Narrative Coaching model is here too as a reminder to continually move through the gateways as you coach so that you remain current with what is unfolding. Ultimately, most coachees will not be able to travel farther in sessions than their coach is willing to go.

Using the Four Gateways as you coach:

- *Open head:* Be curious rather than analyzing or judging what the person is saying
- *Open heart:* Be compassionate rather than pulling away to distance yourself emotionally.
- *Open hara:* Be courageous rather than muting your instincts or taking on what is not yours.
- *Open hips:* Be centered rather than trying to figure out how to fix the person or the situation.

EXAMPLE

How a coach used the Four Gateways to deal more effectively with a challenging coachee:

1. I noticed that I don't voice my concerns to my coachee directly, but instead talk abstractly about them with my supervisor *(head)*.

2. I became aware of what I often feel *(heart)* about myself and the coachee in those moments when I want to speak up.

3. I checked in with my gut *(hara)* to determine what I really want to say to him and notice the strength that arises when I say it directly.

4. I practiced saying it out loud with my coach *(hips)* until my stance, message, and authentic voice were clear.

5. I rehearsed the moment when I will speak to my coachee to ensure that the flow is aligned and anchored and the message works *(head)*.

Both coaches and coachees can use the Four Gateways to help them drop deeper into their embodied experience so they can bring more of their whole self to the process. This is important because your coachees are generally not able to travel farther in sessions than you are willing to go. By working somatically, your inquiry will be more powerful, the conversation will be more informed, and the outcomes will be more transformative. I believe that in the years to come we will gain a much deeper understanding of our body as a whole system. This will enrich our capacity to work with people in a much more integrative manner. For now, we can use the Four Gateways to help people get a better sense of how they are truly doing and what they truly know—so they can make new choices and take new actions.

> **Your coachees are generally not able to travel farther in sessions than you are willing to go.**

Being a Mindful PRO

Accessing the Four Gateways enables each person in coaching to be more aware and better regulate in the course of working together. This is true for them as individuals and as participants in the coaching relationship and process. Another tool you can use to deepen your connection with coachees and enhance the quality of the conversations and outcomes is based in the work of a colleague, Gregory Kramer. He developed and teaches process he developed called Insight Dialogue in which people move between periods of meditation and dialogue—with each deepening the inquiry. The stillness that emerges from the meditation supports a deeper connection and sharing in the dialogue, and what emerges in the dialogue is brought back into meditation to deepen the insights. I have adapted this process for coaching to teach practitioners how to listen and inquire in new ways.

Working this way enables you to be relaxed and alert at the same time—a prerequisite for working narratively with people in coaching. It is easy to be relaxed *or* alert (open), but the real magic happens when you can be both at the same time. In many ways, this is an apt description of what happens when two people mutually regulate well. The more you can pause, relax, and open as you coach, the more awake you will be to what is needed in the moment. It will help you and your coachees to be less reactive and more PROactive. In many ways, narrative coaching can be seen as a form of relational meditation, with the added benefit of facilitating tangible outcomes for people in the process.

This reflects its unique roots in both Eastern and Western psychologies and epistemologies. The following chart brings together the *inner and outer responses* in his core framework (Kramer, 2007), the *energy* associated with each pair of responses, and the *results* that often come from the process (Gallwey, 1981/2009, 2001, 2009). This process is used informally and formally in narrative coaching to enable both parties to engage each other and the coachee's issues at a much deeper level. In so doing, each person becomes more aware of what is happening inside them, their stories and their conversation in the moment.

TOOL

TABLE 7. BEING A MINDFUL PRO

What you gain by working this way:

Internal Response	External Response	Energy	Result
Pause	Listen deeply	Compassion	Deeper connection
Relax	Trust emergence	Consciousness	More clarity
Open	Speak truthfully	Courage	Authentic choices

Inquiring as a Mindful PRO

1. As you listen, notice your own state and breath as a reminder to *Pause* before you inquire so that you can be more clear, conscious and without judgment in the moment. Pausing is at the heart of your ability to self-regulate. It enhances your capabilities as a coach and models for coachees how they can do the same. More than just a welcome respite, pausing and settling into the silence are in themselves transformative. By suspending your habitual reactions and responses, you begin to unbind the neural networks that would otherwise be reinforced, allow any stress to diffuse, and open up more space for what the Buddhists would call lovingkindness. As Kramer (2008) observes, "When *Pause* uncovers difficult matters, it needs the support of *Relax*[12]" (p. 204).

2. The more you can *Relax*, the more you can (a) be awake to and accept what you are experiencing, (b) inquire more deeply and compassionately of coachees and their stories, and (c) form a deeper, more attentive working relationship. This reduces your need for striving as a coach and enables you to more fully trust your presence and the process. Relaxing enables you to ask questions of coachees from a very different space, one that is informed by what is happening in the field and where they are in their process. "Over time, meeting troublesome inner phenomena with stillness means

that they are not fed; their energy begins to drain out of them" (p. 205) as a result.

3. The more you Relax, the more you can courageously Open and speak your truth in the moment, make more authentic choices in the session, and be more accountable for yourself (Kramer, 2007). This enables you to get to the heart of the matter much sooner. In part this is because, as Kramer points out, "Just as the *Pause* is where stillness meets reactivity, in *Relax* love meets suffering. When this happens, healing happens. It happens on the spot" (p. 127)—and *Openness* emerges as a place from which to connect, speak or act in new ways.

Moving Up and Down the Tree

It's not that I'm so smart. But I stay with the questions much longer. . . .
If I had one hour to solve a difficult problem, I'd spend the first 55 minutes
defining the problem. | Albert Einstein

Inquiry in coaching is about helping people surface, explore, and adapt their narratives so they can make the changes in their life or work they have deemed important. As a result, they are not only able to resolve their presenting issues, but they also increase their maturity and capability as a foundation for moving forward. A narrative approach to inquiry is well-aligned with brief methods in this regard. We are not invested in either a need to understand the problem or an assumption that the solution is somehow connected with eliminating the problem (Hoyt, 1996). Instead, we ask questions to increase coachees' clarity about what they most want to be different and how they will know they have been successful (W. O'Hanlon, 1998). In moving between listening and questioning, we are searching for elements in the story that are amenable to challenge, redefinition, or reinterpretation (Coulehan, Friedlander, & Heatherington, 1998), but are close enough to the coachee's current experience and narrative so as to be seen as approachable (Grafaniki & McLeod, 1999). What this means is that narrative coaches ask far fewer questions, particularly in the beginning. In this section we will explore the connections between listening and inquiring, and we will return to the analogy of coaching as a bird circling a tree to describe the types of questions we tend to ask in narrative coaching. The following framework shows the interplay between listening and inquiring as it is used in narrative coaching.

FIGURE 25: DECONSTRUCTIVE AND CONSTRUCTIVE APPROACHES IN COACHING

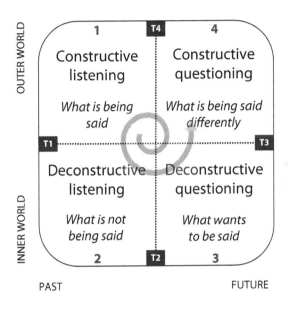

The narrative coaching approach to inquiry incorporates the shift from deconstructive listening to deconstructive questioning in certain forms of psychotherapy. *Deconstructive listening* is about accepting and understanding people's stories as they are—without reifying them—and seeking openings for aspects of their narratives that haven't yet been storied (Freedman & Combs, 1996, p. 46). Once there is enough of a shared understanding, there is a shift to asking questions. *Deconstructive questioning* invites people to see their stories from different perspectives, notice how they are constructed (or even *that* they are constructed), note their limits, and discover there are other possible narratives. I have added *constructive listening* and *constructive questioning* to represent a more complete cycle in coaching. The addition of *constructive listening* is a reminder to stay in *Situate* long enough to get to the real questions; the addition of *constructive questioning* is a reminder to stay in *Sustain* long enough to ensure the outcomes are starting to be integrated. These additions highlight the proposition in narrative coaching that listening drives inquiry, not the other way around. Each of these modes of engaging with coachees relates to one of the four phases of narrative coaching and one of the four elements of the *Narrative Diamond*. As before, these are phases along a spiraling path not necessarily steps in a linear process.

The initial focus in coaching is on the coachee and using *constructive listening* to track what is being said by the person (*Situate*). Next, the focus is on the story and using *deconstructive listening* to help the coachee explore what is not being said in the story (*Search*). Once the coachee has determined what she wants to change, you can shift to *deconstructive questioning* to help her discover what wants to be said and what needs to shift to bring about the change (*Shift*). Lastly, you can use *constructive questioning* based on what is already being said differently to help the coachee prepare for bringing her new story to life (*Sustain*).

EXAMPLE

1. *Constructive listening*—I remained present as the coachee talked about "My team doesn't deliver the results I want."

2. *Deconstructive listening*—I explored with her the insight she had that "I don't think they understand what I want."

3. *Deconstructive questioning*—I invited her to shift perspectives so she could see, "I wonder if I'm not being clear with them."

4. *Constructive questioning*—I guided her in practicing what she could do differently, "I need to make my requests more concrete."

This framework makes some important distinctions about our roles as a coach in different phases of the coaching conversation. For example, when you are forming a question, ask yourself, "What purpose am I hoping it will serve for the coachee and his process?" While this framework mirrors the flow of narrative coaching, feel free to move between these roles based on what best serves the needs of the coachee and the conversation. In so doing, position your questions "on the razor edge between love and power and [seek to] be both supportive and uncompromising" (Heron, 2001, p. 62). This is effective as a technique and as modeling for coachees about how to more authentically and generatively communicate. Otherwise, if you get caught up in listening for too long, coachees may remain stuck in the problem and their own rumination and procrastination. If you rush to questioning too soon, coachees may prematurely choose a project they are not ready for and/or is not at the right level. When in doubt as you move between listening and questioning, return to your breath, to the moment. Come back to presence.

While there is no formula for calculating exactly which question to ask or when, there is a sense in narrative coaching that certain types of questions are better asked at certain points in the conversation. You can draw on the analogy in narrative coaching of a bird circling a tree as a guide to help you do so. Imagine yourself starting with the coachee's experience on a branch in the thick of things as he begins his story, then moving up the tree and into the sky to help him get a better perspective. You can stop on the upward spiral as needed to help him name what he has discovered. Once the implications of the current story and the desires for a new story are clear, imagine yourself moving down into the tree again to help him determine how to put his new story and/or decision into action. The underlying questions are always the same: At what level—relative to the tree—is the coachee right now? What is the next level for him? How can we get there? In doing so, be inspired by the infamous line from Albert Einstein that you can't solve a problem at the level at which it was created.

You can also use the following inquiry process to assess where coachees are relative to their issue and where they need to move next in terms of the level of inquiry. I have included sample questions for each level; I encourage you to find additional ones that work for you. This process was developed as part of my work with a global professional services firm in which I was teaching coaching skills to the partners and directors. I developed a very simple practice in which they paired up and took a short walk, stopping at intervals to ask the next question. As with all of our programs, we wanted to offer them a natural human experience rather than teach than yet another artificial model about how they "should" be talking. Participants found the experience refreshing and surprisingly profound. The message to them was that this is how coaching should feel. In using this tool, start with question #1 at the bottom of the left column and then move up to the top of that column. You can then bridge to question #5 at the top of the right column to take what they have discovered and help them move down through the right column to take action. When you are done, you will have guided the coachee in a complete spiral from *Situate* to *Situate*.

TOOL

FIGURE 26: CIRCLING THE TREE WITH OUR INQUIRY

Moving up the tree

THEN GO HERE.

5. How has it affected you? *(share what it means to you)*

4. What was important about it to you? *(talk about your values)*

3. How do you feel about it? *(notice what emerge)*

2. What do you think about it? *(provide more details)*

1. What happened? *(just give the facts)*

START HERE.

5. What is true and important for you now?

4. What is your motivation to do it differently?

3. How will you remember this new story?

2. What do you need in order to get started?

1. How will you know you're successful?

Moving Down the Tree

Working with Metaphors

This is what keeps you doing things you don't want to do. You do them because you're out of touch with the place where your actions come from. | *James Bugental*

Metaphors and other analogies represent unique opportunities for inquiry in coaching because they act as "side doors" into people's narratives and identities. People tend to be less defended there because metaphors are generally framed as common phrases, images, or experiences that seem innocuous at first. They can be seen as attempts of our unconscious to surface images through which we can notice aspects of ourselves that warrant our attention. It is as if our unconscious and unspoken lives press for recognition in these narrative fragments (Phillips, 1994). They often "mark the living presence of important narratives that constitute one's sense of self" (J.L. Griffith & M.E. Griffith, 1993) and, as such, often reveal larger issues at stake for us. This is why in narrative coaching we work directly with the metaphor itself rather than psychologize it. Like with most questioning in narrative coaching, we inquire *into* it rather than *about* it.

Metaphors and other analogies:

- Provide mental models and linguistic shorthand by which we operate and communicate.

- Bridge the symbolic and literal, emotive and logical, conscious and unconscious.

- Offer hints about issues for which the person has yet to find language.

- Provide access into the coachee's world, into the spaces in-between their stories.

- Invite the coach and the coachee into a realm of serious play in the moment.

Metaphors connect the world as lived *in* the tree and the world as seen from *above* the tree, and they enable people to make associations that they may otherwise not make. They communicate by "juxtaposing two not entirely comparable elements, thereby inducing the hearer to extract from the somewhat discordant image a new vision of the primary element" (Bassler, 1986, p. 158). They sit on the doorstep between worlds and offer people an opportunity to move in and out of perspectives on their situation and/ or themselves. One of the ways you can capitalize on this juxtaposition is by inviting coachees to bring their metaphor to life and immerse themselves in it as if it were real. By animating their metaphors[13]—and often participating in them as coach and/or as character—you can help coachees gain a fuller understanding of their situation, its meaning and significance, and a path to resolution. This often yields more robust outcomes because the whole brain is activated and the whole person is engaged. Even better, "when the metaphor evolves, behavior changes in the client's 'real' world" (Tompkins & Lawley, 1997, p. 1).

For example, with a coachee who felt "stuck in the mud," I pressed her feet down as she tried to walk across the room—to give her a visceral experience of its impact in her life. In processing the experience, we explored how it was that she kept finding herself in this place and what would need to shift for her to walk freely. A workshop participant described himself as a "lone wolf," so I invited him to get up, go stand across the room away from the group, and notice what happened for him and for the group. We all stood there in silence for a minute or two to let his sudden separation from the group sink in. In the dialogue that followed, he began to see where this behavior came from and how he wanted to be more in balance. We also talked with the group about what came up for them in the experience. Bringing metaphors alive in the coaching process is more powerful than just talking about them. It enables coachees to subjectively experience their issue rather than try to objectively explain it. I tend to pause if the coachee uses a metaphor that seems significant and explore it then and there. It often becomes a vehicle through which we can directly access people's issues in new ways.

When you are working with people who are more literal in nature, ground them in the tangible aspect of the metaphor before exploring its symbolic meaning. When you are working with people who are more imaginative in nature, ground them in its symbolic aspect before exploring with them its more literal implications. I enjoy working with metaphors and analogies because they call for serious play and, as such, provide access to the core dynamics of coachees' issues. There is often a point in working with them where you can freeze-frame the moment to capture the essence of the issue. For the "stuck in the mud" person, it was the moment she tried to lift her foot from the floor. For the "lone wolf," it was lifting his head and seeing the group across the room for the first time —and in a new way. Overall, it works best to stay in the ambiguity of the image rather than prematurely rush to an interpretation or objectification. Let it breathe . . .

These experiences can often be quite powerful for people, particularly if they are followed all the way through and people are given the time to fully process them. I recommend not debriefing or discussing big experiences straightaway because it dilutes the energy and the transformative potential. Let the person sit in silence or quietly walk outside so the new awareness can start to settle. Having another person they trust quietly hold space for them as they do so is often appreciated. The changes that began in the process will continue to ripple through the person for quite some time if they are cared for well. For the same reason, I don't make plans with people after big experiences, as it tends to prematurely thrust them back into the world before their new story has gelled. If I offer any instructions at all it is to simply notice what is happening and to nurture themselves.

In this chapter we have looked at inquiry as it is conceptualized and used in narrative coaching. Following the flow of the model, you can use your curiosity and questions to open up and expand new lines of inquiry with people, attend to what emerges as important and in need of attention, and focus the conversation in preparation for implementation. In so doing, you are in essence creating zones of proximal development for people in which they can learn what is required to make the passage across the next threshold and then be guided in doing so. Your coaching can offer them the scaffolding they need as they move into, though, and out of each phase.

We also used the analogy of the bird circling the tree as a frame for thinking about the nature of the questions you ask in coaching. What is important here is the foundation of generative silence and a deep curiosity about what is happening with the person and her process. As a result, your questions neither lead nor follow the conversation, but accompany it as you circle the tree together. You can use Four Gateways and the Mindful PRO as powerful yet simple tools to fine-tune your presence with people, your working relationship, and the "field" in which you work. They will also enhance your ability to tap multiple sources of knowledge as you coach. This same integrative and experiential approach can be seen in how you can work with metaphors that bridge between worlds. In the end, remember that it is your presence that often matters most—more than whether or not you ask the perfect question. Trust that everything you need is right in front of you.

> **It is your presence that often matters most—more than whether or not you ask the perfect question.**

Implications for Your Practice

- Trust that the resolution is already present.

- Let your questions emerge from the silence and what you hear.

- Ask questions to generate experiences not pursue or provide explanations.

- Stay in the story and the present moment even when asking about the past or future.

- Position yourself relative to and in support of the unfolding story.

- Move toward the unknown more than the known with most of your questions.

- Ask open questions to connect and closed questions to invite them to choose.

- Ask one question at a time. Keep them short, simple, and to the point.

- People can only intervene in their life at the level at which they can make distinctions.

- Recognize that your understanding is not essential for their progress.

What are your key insights?
What will you experiment with first?

CONCLUSION

If you ever find yourself in the wrong story, leave. | *Mo Willems*

Narrative coaching draws on rich traditions that predate coaching, incorporates practices that transcend traditional coaching, and offers glimpses into what coaching could become. As I thought about how to conclude this book, I realized that parables and fables have been used as a teaching device for thousands of years because they communicate the moral of the story in simple terms. They are built around two questions: "What is the main message I want you to take away?" and "What common experience can I use as a reference point?" As I thought about this book in those terms, I asked myself: What if we released the word "coaching" and thought in terms of transparent connection, authentic communication, and transformative purpose? What if coaching was a magnificent scenic overlook and there is more road ahead? What if coaching was just the way we lived? These are important questions as more and more people are drawn to incorporate coaching into their work and their lives. It also comes at a time when we are confronted with increasing narrative complexities related to questions about what is means to be a human, a worker, a nation, a planet, and more.

> Here are the main messages I would like you to take away, for yourself and for the people you work with:
> - Be radically present to yourself, the other person, and the conversation.
> - Be open to discover the truths and the illusions in your stories. Both will be liberating.
> - Be willing to pivot in the moment and cross the threshold before you so you can make real change in real time.
>
> The common experience I want to use as a referent point:
> - We have the choice in each moment as to the story we tell ourselves and others. We are responsible for our choices, our stories and their impacts in the world. Our work is to increasingly be radically present so that we choose well and enable our coachees and all those we encounter to do the same.

I would like to conclude by offering a brief summary of what we have covered so far, the six core principles of narrative coaching, and a narrative bill of rights for coachees. At the heart of the process is a commitment to stay in the present moment and within the stories as they are being narrated as much as possible. The first section of the book on **narrative psychologies** outlined how the narrative coaching process is based in a deep understanding of how our brain develops and our mind works, how we form relationships and identities, and how we learn and develop over time. It does so with a deep respect for the preverbal, unconscious, and embodied nature of our identities and stories. The second section on **narrative processes** offered a look at the function and structure of stories, the act of narration and formulation as resources in coaching, and rites of passage as a natural process through our narratives change.

The third section on **narrative practices** explored rites of passage as the underlying structure for narrative coaching. The Narrative Coaching model was introduced with an overview of where it came from, each of the four phases, and how they can be used to achieve optimal results. The fourth section on **narrative practitioners** offered three of the key skills in narrative coaching—holding space, listening, and inquiry—and why each is done differently. The use of silence, the field, and the whole self in coaching are of particular importance. These are important in learning what to listen for in people's stories, advocating for the stories themselves, and seeing narrative coaching as an integrative change process.

The integrative nature of narrative coaching is evident as you look back over the book, and see how each of the four-phase models is based in the same underlying process. Narrative coaching works well because this process mirrors how people naturally tell stories, move through transitions, and learn and develop. Narrative coaching is also unique in that it is organized around the coachee and her stories, not the coach, the methodology, or even the problem/solution. It is based in the premise that, as David K. Reynolds (1986) noted, "I can take my life in a new direction at any time, merely by stepping into this moment in a new way."

To borrow from the traditions of the indigenous peoples of Australia, coachees have arrived where they are right now along the "songline" of their own life and the lives of those who came before them. It could be no other way. The choice for them now is, "Which stories will I continue to tell? Which stories will I change or release? What new stories might I bring to my life?" At the same time, it is also important to acknowledge that their stories are formed out of material from larger narratives that existed before they were born and will continue on in some form after they die. Narrative coaching is one of the few methodologies that moves beyond the individual to address these larger narratives and the forces that shape our identities, mindsets, and behaviors. It offers a process through which people can awaken more fully and achieve more of what matters most as a result. I would invite you to imagine yourself as a channel for wisdom and energy that is passing *through* you in service of the process and the person. The more you develop yourself, the stronger your channel will become and the more powerful yet simple your coaching will be.

Narrative coaching works well because it doesn't need certitudes; instead, it precipitates an acceleration of consciousness (Paris, 2007). It does so not by offering a prescriptive methodology, but by grounding itself in an integrative philosophy and a set of clear principles. I believe that the time has come for narrative coaching to really shine. There is a greater awareness of the power of narrative and the need for more advanced and integrative forms of practice. I believe this will be increasingly important as we move into a difficult period of transition as a planet. Now more than ever, with so much up in the air, we need to develop new ways to stay connected with and in conversation with one another. Narrative coaching has always been a pioneer in our field in this regard and will continue to do so because:

- It is based in natural human processes through which coaches can develop themselves.

- It is based on the broader applied Narrative Design platform such that it can be scaled to any size[14.]

- It connects the deeply systemic and the deeply personal to support more sustainable change.

- It has a strong academic foundation, yet it is accessible to anyone and can be used in any moment.

- It draws on attachment theory and applied mindfulness to increase people's capacities to cope, connect, create, and contribute.

Coda: The Six Principles

Narrative coaching is built around a robust model, and it offers a distinct and powerful methodology. Fundamentally, though, it is a philosophy and set of principles for purposeful conversations. One of the things participants most appreciate is how this work enables them to integrate their prior knowledge, experience, and modalities—and at a higher level. They find that they can let go of a lot of what they thought coaching had to include and, as a result, they end up de-cluttering the way they work. They come to see the wisdom in only adding to the coaching conversation when it feels essential to do so. One colleague described what I am doing with narrative coaching as "helping people re-boot their human operating system." Another one remarked in the midst of a Lab, "It can't be this simple, can it?"—and then affirmatively answered her own question a few minutes later as she moved through the exercise.

Narrative coaching can work this way because it is based in the following six core principles of narrative coaching:

- *Trust that everything you need is right in front of you.*

   This is the cornerstone of narrative coaching. It means staying out of our heads—worried about what to do next—and trusting that the resources and resolution are already there. It means moving toward the unknown and letting go of our need to be in control or clever so that we can:

- *Be fully present to what IS without judgment.*

   This is about being radically present even as we observe what is unfolding using our expertise and wisdom. It means serving as a loving witness and accepting what is true for coachees before attempting to make changes—so they can do the same for themselves. Therefore:

- *Speak only when you can improve on silence.*

   This is about using the power of generative silence to build rapport, activate the field, and make more space for the whole story. It means staying in the moment, listening at many levels, and being guided more by what we hear and sense than what we say. From that place we can:

- *Focus on generating experiences not explanations.*

   This is about bringing people's stories into the room through serious play and compassionate direct inquiry. It means inviting them to take new action now—rather than analyzing and planning for later. This allows them to experiment with trying out new ways of being, acting or speaking. To do so:

- *Work directly with the narrative elements in the field.*

  This is about inviting people to reconfigure elements in their stories to elicit insights and move closer to their aspiration. It means staying within their frame and language so that changes are more likely to stick. This is especially important when we are called to:

- *Stand at the threshold when a new story is emerging.*

  This is about noticing when people are approaching a developmental breakthrough and/or choice point—either of which may come first. It means ensuring they are prepared to cross, safeguarding their traverse, and welcoming them and their new story on the other side.

A story is just a story. A story is way more than a story.

Working from these principles requires a commitment to a strong ethic in relation to people and their stories. This is reflected in the fact that people often comment on how respectful narrative coaching feels. It is because we realize that while a story is just a story, a story is way more than a story. We important because we often have far more invested in and tied up with our stories than we realize at first. Much of this comes down to working in the spaces where reality and story meet with compassionate candor. Therefore, in narrative coaching we tend to move slowly at first and, as such, recognize their true significance. It gives people the time and space to soften their grip on their stories before they release or reconfigure them. This reflects the centrality of a non-judgmental respect that is at the core of narrative coaching.

The next frontier for this work is to explore how these principles can be used outside of coaching as well. It is for this reason that I founded the Moment Institute in 2017. I came to increasingly appreciate the observation by the

American naturalist John Muir, "When we try to pick out anything by itself, we find it hitched to everything else in the Universe." We live in a time when coaches and others need to step up into new ways of working in order to meet the complex needs we face. However, in doing so, we can be guided by the same philosophy and principles that are at the heart of narrative coaching. These are reflected in the following set of ethical guidelines[15] I use when I am coaching or developing coaches. They are based in a fundamental belief that when you coach people you are a guest in their narrative "home"—whether that is with one person, one neighborhood or one organization.

A narrative bill of rights in coaching:

- People have the right to a safe space for their storytelling. Respect them and their stories above anything else.
- People have the right to be heard in a nonjudgmental and non-assumptive manner. As part of this, take their communal and cultural stories seriously.
- People have the right to tell their own story their own way. They are accountable for the impact of their stories on themselves and others.
- People have the right to understand and interpret their own stories. They are responsible for changing their stories, lives, and selves if/as they so choose.
- People have the right to expect coaches to manage their own stories, agendas, and participation. Be an exemplary steward of the process and the field.
- People have the right to make sense and meaning of what happens in coaching. They are responsible for what they choose to do as a result.

This book is a culmination of a long personal and professional journey. It is also an invitation to you to help create what comes next with this work. I hope that reading this book has been a rich and rewarding experience and inspired you to go further with narrative coaching. If so, check out our retreats and mastermind groups at www.momentinstitute.org and our training program through WBECS at www.narrativecoach.com. In the end, narrative coaching is about helping people to:

- Become more aware of and awake to their own stories.
- Recognize that their stories are personally and socially constructed.
- Recognize that their stories are formed in relation to larger narratives.
- Understand how their stories shape their identity and behavior.
- Be more authentic and authorial in how they narrate and live.
- Relate to themselves and others with a wider window of tolerance so they can grow.
- Find ways to be an activist for new narratives that are more inclusive, empowering and sustainable for generations to come.

I hope this book has opened your heart and mind to new ways of working with people and their stories in coaching. I invite you to look around and see where this work is most needed and you have the greatest gifts and passion. This work is a powerful resource for your own growth as a human being and as a practitioner. As you've seen by now, there is a tremendous depth to this work in terms of its foundations and fundamentals. At the same time, each of the versions of the core model attest to the fact that it is in the end a profoundly human process of change. The beauty of it is that you can use it in most any moment of your life to pivot toward a new story that is more affirming and generative. I invite you to seek out opportunities each day to practice and open the door a bit wider to what is possible. I will close with a piece of gratitude from one of our students that captures the spirit of this work so well: "Thank you for showing us this humble magic in action." *What new stories do you want to bring to life?*

Implications for Your Practice

What are your key insights?
What will you experiment with first?

ENDNOTES

1. If you want to know more about the concept of the "field" in coaching, look ahead to p. 254. The term is most often used in this book to describe the energetic space between and around a coach and coachee when they work together.

2. Personal communication: (Francis, 2012).

3. I will alternate between feminine and masculine pronouns throughout the book.

4. Sometimes described as Fearful or Disorganized in the literature.

5. Sources: Begley, 2007; Cozolino, 2002; Drake, 2009d, Mikulincer & Shaver, 2007; Siegel, 2007.

6. Primary sources: Cozolino, 2002, 2006, 2010; Siegel 2007.

7. As they both do in later writings.

8. Cited in de Geus, 1997, p. 36.

9. These four types were identified by Daniel Stern and others from the Change Process Study Group; the fourth term was adapted from "Open space" by David Drake. Benefits adapted from Keenan & Miehls' (2008) work on third spaces.

10. A version of this case first appeared in Drake & Stelter, 2014, pp. 83–87.

11. BEAM: The four elements in the integrative approach to change and development used in narrative coaching: Behavior, Environment, Aspiration, and Mindset.

12. Italics added.

13. I will use the term "metaphors" to encompass all such forms in line with the popular usage of the term.

14. This work has been scaled from 1-50,000+ in support of change.

15. I am grateful for the powerful work of Paul Costello in this space.

REFERENCES

Ainsworth, Mary, & Bowlby, John J. (1991). An ethological approach to personality development. *American Psychologist, 46*, 331–341.

Alexander, Bobby C. (1991). Victor Turner revisited: Ritual as social change (Vol. 74). Atlanta, GA: Scholars Press.

Alexander, Franz Gabriel (1961). *The Scope of Psychoanalysis*. New York: Ronald Press.

Allport, Gordon. (1955/1968). *Becoming: Basic Considerations for a Psychology of Personality*. New Haven, CT: Yale University Press.

Amabile, Teresa M., & Kramer, Steven J. (2012). The power of small wins. *Harvard Business Review, 7*. Retrieved from http://hbr.org/2011/05/the-power-of-small-wins/ar/1.

Anderson, Timothy. (2004). "To tell my story": Configuring interpersonal relations within narrative process. In Lynne E. Angus & John McLeod (Eds.), *Handbook of Narrative and Psychotherapy: Practice, Theory, and Research* (pp. 315–329). Thousand Oaks, CA: Sage.

Angus, Lynne E., and John McLeod, eds. 2004. *The handbook of narrative and psychotherapy: Practice, theory and research*. Thousand Oaks, CA: Sage.

Anzaldua, Gloria. (1987). *Borderlands | La frontera: The New Mestiza*. San Francisco: Aunt Lute Books.

Ashton, Paul W. 2007. *From the brink: Experiences of the void from the depth psychology perspective*. London, UK: Karnac. Augustine, Saint. (400/2009). *Confessions* (Henry Chadwick, Trans.). Oxford: Oxford University Press.

Austin, James T., & Vancouver, Jeffrey B. (1996). Goal constructs in psychology: Structure, process, and content. *Psychological Bulletin, 120*(3), 338–375.

Badenoch, Bonnie. (2008). *Being a Brain-Wise Therapist: A Practical Guide to Interpersonal neurobiology*. New York: W.W. Norton.

Bakan, David. (1966). *The Duality of Human Existence: Isolation and Communion in Western Man*. Boston: Beacon.

Baker, Ann C. 2002. "Receptive spaces for conversational learning." In *Conversation learning: An experiential approach to knowledge creation*, edited by Ann C. Baker, Patricia J. Jensen and David A. Kolb, 101-123. Westport, CT: Quorum.

Barrett, Terry, Cashman, Diane, & Moore, Diane. (2011). Designing problems and triggers in different media. In Terry Barrett & Sarah Moore (Eds.), *New Approaches to Problem-Based Learning* (pp. 18–35). New York: Routledge.

Barry, David. 1997. "Telling changes: from narrative therapy to organizational change and development." *Journal of Organizational Change Management* 10 (1):30-46.

Bartel, C., & Dutton, Jane E. (2001). Ambiguous organizational memberships: Constructing organizational identities in interactions with others. In M. A. Hogg & D. J. Terry (Eds.), *Social Identity Processes in Organizational Contexts* (pp. 115–130). Philadelphia: Psychology Press.

Bassler, Jouette M. (1986). The parable of the loaves. *The Journal of Religion*, 66(2), 157–172.

Bateson, Gregory. (1972). *Steps to an Ecology of Mind*. New York: Ballantine Books.

Bateson, Gregory. (1982). Difference, double description and the interactive designation of self. In F. Allan Hanson (Ed.), *Studies in Symbolism and Cultural Communication* (Vol. 14, pp. 3–8). Lawrence: University of Kansas.

Baumeister, R. F., Bratslavsky, E., Muraven, M., & Tice, D. M. (1998). Ego depletion: Is the active self a limited resource? *Journal of Personality and Social Psychology*, 74(5), 1252.

Begley, Sharon. (2007). *Train Your Mind, Change Your Brain*. New York: Ballantine Books.

Beisser, Arnold. 1970. "The paradoxical theory of change." In *Gestalt therapy now*, edited by J Fagan and I Lee, 77-80. New York, NY: Harper Calophon.

Berger, Peter L. (1963). *Invitation to Sociology*. New York: Doubleday.

Berger, Peter L., & Luckmann, Thomas. (1966). *The Social Construction of Reality*. New York: Doubleday.

Bergum, Vangie. (1997). *A Child on Her Mind: The Experience of Becoming a Mother*. Westport, CT: Bergin & Garvey.

Bernstein, Jerome S. (2005). *Living in the Borderland*. New York: Routledge.

Bion, Wilfred R. (1961). *Experiences in Groups and Other Papers*. London: Tavistock.

Bion, Wilfred R. (1967). Notes on memory and desire. *Psychoanalytic Forum*, 2(3), 271–280.

Bird, Johnella. 2000. *The Heart's Narrative: Therapy and Navigating Life's contradictions*. Auckland, NZ: Edge Press.

Block, Jack. 1982. "Assimilation, accommodation, and the dynamics of personality development." *Child Development* 53:281-295.

Bluckert, Peter. (2010). The Gestalt approach to coaching. In Elaine Cox, Tatiana Bachkirova, & David A. Clutterbuck (Eds.), *The Complete Handbook of Coaching* (pp. 80–93). London: Sage.

Bly, Robert. (1988). *A Little Book on the Human Shadow*. New York: HarperCollins Publishers.

Boa, F. (1988). *The Way of the Dream: Conversations on Jungian Dream Interpretation with Marie-Louise von Franz*. Boston: Shambhala.

Boje, David M. (1998). The postmodern turn from stories-as-objects to stories-in-context methods. Research Methods Forum. Retrieved from http://www.aom.pace.edu/rmd/1998_forum_postmodern_stories.html

Boje, David M. 2001. "What is antenarrative?", accessed January 7. http://cbae.nmsu.edu/~dboje/papers/what_is_antenarative.htm

Boscolo, Luigi, & Bertrando, Paolo. (1992). The reflexive loop of past, present, and future in systemic therapy and consultation. *Family Process*, 31, 119–130.

Botella, Luis, & Herrero, Loga. (2000). A relational constructivist approach to narrative therapy. *European Journal of Psychotherapy, Counselling & Health*, 3(3), 407–418.

Bowlby, John. (1969). *Attachment* (2nd ed. Vol. 1). New York: Basic Books.

Bowlby, John. (1973). *Separation: Anxiety and Anger* (Vol. 2). New York: Basic Books.

Bowlby, John. (1982). *Loss: Sadness and Depression* (Vol. 3). New York: Basic Books.

Bowlby, John. (1988). *A Secure Base: Clinical Applications of Attachment Theory*. London: Routledge.

Boyd, Brian. (2009). *On the Origin of Stories*. Cambridge, MA: Harvard University Press.

Brehony, Kathleen A. (1996). *Awakening at Midlife*. New York: Riverhead Books.

Bretherton, Inge, and Kristine A. Munholland. 2008. "Internal working models in attachment relationships; Elaborating a central construct in attachment theory." In *Handbook of Attachment: Theory, Research and Clinical Applications*, edited by Jude Cassidy and Phillip R. Shaver, 102-127. New York, NY: Guilford Press.

Bridges, William. (2001). *The Way of Transition: Embracing Life's Most Difficult Moments*. Cambridge, MA: De Capo Press.

Bridges, William. (1980). *Transitions: Making Sense of Life's Transitions*. Reading: Addison-Wesley.

Brimhall, Andrew S., Gardner, Brandt C., & Henline, Branden H. (2003). Enhancing narrative couple therapy process with an enactment scaffolding. *Contemporary Family Therapy*, 25(4), 391–414.

Brown, Molly Young. (2004). *Unfolding the Self: The Practice of Psychosynthesis*. New York: Helios.

Brown, T. (2009). *Change by Design: How Design Thinking Transforms Organizations and Inspires Innovation*. New York: HarperBusiness.

Bruner, Jerome. (1986). *Actual Minds, Possible Worlds*. Cambridge, MA: Harvard University Press.

Bruner, Jerome. 1990. *Acts of meaning*. Cambridge, MA: Harvard University Press.

Chang, Jeff, and Michele Phillips. 1993. "Michael White and Steve de Shazer: New directions in family therapy." In *Therapeutic Conversations*, edited by Stephen Gilligan and Reese Price, 95-135. New York, NY: W.W. Norton.

Bruner, Jerome. (2002). *Making Stories: Law, Literature, Life*. Cambridge, MA: Harvard University Press.

Bruner, Jerome, & Luciarello, J. (1989). Monologue as narrative recreation of the world. In K. Nelson (Ed.), *Narratives from the Crib*. Cambridge, MA: Harvard University Press.

Buck, Stephanie. (2004). Home, hearth, and grace: The archetypal symbol of threshold on the road to self. Paper presented at the 2004 International Conference: Jungian Society for Scholarly Studies, Newport, RI.

Bugental, James, F.T. (1990). *Intimate Journeys: Stories for Life-Changing Therapy*. San Francisco: Jossey-Bass.

Burke, Kenneth. (1969). *A Grammar of Motives*. Berkeley, CA: University of California Press.

Bynum, Caroline Walker. (1984). Women's stories, women's symbols: A critique of Victor Turner's theory of liminality. In R. L. Moore & Frank E. Reynolds (Eds.), *Anthropology and the Study of Religion*. Chicago: Center for the Scientific Study of Religion.

Campbell, Joseph. (1968). *The Masks of God: Creative Mythology*. New York: Viking.

Campbell, Joseph. (1973). *The Hero with a Thousand Faces*. Princeton: Princeton University Press.

Carey, Maggie, Walther, Sarah, & Russell, Shona. (2009). The absent but implicit: A map to support therapeutic enquiry. *Family Process*, 48(3), 319–331.

Carnabucci, Karen, & Anderson, Ronald. (2012). *Integrating Psychodrama and Systemic Constellation Work*. London: Jessica Kingsley.

Carotenuto, Aldo. (1979). *The Spiral Way: A Woman's Healing Journey* (John Shepley, Trans.). Toronto: Inner City Books.

Carotenuto, Aldo. (1985). *The Vertical Labyrinth: Individuation in Jungian Psychology*. Toronto: Inner City Books.

Carr, David. (1986). *Time, Narrative, and History*. Bloomington, IN: Indiana University Press.

Carson, Timothy L. (1997). *Liminal Reality and Transformational Power*. Lanham, MD: University Press of America.

Casement, Patrick. (1991). *Learning from the Patient.* New York: Guilford Press.

Cavanagh, Michael J., & Spence, Gordon B. (2013). Mindfulness in coaching: Philosophy, psychology or just a useful skill? In Jonathan Passmore, David B. Peterson, & Teresa Freire (Eds.), *The Wiley-Blackwell Handbook of the Psychology of Coaching and Mentoring* (pp. 112–134). West Sussex, UK: John Wiley & Sons.

Chafe, Wallace. (1990). Some things that narratives tell us about the mind. In Bruce K. Britton & A.D. Pellegrini (Eds.), *Narrative Thought and Narrative Language* (pp. 79–98). Hillsdale, NJ: Lawrence Erlbaum.

Chaiklin, Seth. (2003). The zone of proximal development in Vygotsky's analysis of learning and instruction. In A. Kozulin, B. Gindis, V. Ageyev, & S. Miller (Eds.), *Vygotsky's Educational Theory and Practice in Cultural Context* (pp. 39–64). Cambridge: Cambridge University Press.

Charon, Rita. (2006). *Narrative Medicine: Honoring the Stories of Illness.* New York: Oxford University Press.

Chiron, C., Jambaque, I., Nabbout, R., Lounes, R., Syrota, A., & Dulac, O. (1997). The right hemisphere is dominant in human infants. *Brain* (120), 1057–1065.

Chittister, Joan. (2010). *Illuminated Life: Monastic Wisdom for Seekers of Light.* Maryknoll, NY: Orbis Books.

Chödrön, Pema. 1997. *When things fall apart: Heart advice for difficult times.* Boston, MA: Shambhala.

Clandinin, D. Jean, & Connelly, F. Michael. (2000). *Narrative Inquiry: Experience and Story in Qualitative Research.* San Francisco: Jossey-Bass.

Clutterbuck, David, & David, Susan A. (2013). Goals in coaching and mentoring. In Susan David, David Clutterbuck, & David Megginson (Eds.), *Beyond Goals: Effective Strategies for Coaching and Mentoring* (pp. 21–34). Farnham, UK: Gower.

Corrie, Sarah, Drake, David B., & Lane, David A. (2010). Creating stories for complex times. In Sarah Corrie & David Lane (Eds.), *Constructing Stories, Telling Tales: A Guide to Formulation in Applied Psychology* (pp. 320–352). London: Karnac.

Coulehan, Robin, Friedlander, Myrna L., & Heatherington, Laurie. (1998). Transforming narratives: A change event in constructivist family therapy. *Family Process*, 37, 17–33.

Coyote, Peter. (2014, August 12). Robin Williams' last gift. Retrieved from https://www.facebook.com/peter.coyote.3?fref=photo

Cozolino, Louis. (2002). *The Neuroscience of Psychotherapy: Building and Rebuilding the Human Brain*. New York, NY: W.W. Norton.

Cozolino, Louis. (2006). *The Neuroscience of Human Relationships: Attachment and the Developing Brain*. New York: W.W. Norton.

Cozolino, Louis. (2010). *The Neuroscience of Psychotherapy: Healing the Social Brain* (Second ed.). New York: W.W. Norton.

Cross, Susan, & Markus, Hazel. (1991). Possible selves across the lifespan. *Human Development*, 34, 230–255.

Crossley, Michelle L. (2002). Introducing narrative psychology. In *Narrative, Memory and Life Transitions* (pp. 1–13). Huddersfield: University of Huddersfield.

Czarniawska, Barbara. (1998). *A Narrative Approach to Organization Studies*. Thousand Oaks, CA: Sage.

Czarniawska, Barbara. (2004). *Narratives in Social Science Research*. London: Sage

Day, David D., Harrison, Michelle M., & Halpin, Stanley M. (2009). *An Integrative Approach to Leader Development: Connecting Adult Development, Identity, and Expertise*. New York: Psychology Press.

Dayton, Tian. (2005). *The Living Stage: A Step-By-Step Guide to Psychodrama, Sociometry and Experiential Group Therapy*. Deerfield Beach, FL: Health Communications, Inc.

de Shazer, Steve. (1988). *Clues: Investigating Solutions in Brief Therapy*. New York: W.W. Norton.

Deegan, Mary Jo, & Hill, Michael R. (1991). Doctoral dissertations as liminal journeys of the self: Betwixt and between in graduate sociology programs. *Teaching Sociology*, 19, 322–332.

Depraz, Natalie, Varela, Francisco J., & Vermersch, Pierre. (2000). The gesture of awareness: An account of structural dynamics. In Max Velmans (Ed.), *Investigating Phenomenal Consciousness: New Methodologies and Maps* (pp. 121–138). Amsterdam, Netherlands: John Benjamins.

Dijkstra, Katinka, Michael P. Kaschak, and Rolf A. Zwaan. 2007. "Body posture facilitates retrieval of autobiographical memories." *Cognition* 102:139-149.

Doige, Norman. (2007). *The Brain that Changes Itself: Stories of Personal Triumph from the Frontiers of Brain Science.* New York: Penguin Group.

Doige, N. (2015). *The Brain's Way of Healing: Remarkable Discoveries and Recoveries from the Frontiers of Neuroplasticity.* New York: Viking.

Dougherty, Nancy J., & West, Jacqueline J. (2007). *The Matrix and Meaning of Character: An Archetypal and Developmental Approach.* London: Routledge.

Drake, David B. (2003). How stories change: A narrative analysis of liminal experiences and transitions in identity. (dissertation), Fielding Graduate Institute, Santa Barbara.

Drake, David B. (2004a). Creating third space: The use of narrative liminality in coaching. In Irene Stein, Francine Campone, & Linda J. Page (Eds.), *Second ICF Coaching Research Symposium* (pp. 50–59). Quebec City, Canada: International Coaching Federation.

Drake, David B. (2004b). Creating third space: The use of narrative liminality in research and practice. Paper presented at the Narrative Matters Conference, Fredericton, Canada.

Drake, David B. (2004c). Once upon a time: Depression as an expression of untold narratives. Paper presented at the Narrative Matters Conference, Fredericton, Canada.

Drake, David B. (2005a). Creating third spaces: The use of narrative liminality in organizational coaching. Paper presented at the Western States Communication Association Convention, San Francisco, CA.

Drake, David B. (2005b). Narrative coaching: A psychosocial method for working with clients' stories to support transformative results. Paper presented at the Second Australia Conference on Evidence-Based Coaching, Sydney, Australia.

Drake, David B. (2007). The art of thinking narratively: Implications for coaching psychology and practice. *Australian Psychologist,* 42(4), 283-294.

Drake, David B. (2008a). Finding our way home: Coaching's search for identity in a new era. *Coaching: An International Journal of Theory, Research and Practice*, 1(1), 15–26.

Drake, David B. (2008b). Thrice upon a time: Narrative structure and psychology as a platform for coaching. In David B. Drake, Diane Brennan, & Kim Gørtz (Eds.), *The Philosophy and Practice of Coaching: Issues and Insights for a New Era* (pp. 51–71). San Francisco: Jossey-Bass.

Drake, David B. (2009a). Evidence is a verb: A relational view of knowledge and mastery in coaching. *International Journal of Evidence Based Coaching and Mentoring*, 7(1), 1–12.

Drake, David B. (2009b). Identity, liminality, and development through coaching: An intrapersonal view of intercultural sensitivity. In Michel Moral & Geoff Abbott (Eds.), *The Routledge Companion to International Business Coaching* (pp. 61–74). London: Routledge.

Drake, David B. (2009c). Narrative coaching. In Elaine Cox, Tatiana Bachkirova, & David Clutterbuck (Eds.), *The Sage Handbook of Coaching* (pp. 120–131). London: Sage.

Drake, David B. (2009d). Using attachment theory in coaching leaders: The search for a coherent narrative. *International Coaching Psychology Review*, 4(1), 49–58.

Drake, David B. (2010). What story are you in? Four elements of a narrative approach to formulation in coaching. In Sarah Corrie & David Lane (Eds.), *Constructing Stories, Telling Tales: A Guide to Formulation in Applied Psychology* (pp. 239–258). London: Karnac.

Drake, David B. (2011b). Moving from good to great: A narrative perspective on strengths. Paper presented at the Positive 2012, Wollongong, Australia. http://www.uow.edu.au/content/groups/public/@web/@gsb/documents/doc/uow122223.pdf

Drake, David B. (2011c). A narrative approach to coaching. In Leni Wildflower & Diane Brennan (Eds.), *The Handbook of Knowledge-Based Coaching: From Theory to Practice* (pp. 271–278). San Francisco: Jossey-Bass.

Drake, David B. (2011d). Using the five elements of mastery to develop ourselves as supervisors. Paper presented at the ANSE Summer Institute, Stavanger, Norway.

Drake, David B. (2011e). What do coaches need to know? Using the Mastery Window to assess and develop expertise. *Coaching: An International Journal of Theory, Research & Practice*, 4(2), 138–155.

Drake, David B. (2014b). Narrative coaching. In Elaine Cox, Tatiana Bachkirova, & David A. Clutterbuck (Eds.), *The Sage Handbook of Coaching* (2nd ed., pp. 117–130). London: Sage.

Drake, David B. (2014c). Three windows of development: A postprofessional perspective on supervision. *International Coaching Psychology Review*, 9(1), 36–48.

Drake, D. B. (2015). *Narrative Coaching: Bringing Our New Stories to Life*. Petaluma, CA: CNC Press.

Drake, D. B. (2016). Working with narratives in coaching. In T. Bachkirova, G. Spence, & D. Drake (Eds.), *Handbook of Coaching* (pp. 291-309). London: Sage.

Drake, David B. 2017. "Using the four gateways to tell new stories and make new choices." *The Coaching Psychologist* 13 (1):22-26.

Drake, David B., and Pritchard, James. 2016. "Coaching and the development of organisations." In *Handbook of coaching*, edited by Tatiana Bachkirova, Gordon Spence and David Drake, 159-175. London, UK: Sage.

Drake, David B., & Stelter, Reinhard. (2014). Narrative coaching. In Jonathan Passmore (Ed.), *Mastery in Coaching: A Complete Psychological Toolkit for Advanced Coaching* (pp. 65–96). London, UK: Kogan Page.

Drake, David B., & Stober, Dianne R. (2005). The rise of the postprofessional: Lessons learned in thinking about coaching as an evidence-based practice. Paper presented at the Australia Conference on Evidence-Based Coaching, Sydney, Australia.

Duhigg, C. (2013). *The Power of Habit: Why We Do What We Do and How to Change*. New York: Random House.

Durrell, Lawrence. (1988). *The Alexandria Quartet* (8th ed.). London: Faber.

Dweck, Carol S. (2008). *Mindset: The Psychology of Success.* New York: Ballantine Books.

Edelson, Marshall. (1993). Telling and enacting stories in psychoanalysis and psychotherapy. *The Psychoanalytic Study of the Child,* 48, 293–325.

Eliade, Mircea. (1959). *The Sacred and Profane: The Nature of Religion.* New York: Harcourt.

Ellis, M.J. (1973). *Why People Play.* New York: Prentice Hall.

Emunah, R. (1994). *Acting for Real: Drama Therapy Process, Technique, and Performance.* New York: Routledge.

Epston, David, and Michael White. 1992. "Consulting your consultants: The documentation of alternative knowledges." In *Experience, contradiction, and narrative imagination: Selected papers of David Epston and Michael White (1989-91),* edited by Michael White and David Epston. Adelaide: Dulwich Centre Publications.

Epston, David, and Michael White. 1995. "Constructivism in psychotherapy." In *Constructivism in psychotherapy,* edited by Robert A Neimeyer and Michael J. Mahony, 339-354. Washington DC: American Psychological Association.

Ericsson, K. Anders, & Charness, Neil. (1994). Expert performance: Its structure and acquisition. *American Psychologist,* 49(8), 725–747.

Ericsson, K. Anders, Krampe, Ralf, & Tesch-Römer, Clemens. (1993). The role of deliberate practice in the acquisition of expert performance. *Psychological Review,* 100(3), 363–406.

Erikson, Erik H. (1950). *Childhood and Society.* New York, NY: W.W. Norton.

Eron, Joseph B., & Lund, Thomas W. (1996). *Narrative Solutions in Brief Therapy.* New York: Guilford Press.

Evanoff, Richard. (2000). The concept of "third cultures" in intercultural ethics. *Eubios Journal of Asian and International Bioethics,* 10, 126–129.

Feinstein, David, Stanley Krippner, and D. Granger. 1988a. "Mythmaking and human development." *Journal of Humanistic Psychology* 28 (3):23-50.

Feldenkrais, Moshe. (1972). *Awareness through Movement.* New York: Harper & Row.

Feldenkrais, Moshe. (2005/1949). *Body & Mature Behavior.* Berkeley, CA: Frog Books

Fitzgerald, Stephen P., Oliver, Christine, & Hoxsey, Joan C. (2010). Appreciative Inquiry as a shadow process. *Journal of Management Inquiry,* 19(3), 220–233.

Fosha, Diana. (2003). Dyadic regulation and experiential work with emotion and relatedness in trauma and disorganised attachment. In M. F. Solomon & D. J. Siegel (Eds.), *Healing Trauma: Attachment, Mind, Body, and Brain* (pp. 221–281). New York: W.W. Norton.

Foss, Sonja K., & Foss, Karen A. (2003). *Inviting Transformation: Presentational Speaking for a Changing World* (2nd ed.). Prospect Heights, IL: Waveland Press.

Foucault, Michel. 1965. *Madness and Civilization: A History of Insanity in the Age of Reason.* vols. New York, NY: Random House.

Fox, Hugh. (2003). Using therapeutic documents: A review. *International Journal of Narrative Therapy and Community Work,* 4, 26–36.

Francis, Sophie (2012, September 15). [personal communication].

Frank, Arthur W. (2010). *Letting Stories Breathe: A Socio-Narratology.* Chicago: University of Chicago Press.

Fraser, J Scott, and Andrew D Solovey. 2007. *Second-order change in psychotherapy: The golden thread that unifies effective treatments.* Washington, DC: American Psychological Association.

Frederickson, Barbara. (2006). The broaden and build theory of positive emotions. In M. Csikszentmihalyi & I. Csikszentmihalyi (Eds.), *A Life Worth Living: Contributions to Positive Psychology.* New York: Oxford University Press.

Freedman, Jill, & Combs, Gene (1996). New York: W.W. Norton.

Freeman, John. (1964). Introduction: *Man and His Symbols* (pp. x). New York: Doubleday.

Freire, Paolo. (1970). Pedagogy of the oppressed. New York: Seabury Press.

Freud, Sigmund. 1912/1958. "Recommendations to physicians practicing psychoanalysis." In *The Standard Edition of the Complete Works of Sigmund Freud*, edited by J. Strachey, 109-120. London: Hogarth Press.

Frye, Northrop. (1957). *Anatomy of Criticism: Four Essays*. Princeton: Princeton University Press.

Fulton, Paul R., & Siegel, Ronald D. (2005). Buddhist and western psychology. In Christopher K. Germer, Ronald D. Siegel, & Paul R. Fulton (Eds.), *Mindfulness and Psychotherapy* (pp. 28–51). New York: Guilford Press.

Gagan, Jeannette M. (1998). *Journeying: Where Shamanism and Psychology Meet*. Santa Fe, NM: Rio Chama Publications.

Gallwey, Timothy. (1981/2009). *The Inner Game of Golf*. New York: Random House.

Gallwey, Timothy. (2001). *The Inner Game of Work*. New York: Random House.

Gallwey, Timothy. (2009). *The Inner Game of Stress*. New York: Random House.

Geertz, Clifford. 1978. *The interpretation of cultures*. New York, NY: Basic Books.

Gergen, Kenneth J. (1973). Social psychology as history. *Journal of Personality and Social Psychology*, 26(2), 309–320.

Gergen, Kenneth J. (1994). *Realities and Relationships*. Cambridge, MA: Harvard University Press.

Gergen, Kenneth J., & Kaye, John. (1993). Beyond narrative in the negotiation of therapeutic meaning. In Kenneth J. Gergen (Ed.), *Refiguring Self and Psychology*. Aldershot, UK: Dartmouth.

Gergen, Mary, & Davis, Sara N. (2005). Dialogic pedagogy: Developing narrative research perspectives through conversation. In Ruthellen Josselson, Amia Lieblich, & Dan P. McAdams (Eds.), *Up Close and Personal: The Teaching and Learning of Narrative Research* (pp. 239–257). Washington, DC: American Psychological Association.

Gergen, Mary M., & Gergen, Kenneth J. (2006). Narratives in action. *Narrative Inquiry*, 16(1), 112–121.

Germer, Christopher K. 2005. "Mindfulness: What is it? What does it matter?" In *Mindfulness and psychotherapy*, edited by Christopher K. Germer, Ronald D. Siegel and Paul R. Fulton, 3-27. New York, NY: Guilford Press.

Giddens, Anthony. (1991). *Modernity and Self-Identity: Self and Society in the Late Modern Age*. Stanford: Stanford University Press.

Gilligan, Carol. (1982). *In a Different Voice: Psychological Theory and Women's Development*. Cambridge, MA: Harvard Business School Press.

Gilligan, Carol, & Brown, Lyn Mikel. (1991). Listening for voice in narratives of relationships. In Mark B. Tappan & Martin J. Packer (Eds.), *Narrative and Storytelling: Implications for Understanding Moral Development* (Vol. 54, pp. 43). San Francisco: Jossey-Bass.

Gioia, Dennis A. (1986). Symbols, scripts, and sensemaking. In Henry P. Sims Jr. & Dennis A. Gioia (Eds.), *The Thinking Organization* (pp. 49–74). San Francisco: Jossey-Bass.

Gluckman, Max. (1962). Les rites de passage. In Max Gluckman (Ed.), *Essays on the Ritual of Social Relations* (pp. 1–52). Manchester: University Press.

Goffman, Erving. (1959). *The Presentation of Self in Everyday Life*. New York: Doubleday.

Goldhaber, Dale E. (2000). *Theories of Human Development: Integrative Perspectives*. Mountain View, CA: Mayfield Publishing.

Goldstein, Kurt. (1939). *The Organism*. New York: American Books.

Grafanaki, Soti, and John McLeod. 1999. "Narrative processes in the construction of helpful and hindering events in experiential psychotherapy." *Psychotherapy Research* 9 (3):289-303.

Graham, Linda. (2013). *Bouncing Back: Rewiring Your Brain for Maximum Resilience and Well-Being*. Novato, CA: New World Library.

Grant, A. M. (2012). An integrated model of goal-focused coaching: An evidence-based framework for teaching and practice. *International Coaching Psychology Review*, 7(2), 146–164.

Greenberg, L. S. (2002). *Emotion-Focused Therapy: Coaching Clients to Work through Their Feelings*. Washington, DC: American Psychological Association.

Griffith, James L., & Griffith, Melissa E. (1993). Language solutions for mind-body problems. In Reese Price & Stephen Gilligan (Eds.), *Therapeutic Conversations* (pp. 309–329). New York: W.W. Norton.

Griffith, James L., & Griffith, Melissa Elliot. (1993). Language solutions for mind–body problems. In Stephen Gilligan & Reese Price (Eds.), *Therapeutic Conversations* (pp. 309–329). New York: W.W. Norton.

Haidet, Paul, & Paterniti, Debora. (2003). "Building" a history rather than "taking" one: A perspective on information sharing during the medical interview. *Archives of Internal Medicine*, 163, 1134–1140.

Halifax, Joan. (1993). *The Fruitful Darkness: A Journey through Buddhist Practice and Tribal Wisdom*. New York: Grove Press.

Hall, Douglas T. (1971). A theoretical model of career subidentity development in organizational settings. *Organizational Behavior and Human Performance*, 6, 50–76.

Hänninen, Vilma. (2004). A model of narrative circulation. *Narrative Inquiry*, 14(1), 69–85.

Harris, Russell. (2006). Embracing your demons: An overview of Acceptance and Commitment Therapy. *Psychotherapy in Australia*, 12(4), 1–8.

Hayes, Steven C. (2004). Acceptance and Commitment Therapy and the new behavior therapies: Mindfulness, commitment, and relationship. In Steven C. Hayes, Victoria M. Follette, & Marsha M. Linehan (Eds.), *Mindfulness and Acceptance: Expanding the Cognitive Tradition* (pp. 1–29). New York: Guilford Press.

Hebb, Donald O. (1949). *The Organization of Behavior: A Neuropsychological Theory*. New York: Wiley.

Heidegger, Martin. (1927/1996). *Being in Time* (Joan Stambaugh, Trans. Vol. 2). London: State University of New York Press.

Hellinger, Bert. (1998). *Love's Hidden Symmetry*. Phoenix, AZ: Zeig, Tucker & Theisen.

Hermans, Hubert J.M. 2004. "The innovation of self-narratives: A dialogical approach." In *Handbook of narrative and psychotherapy: Practice, theory, and research*, edited by Lynne E. Angus and John McLeod, 175–191. Thousand Oaks, CA: Sage.

Hernadi, Paul 1987. "Literary interpretation and the rhetoric of the human sciences." In *The rhetoric of the human sciences*, edited by John S. Nelson, 263-275. Madison, WI: University of Wisconsin Press.

Heron, John. (2001). *Helping the Client: A Creative Practical Guide*. London: Sage.

Hewson, Daphne. (1991). From laboratory to therapy room: Prediction questions for reconstructing the 'new-old' story. Dulwich Centre Newsletter, 3, 5–12.

Hillman, James. (1975a). The fiction of case history: A round. In James B. Wiggins (Ed.), *Religion as Story* (pp. 123–173). New York: Harper & Row.

Hillman, James. (1975b). *Re-visioning Psychology*. New York: Harper & Row.

Hillman, James. (1983). *Healing Fiction*. Woodstock, NY: Spring.

Hillman, James. (1996). *The Soul's Code*. New York: Random House.

Holland, John H. (1995). *Hidden Order*. Reading, MA: Addison-Wesley.

Hollis, James. (2004). *Mythologems: Incarnations of the Invisible World*. Toronto: Inner City Books.

Hollis, James. 2010. *What matters most: Living a more considered life*. New York, NY: Penguin Group.

Hollis, James. (2013). *Hauntings: Dispelling the Ghosts Who Run Our Lives*. Asheville, NC: Chiron.

Holmes, Jeremy. (1999). Narrative, attachment and the therapeutic process. In Chris Mace (Ed.), *Heart and Soul: The Therapeutic Face of Philosophy* (pp. 147–162). London: Routledge.

Holmes, Jeremy. (2001). *The Search for the Secure Base: Attachment Theory and Psychotherapy*. London: Routledge.

Horney, Karen. (1945). *Our Inner Conflicts: A Constructive Theory of Neurosis*. New York: W.W. Norton.

Howe, David. 2011. *Attachment across the lifecourse: A brief introduction*. New York, NY: Palgrave Macmillan.

Hoyt, Michael F. (1996). Introduction: Some stories are better than others. In Michael F. Hoyt (Ed.), *Constructive Therapies* (Vol. 2, pp. 1–32). New York: Guilford Press.

Husserl, Edmund. (1931). *Ideas: General Introduction to Pure Phenomenology*. London: George Allen & Unwin.

Ibarra, Herminia. 1999. "Provisional selves: Experimenting with image and identity in professional adaptation." *Administrative Science Quarterly* 44 (4):764-791.

Ibarra, Herminia, & Linebeck, Kent. (2005, January). What's your story? *Harvard Business Review*, 65–71.

Ibarra, Herminia, & Petriglieri, Jennifer Louise. (2010). Identity work and play. Journal of Organizational Change Management, 23(1), 10–25.

Ihde, Don. (1977). *Experimental Phenomenology: An Introduction*. New York: Putnam.

Illeris, Knud. (2004). *Adult Education and Adult Learning*. Malabar, FL: Krieger Publishing Company.

James, William. (1890/1950). *The Principles of Psychology* (Vol. 1). New York: Dover.

James, William. (1892/1927). *Psychology: Briefer Course*. New York: Henry Holt.

Johnson, Robert. (1986). *Inner Work*. New York: Harper & Row.

Johnstone, Keith. (1981). *Impro: Improvisation and the Theatre*. New York: Routledge.

Johnstone, Keith. (1999). *Impro for Storytellers*. New York: Routledge.

Josselson, Ruthellen. 2004. "On becoming the narrator of one's own life." In *Healing plots: The narrative basis for psychotherapy*, edited by Amia Lieblich, Dan P. McAdams and Ruthellen Josselson, 111-127. Washington, DC: American Psychological Association.

Jung, Carl G. (1964). *Man and His Symbols*. New York: Doubleday.

Jung, Carl G. (1967). *Alchemical Studies* (R.F.C. Hull, Trans. Vol. 13). Princeton: Princeton University Press.

Jung, Carl G. (1969). *The Structure and Dynamics of the Psyche* (R.F.C. Hull, Trans. Vol. 8). Princeton: Princeton University Press.

Jung, Carl G. (1970). *Psychological Reflections*. Princeton: Princeton University Press.

Jung, Carl G. (1972). *Two Essays on Analytical Psychology* (Gerhard Adler & R.F.C. Hull, Trans. Vol. 7). Princeton, NJ: Princeton University Press.

Kailo, Kaarina. (1997). Integrative feminist pedagogy, C.G. Jung, and the politics of visualization. In Sharon Todd (Ed.), *Learning Desire: Perspectives on Pedagogy, Culture, and the Unsaid.* New York: Routledge.

Kaplan, Allan. (2002). *Development Practitioners and Social Process*: Artists of the Invisible. London: Pluto Press.

Kay, John. (2010). *Obliquity: Why Our Goals Are Best Achieved Indirectly.* New York: Penguin Group.

Kearney, Richard. 2002. *On stories.* New York, NY: Routledge.

Kegan, Robert. (1994). *In Over Our Heads: The Mental Demands of Modern Life.* Cambridge, MA: Harvard University Press.

Kelly, G.A. (1955). *The Psychology of Personal Constructs* (Vol. 1). New York: W.W. Norton.

Kenyon, Gary M., & Randall, William L. (1997). *Restorying Our Lives: Personal Growth through Autobiographical Reflection.* Westport, CT: Praeger.

Kleinman, Arthur. 1988. *The illness narratives: Suffering, healing and the human condition.* New York, NY: Basic Books.

Kolb, Alice Y., & Kolb, David A. (2010). Learning to play, playing to learn: A case study of a ludic learning space. *Journal of Organizational Change Management*, 32(1), 26–50.

Kohut, Heinz. 1971. *The analysis of the self.* Chicago, IL: University of Chicago Press.

Kolb, David A. (1984). *Experiential Learning: Experience as the Source of Learning and Development.* Englewood Cliffs, NJ: Prentice-Hall.

Kolodziejski, Karin. (2004). The organization shadow: Exploring the untapped, trapped potential in organizational setting. *Dissertation Abstracts International*, 66, DAI-B, (UMI No. AAT-3166383).

Kramer, Gregory. (2007). *Insight Dialogue: The Interpersonal Path to Freedom.* Boston: Shambhala.

Kramer, Gregory, Meleo-Meyer, Florence, & Turner, Martha Lee. (2008). Cultivating mindfulness in relationship. In Steven F. Hick & Thomas

Bien (Eds.), *Mindfulness and Therapeutic Relationship* (pp. 195–214). New York: Guilford Press.

Kraus, Wolfgang. (2006). The narrative negotiation of identity and belonging. *Narrative Inquiry*, 16, 103–111.

Labov, William. (1982). Speech actions and reactions in personal narrative. In Deborah Tannen (Ed.), *Analyzing Discourse: Text and Talk*. Washington, DC: Georgetown University Press.

Lane, David A., & Corrie, Sarah. (2006). *The Modern Scientist-Practitioner: A Guide to Practice in Psychology*. London; New York: Routledge.

Langer, Ellen J. (1997). *The Power of Mindful Learning*. Reading, PA: Addison-Wesley.

Lave, Jean, & Wenger, Etienne. (1991). *Situated Learning: Legitimate Peripheral Participation*. Cambridge: Cambridge University Press.

Law, Ho C. (2007). Narrative coaching and psychology of learning from multicultural perspectives. In S. Palmer & A. Whybrow (Eds.), *Handbook of Coaching Psychology* (pp. 174–192). East Sussex, UK: Routledge.

Lawley, James, & Tompkins, Penny. (2000). *Metaphors in Mind: Transformation through Symbolic Modeling*. London: Developing Company Press.

LeCompte, Margaret D. (1993). A framework for hearing silence: What does telling stories mean when we are supposed to be doing science? In Daniel McLaughlin & William G. Tierney (Eds.), *Naming Silenced Lives: Personal Narratives and Processes of Educational Change* (pp. 9–27). New York, NY: Routledge.

Lefebvre, Henri. (1980). *La Presence et l'Absence*. Paris, France: Casterman.

Leonard, George. (1992). *Mastery: The Keys to Success and Long-Term Fulfillment*. New York: Penguin Group.

Levine, Peter. (2010). *In an Unspoken Voice: How the Body Releases Trauma and Restores Goodness*. Berkeley, CA: North Atlantic Books.

Lewin, Kurt. (1951). *Field Theory in Social Science: Selected Papers on Group Dynamics* (G.W. Lewin Ed.). New York, NY: Harper & Brothers.

Liedtka, J., & Ogilvie, T. (2011). *Designing for Growth: A Design Thinking Tool Kit for Managers*. New York: Columbia Business School Press.

Linde, Charlotte. (1993). *Life Stories: The Creation of Coherence*. New York: Cambridge University Press.

Locke, Edwin A. (1996). Motivation through conscious goal setting. *Applied and Preventative Psychology*, 5, 117–124.

Loehr, Jim. 2007. *The power of story*. New York: Free Press.

MacIntyre, Alasdair. (1981). *After Virtue*. New York: University of Notre Dame Press.

Maddi, Salvatore R. (1988). On the problem of accepting facticity and pursuing possibility. In S. Messer, L. Sass, & R. Woolfolk (Eds.), *Hermeneutics and Psychological Theory*. New Brunswick, NJ: Rutgers University Press.

Madigan, Stephen (1996). The politics of identity: Considering community discourse in the externalizing of internalized problem conversations. *Journal of Systematic Therapies*, 15(1), 47–62.

Mahony, Michael J. (2003). *Constructive Pyschotherapy: A Practical Guide*. New York: Guilford Press.

Main, Mary. (1995). Recent studies in attachment: Overview, with selected implications for clinical work. In Susan Goldberg, Roy Muir, & John Kerr (Eds.), *Attachment Theory: Social, Developmental, and Clinical Perspectives* (pp. 407–474). Hillsdale, NJ: Analytic Press.

Mainemelis, C., & Ronson, S. (2006). Ideas are born in fields of play: Towards a theory of play and creativity in organizational settings. *Research in Organizational Behavior*, 27, 69–81.

Mancuso, James C., & Sarbin, Theodore R. (1983). The self-narrative in the enactment of roles. In Theodore R. Sarbin & Karl E. Scheibe (Eds.), *Studies in Social Identity* (pp. 233–253). Westport, CT: Praeger.

Mandler, Jean. (1984). *Stories, Scripts, and Scenes: Aspects of Schema Theory*. Hillsdale, NJ: Lawrence Erlbaum.

Mar, Raymond A. (2004). The neuropsychology of narrative: Story comprehension, story production and their interrelation. *Neuropsychologia*, 42, 1414–1434.

March, James G. (1976). The technology of foolishness. In John G. March & J.P. Olsen (Eds.), *Ambiguity and Choice in Organizations* (pp. 81). Bergen: Universitetsforlaget.

Markus, Hazel, & Nurius, Paula. (1986). Possible selves. *American Psychologist*, 41(9), 954–969.

Marshak, Robert J. (1993). Managing the metaphors of change. *Organizational Dynamics* (Summer), 44–56.

Martin, R. (2009). *The Design of Business: Why Design Thinking Is the Next Competitive Advantage*. Boston: Harvard Business Press.

Maslow, Abraham H. (1954). *Motivation and Personality*. New York: Harper.

Mattingly, Cheryl. (1998). *Healing Dramas and Clinical Plots: The Narrative Structure of Experience*. New York: Cambridge University Press.

McAdams, Dan P. (1985). *Power, Intimacy, and the Life Story*. Belmont, CA: The Dorsey Press.

McAdams, Dan P. (2003). Identity and life story. In Robyn Fivush & Catherine A. Haden (Eds.), *Autobiographical Memory and the Construction of a Narrative Self* (pp. 187–207). Mahweh, NJ: Lawrence Erlbaum.

McAdams, Dan P., A. Diamond, E. de St. Aubin, and E. Mansfield. 1997. "Stories of commitment: The psychosocial construction of generative lives." *Journal of Personality and Social Psychology* 72:678-694.

McKee, Robert. (1997). *Story: Substance, Structure, Style and the Principles of Screenwriting*. New York: HarperCollins.

McKee, Robert (2004, September 10–12). [Story seminar].

McLaren, Peter. (1993). Border disputes: Multicultural narrative, identity formation, and critical pedagogy in postmodern America. In Daniel McLaughlin & William G. Tierney (Eds.), *Naming Silenced Lives: Personal Narratives and Processes of Educational Change* (pp. 201–235). New York: Routledge.

McLeod, John. (2004). The significance of narrative and storytelling in postpsychological counseling and psychotherapy. In Amia Lieblich, Dan P. McAdams, & Ruthellen Josselson (Eds.), *Healing Plots: The Narrative Basis for Psychotherapy* (pp. 11–27). Washington, DC: American Psychological Association.

McLeod, John. (2006). *Narrative and Psychotherapy*. London: Sage.

McMahon, Mary L., & Patton, Wendy A. (2006). The systems theory framework: A conceptual and practical map for career counseling. In M. McMahon & W. Patton (Eds.), *Career Counseling: Constructivist Approaches* (pp. 94–109). London: Routledge.

McNamara, Olwen, Roberts, Lorna, Basit, Tehmina N., & Brown, Tony. (2002). Rites of passage in initial teacher training. *British Educational Research Journal*, 28(6), 863–878.

McWhinney, Will, & Markos, Laura. (2003). Transformative education: Across the threshold. *Journal of Transformative Education*, 1(1), 16–37.

McWilliams, Nancy. (1994). *Psychoanalyic Diagnosis: Understanding Personality Structure in the Clinical Process*. New York: Guilford.

Mead, George Herbert. (1934/1967). *Mind, Self, and Society* (Charles W. Morris Ed.). Chicago: University of Chicago Press.

Meade, Michael. (2006). *The Water of Life: Initiation and the Tempering of the Soul*. Seattle, WA: Greenfire Press.

Mehl-Madrona, Lewis. (2010). *Healing the Mind through the Power of Story: The Promise of Narrative Psychiatry*. Rochester, VT: Bear & Company.

Mellou, Eleni. (1994). Play theories: A contemporary review. *Early Childhood Development and Care,* 102, 91–100.

Merleau-Ponty, Maurice. (1945/2013). *Phenomenology of Perception*. London: Routledge.

Metzger, Deena. (1992). *Writing for Your Life: A Guide and Companion to the Inner Worlds*. New York: HarperSanFrancisco.

Mezirow, Jack. (1991). *Transformative Dimensions of Adult Learning*. San Francisco: Jossey-Bass.

Mezirow, Jack (Ed.) (2000*). Learning as Transformation: Critical Perspectives on a Theory in Progress*. San Francisco: Jossey-Bass.

Mikulincer, Mario, & Shaver, Phillip R. (2007). *Attachment in Adulthood: Structure, Dynamics, and Change*. New York: Guilford Press.

Miller, Richard, and Iona Miller. 1994. *The modern alchemist*. Phanes Press: Grand Rapids, MI.

Milton, M., and Sarah Corrie. 2002. "Exploring the place of technical and implicit knowledge in therapy." *The Journal of Critical Psychology,*

Counselling and Psychotherapy 2 (3):188-195.

Mink, Louis A. (1969). History and fiction as modes of comprehension. *New Literary History*, 1, 556–569.

Mishler, Eliot G. (1992). Work, identity, and narrative: An artist-craftsman's story. In George C. Rosenwald & Richard L. Ochberg (Eds.), *Storied Lives: The Cultural Politics of Self-Understanding* (pp. 21–39). New Haven, CT: Yale University Press.

Mishler, Eliot G. (1999). *Storylines: Craftartist's Narratives of Identity*. Cambridge, MA: Harvard University Press.

Mishler, Eliot G. (2000). Narrative and the paradox of temporal ordering: How ends beget beginnings. Paper presented at the Discourse and Identity Conference, Clark University.

Moody, Harry R., and David Carroll. 1997. *The five stages of the soul*. New York: Anchor Books.

Moore, Margaret, Drake, David B., Tschannen-Moran, Bob, Campone, Francine, & Kauffman, Carol. (2005). Relational flow: A theoretical model for the intuitive dance. In Francine Campone & John Bennett (Eds.), *Proceedings of the Third ICF Coaching Research Symposium* (pp. 79–91). San Jose, CA: International Coach Federation.

Moore, Robert L. (1987). The liminal and the liminoid in ritual process and analytical practice. (diplomate paper), C.G. Jung Institute, Chicago.

Moore, Thomas. (2000). *Original Self*. New York: HarperCollins.

Moreno, Jacob Levy. 2008. *The essential Moreno: Writings on psychodrama, group method, and spontaneity*. New Paltz, NY: Tusitala Publishing.

Morgan, Stephanie P. (2005). Depression: Turning toward ife. In Christopher K. Germer, Ronald D. Siegel, & Paul R. Fulton (Eds.), *Mindfulness and Psychotherapy* (pp. 130–151). New York: Guilford Press.

Morton, Nelle. (1985). *The Journey Is Home*. Boston: Beacon Press.

Muller, Michael J. (2001). Participatory design: The third space in HCI. Retrieved from Cambridge, MA.

Nachmanovitch, S. (1990). *Free Play*. Los Angeles: Jeremy P. Tarcher.

Nepo, M. (1998). Because of my not knowing. In S. M. Intrator (Ed.), *Living the Questions: Essays Inspired by the Work and Life of Parker J. Palmer* (pp. 73-80). San Francisco: Jossey-Bass.

Nicolopoulou, Angeliki. 2008. "The elementary forms of narrative coherence in young children's storytellling." *Narrative Inquiry* 18 (2):299-325.

Nouwen, Henri. (1998). *Reaching Out*. Grand Rapids, MI: Zondervan.

Novitz, David. (1997). Art, narrative, and human nature. In Lewis P. Hinchman & Sandra Hinchman (Eds.), *Memory, Identity, Community* (pp. 143–160). Albany, NY: State University of New York Press.

O'Donohue, J. (2008). *To Bless the Space between Us*. New York: Doubleday.

O'Hanlon, Bill. (2000). *Do One Thing Different: Ten Simple Ways to Change Your Life*. New York: HarperCollins.

O'Hanlon, William. (1998). Possibility therapy: An inclusive, collaborative, solution-based model of psychotherapy. In Michael F. Hoyt (Ed.), *The Handbook of Constructive Therapies: Innovative Approaches from Leading Practitioners* (pp. 137–158). San Francisco: Jossey-Bass.

O'Reilley, M. R. (1998). *Radical Presence: Teaching as Contemplative Practice*. Portsmouth, NH: Boynton/Cook Publishers.

Ochs, Elinor, & Capps, Lisa. (1996). Narrating the self. *Annual Review of Anthropology*, 25, 19–43.

Ogden, Thomas A. (1999). The analytic third: An overview. *fort da*, 5(1).

Oldenburg, Ray. (1989). *The Great Good Place*. New York: Marlow.

Ollerenshaw, Jo Anne, & Creswell, John W. (2002). Narrative research: A comparison of two restorying data analysis approaches. *Qualitative Inquiry*, 8(3), 329–347.

Ordóñez, Lisa .D., Schweitzer, Maurice E., Galinsky, Adam E., & Bazerman, Max H. (2009). Goals gone wild: The systemic side effects of overprescribing goal setting. *Academy of Management Perspectives*, 23(1), 6–16.

Osatuke, Katerine, Glick, Merideth J., Gray, Michael A., Reynolds, Jr., D'Arcy J., Humphreys, Carol, Salvi, Lisa M., & Siles, William B. (2004). Assimilation and narrative: Stories as meaning bridges. In-

Lynne E. Angus & John McLeod (Eds.), *Handbook of Narrative and Psychotherapy: Practice, Theory, and Research* (pp. 193–210). Thousand Oaks, CA: Sage.

Oyserman, Daphna, & Markus, Hazel. (1993). The sociocultural self. In Jerry Suls (Ed.), *Psychological Perspectives on the Self* (Vol. 4, pp. 187–220). Hillsdale, NJ: Lawrence Erlbaum.

Page, Steve. (1999). *The Shadow and the Counsellor: Working with Darker Aspects of the Person, Role and Profession*. London, UK: Routledge.

Paris, Ginette. (2007). *Wisdom of the Psyche: Depth Psychology after Neuroscience*. London, UK: Routledge.

Paris, Ginette. (2011). *Heartbreak: New Approaches to Healing*. Minneapolis: Mill City Press.

Pearce, W. Barnett, & Pearce, Kimberley A. (2001). [Transcendent storytelling: Abilities for systemic practitioners and their clients].

Penuel, William R., & Wertsch, James V. (1995). Vygotsky and identity formation: A sociocultural approach. *Educational Psychologist*, 30(2), 83–92.

Perls, Frederick S. (1992/1969). *Gestalt Therapy Verbatim*. Gouldsboro, ME: The Gestalt Journal Press.

Perls, Fritz S., Hefferline, R. , & Goodman, P. (1994/1951). *Gestalt Therapy: Excitement and Growth in the Human Personality*. Gouldsboro, ME: The Gestalt Journal Press.

Petriglieri, Gianpiero, & Petriglieri, Jennifer Louise. (2010). Identity workspaces: The case of business schools. *Academy of Management Learning & Education*, 9(1), 44–60.

Phillips, Adam. (1994). *On Flirtation*. Cambridge, MA: Harvard University Press.

Piaget, Jean. (1954). *The Construction of Reality in the Child*. New York: Basic Books.

Piaget, Jean. (1962). *Play, Dreams and Imitation in Childhood* (C. Gattegno & F.M. Hodgson, Trans.). New York: W.W. Norton.

Picard, Max. (2002). *The World of Silence*. Wichita, KS: Eighth Day Press.

Pinker, Steven. (2009). *How the Mind Works*. New York: W.W. Norton.

Plett, Heather. (2015). What it means to 'hold space' for people, plus eight tips on how to do it well. Retrieved from http://heatherplett.com/2015/03/hold-space/

Poincaré, Henri. (1952). *Science and Method*. Mineola, NY: Dover.

Polkinghorne, Donald E. (1988). *Narrative Knowing and the Human Sciences*. Albany, NY: State University of New York Press.

Polkinghorne, Donald E. (1991). Narrative and self-concept. *Journal of Narrative and Life History*, 1(2&3), 135–153.

Polkinghorne, Donald E. (1995). Narrative configuration in qualitative analysis. In J. Amos Hatch & Richard Wisniewski (Eds.), *Life History and Narrative* (pp. 5–23). Washington, DC: The Falmer Press.

Polkinghorne, Donald E. (2001). The self and humanistic psychology. In Kirk J. Schneider, James F.T. Bugental, & J. Fraser Pierson (Eds.), *The Handbook of Humanistic Psychology* (pp. 81–99). Thousand Oaks, CA: Sage.

Polkinghorne, Donald E. (2004). Narrative therapy and postmodernism. In Lynne E. Angus & John McLeod (Eds.), *Handbook of Narrative and Psychotherapy: Practice, Theory, and Research* (pp. 53–67). Thousand Oaks, CA: Sage.

Post, Robert M., Weiss, S.R.B., Li, H., Smith, M.A., Zhang, L.X., & Xing, G. (1998). Neural plasticity and emotional memory. *Development and Psychopathology*, 10, 829–856.

Pressfield, Steven. 2011. *Do the work!: Overcome resistance and get out of your own way*: Do You Zoom.

Prochaska, James O., & Norcross, John C. (2002). Stages of change. In John C. Norcross (Ed.), *Psychotherapy Relationships that Work: Therapist Contributions and Responsiveness in Patients* (pp. 303–313). New York: Oxford University Press.

Propp, Vladimir. (1968). *Morphology of the Folktale* (Laurence Scott, Trans.). Austin: University of Texas Press.

Raff, Jeffrey. (2000). *Jung and the Alchemical Imagination*. Berwick, ME: Nicolas-Hays.

Ramsey, Caroline. 2005. "Narrative: From learning in reflection to learning in performance." *Management Learning* 36 (2):219-235.

Randall, William L. (1995). *The Stories We Are: An Essay on Self-Creation*. Toronto: University of Toronto Press.

Rappaport, Julian. (1995). Empowerment meets narrative: Listening to stories and creating settings. *American Journal of Community Psychology*, 23(5), 795–807.

Reik, Theodor. 1948. *Listening with the third ear: The inner experience of a psychoanalyst*. Twelfth ed. New York: Farrar, Strauss and Giroux. Original edition, 1948.

Rennie, David L. (1994). Storytelling in psychotherapy: The client's subjective experience. *Psychotherapy*, 31(2), 234–243.

Ricoeur, Paul. (1984). *Time and Narrative* (Kathleen McLaughlin & David Pellauer, Trans. Vol. 1). Chicago: University of Chicago Press.

Ricoeur, Paul. (1988). *Time and Narrative* (Vol. 3). Chicago: University of Chicago Press.

Ricoeur, Paul. (1992). *Oneself as Another* (Kathleen Blamey, Trans.). Chicago: University of Chicago Press.

Riessman, Catherine K. (1993). *Narrative Analysis* (Vol. 30). Newbury Park, CA: Sage.

Riessman, Catherine K. (2002). Analysis of personal narrative. In Jaber F. Gubrium & James A. Holstein (Eds.), *Handbook of Interview Research* (pp. 695–710). Thousand Oaks, CA: Sage.

Rimmon-Kenan, Shlomith. (1983). *Narrative Fiction: Contemporary Poetics*. London: Methuen.

Rogers, Carl R. (1961). *On Becoming a Person*. Boston: Houghton Mifflin.

Ross, Michael, & Conway, Michael. (1986). Remembering one's own past: the construction of personal histories. In R. Sorrentino & E. Higgins (Eds.), *Handbook of Motivation and Cognition*. New York: Guilford Press.

Rossiter, Marsha. (1999). Understanding adult development as narrative. *New Directions for Adult and Continuing Education* (84), 77–85.

Rubin, Harriet. (2000, October). Living dangerously. *Fast Company*, 340.

Russell, Robert L., & van Den Broek, Paul. (1992). Changing narrative schemas in psychotherapy. *Psychotherapy*, 29(3), 344–354.

Rycroft-Malone, Jo, Seers, Kate, Titchen, Angie, Harvey, Gill, Kitson, Alison, & McCormack, Brendan. (2004). What counts as evidence in evidence-based medicine? *Journal of Advanced Nursing*, 47(1), 81–90.

Sarbin, Theodore R. (1986a). The narrative as a root metaphor for psychology. In Theodore R. Sarbin (Ed.), *Narrative Psychology: The Storied Nature of Human Conduct* (pp. 3–21). Wellesley, MA: Praeger.

Sarbin, Theodore R. (Ed.) (1986b). *Narrative Psychology: The Storied Nature of Human Conduct*. Westport, CT: Praeger.

Satir, Virginia, Banmen, John, Gerber, Jane, & Gomori, Maria. (1991/2006). *The Satir Model: Family Therapy and Beyond*. Palo Alto, CA: Science and Behavior Books.

Schachtel, Ernest G. (1959). *Metamorphosis*. New York: Basic Books.

Schank, Roger. (1990). *Tell Me a Story: A New Look at Real and Artificial Memory*. New York: Scribner.

Schank, Roger, & Abelson, Robert P. (1995). Knowledge and memory: The real story. In Jr. Wyer, Robert S. (Ed.), *Knowledge and Memory: The Real Story* (pp. 1–86). Hillsdale, NJ: Lawrence Erlbaum.

Scharmer, Otto. (2007). *Theory U: Leading from the Future as It Emerges*. Boston: Society for Organizational Learning.

Scholes, Robert, & Kellogg, Robert. (1966). *The Nature of Narrative*. London: Oxford University Press.

Schön, Donald A. (1983). *The Reflective Practitioner*. New York: Basic Books.

Schwartz-Salant, Nathan. (1998). *The Mystery of Human Relationship: Alchemy and the Transformation of the Self*. New York: Routledge.

Schwartz-Salant, Nathan. (2007). *The Black Nightgown: The Fusional Complex and the Unlived Life*. Wilmette, IL: Chiron.

Seel, Richard. (2003). Story & conversation in organisations: A survey. Retrieved from http://www.new-paradigm.co.uk/story_&_conversation.htm.

Seligman, M. E. P., & Tierney, J. (2017). We aren't built to live in the moment. *New York Times*. Retrieved from https://www.nytimes.com/2017/05/19/opinion/sunday/why-the-future-is-always-on-your-mind.html?_r=0.

Sennett, Richard. (2008). *The Craftsman*. New Haven, CT: Yale University Press.

Sheldrake, Rupert. (2009). *Morphic Resonance: The Nature of Formative Causation* (4th ed.). South Paris, ME: Park Street Press.

Shenk, Joshua Wolf. 2005. *Lincoln's melancholy: How depression challenged a president and fueled his greatness*. New York, NY: Houghton Mifflin.

Sherman, Howard, & Schultz, Ron. (1998). *Open Boundaries*. Reading, MA: Perseus Publishing.

Sherman, Steven J., Skov, Richard B., Hervitz, Esther F., & Stock, Caryl B. (1981). The effects of explaining hypothetical future events: from possibility to probability to actuality and beyond. *Journal of Experimental Social Psychology*, 17, 142–158.

Siegel, Daniel J. (2007). *The Mindful Brain: Reflection and Attunement in the Cultivation of Well-Being*. New York: W.W. Norton.

Silsbee, Doug. (2008). *Presence-Based Coaching: Cultivating Self-Generative Leaders through Mind, Body and Heart*. San Francisco: Jossey-Bass.

Singer, Jefferson A. (1996). The story of your life: A process perspective on narrative and emotion in adult development. In Carol Magai & Susan H. McFadden (Eds.), *Handbook of Emotion, Adult Development, and Aging* (pp. 443–463). San Diego: Academic Press.

Singer, Jefferson A. (2001). Living in the amber cloud: A life story analysis. In Dan P. McAdams, Ruthellen Josselson, & Amia Lieblich (Eds.), *Turns in the Road: Narrative Studies of Lives in Transition* (pp. 253–277). Washington, DC: American Psychological Association.

Singer, Jefferson A. (2005a). *Memories that Matter: How to Use Self-Defining Memories to Understand & Change Your Life*. Oakland, CA: New Harbinger.

Singer, Jefferson A. (2005b). *Personality and Psychotherapy: Treating the Whole Person*. New York: Guilford Press.

Singer, Jefferson A., and Blerim Rexhaj. 2006. "Narrative coherence and psychotherapy: A commentary." *Journal of Constructivst Psychology* 19 (2):209-217.

Sitkin, Sim B. (1992). Learning through failure: The strategy of small losses. Research in *Organizational Behavior*, 14, 231–266.

Slade, Arietta. 2008. "The implications of attachment theory and research for adult psychotherapy." In *Handbook of attachment: Theory, research and clinical applications*, edited by Jude Cassidy and Phillip R. Shaver, 762-782. New York, NY: Guilford Press.

Slingerland, Arthur. (2014). *Trying Not to Try: The Art and Science of Spontaneity*. New York: Crown.

Sorell, Gwendolyn T., & Montgomery, Marilyn J. (2001). Feminist perspectives on Erikson's theory: Their relevance for contemporary identity development research. *Identity*, 1(2), 97–128.

Spinelli, Ernesto. (2010). Existential coaching. In Elaine Cox, Tatiana Bachkirova, & David Clutterbuck (Eds.), *The Complete Handbook of Coaching* (pp. 94–106). London: Sage.

Spolin, Viola. (1999). *Improvisation for the Theater* (3rd ed.). Evanston, IL: Northwestern University Press.

Stadter, Michael, & Scharff, David E. (2000). Object relations brief therapy. In Jon Carlson & Len Sperry (Eds.), *Brief Therapy with Individuals and Couples* (pp. 191–209). Phoenix, AZ: Zeig, Tucker & Theisen.

Stanislavsky, Konstantin. (1936/1989). *An Actor Prepares*. New York: Routledge.

Stein, Jan O., & Stein, Murray. (1987). Psychotherapy, initiation and the midlife transition. In L.C. Mahdi, S. Foster, & M. Little (Eds.), *Betwixt & Between: Patterns of Masculine and Feminine Initiation* (pp. 287–303). La Salle, IL: Open Court.

Stein, Nancy L., & Glenn, Christine G. (1979). An analysis of story comprehension in elementary school children. In Roy O. Freedle (Ed.), *New Directions in Discourse Processing* (Vol. 2, pp. 53–120). Greenwich, CT: Ablex.

Stelter, Reinhard. (2007). Coaching: A process of personal and social meaning making. *International Coaching Psychology Review*, 2(2), 191–201.

Stelter, Reinhard. (2009). Coaching as a reflective space in a society of growing diversity: Towards a narrative, postmodern paradigm. *International Coaching Psychology Review*, 4(2), 207–217.

Stelter, Reinhard. (2013). Narrative approaches. In Jonathan Passmore, David B. Peterson, & Teresa Freire (Eds.), *The Wiley-Blackwell Handbook of the Psychology of Coaching and Mentoring* (pp. 407–425). London: Wiley.

Stelter, Reinhard. (2014a). *A Guide to Third Generation Coaching: Narrative-Collaborative Theory and Practice.* New York: Springer.

Stelter, Reinhard. (2014b). Reconstructing dialogues through collaborative practice and a focus on values. *International Coaching Psychology Review,* 9(1), 51–66.

Stern, Daniel N. (1985). *The Interpersonal World of the Infant.* New York: Basic Books.

Stern, Daniel N. 2004. *The present moment in psychotherapy and everyday life.* New York, NY: W.W. Norton.

Stevens-Long, Judy. (2000). The prism self: Multiplicity on the path to transcendence. In Polly Young-Eisendrath & Melvin E. Miller (Eds.), *The Psychology of Mature Spirituality: Integrity, Wisdom, Transcendence* (pp. 161–174). Philadelphia, PA: Routledge.

Stevenson, Herb. (2005). Gestalt coaching. *OD Practitioner,* 37(4), 35–40.

Strauss, Anselm L. (1997). *Mirrors and Masks: The Search for Identity* (Second ed.). New Brunswick, NJ: Transaction Publishers.

Strupp, Hans H., & Binder, Jeffrey L. (1984). *Psychotherapy in a New Key: A Guide to Time-Limited Dynamic Psychotherapy.* New York: Basic Books.

Stryker, Sheldon. (1987). Identity theory: Developments and extensions. In K. Yardley & T. Honess (Eds.), *Self and Identity.* New York: Wiley.

Sull, Donald N., & Eisenhardt, Kathleen M. (2012). Simple rules for a complex world. *Harvard Business Review,* (September), 6. Retrieved from http://hbr.org/2012/09/simple-rules-for-a-complex-world/ar/1.

Swann, William B., Jr., & Read, Stephen. J. (1981). Self-verification processes: How we sustain our self-conceptions. *Journal of Experimental Social Psychology,* 17, 351–372.

Tammi, Pekka. (2005). Against narrative: A boring story. Paper presented at the Narrative as a way of thinking: International symposium in honor of Shlomith Rimmon-Kenan, Jerusalem, Israel.

Tarrant, John. 1998. *The light inside the dark*. New York, NY: HarperCollins.

Thaler, Richard, & Sunstein, Cass. (2008). *Nudge: Improving Decisions about Health, Wealth and Happiness*. New Haven, CT: Yale University Press.

Tillich, Paul. (1965). Frontiers. *Journal of the American Academy of Religion*, XXXIII(1), 17–23.

Todorov, Tzvetan. (1971/1977). *The Poetics of Prose*. Oxford, UK: Blackwell.

Tompkins, Penny, & Lawley, James. (1997). Less is more…The art of clean language. *Rapport: The Magazine for NLP Professionals*, 35, 36–40.

Tompkins, Penny, & Lawley, James. (2011). Self-nudge: Unconscious decision-making and how we can bias the future self. Retrieved from http://w w w.cleanlang uage.co.uk /articles/articles/312/1 /Self-nudge/ Page1.html.

Turner, Victor. (1967). Betwixt and between: The liminal period in rites of passage. In *The Forest of Symbols* (pp. 93–111). Ithica, NY: Cornell University Press.

Turner, Victor. (1969). *The Ritual Process: Structure and Anti-Structure*. New York: Aldine Publishing Co.

Turner, Victor. (1974). *Dramas, Fields and Metaphors*. Ithica, NY: Cornell University Press.

Turner, Victor. (1978). [Foreword]. In B. Meyerhoff, *Number Our Days* (pp. xiii–xvii). New York: Dutton.

Turner, Victor. (1982). Liminality and the performative genres. In F. Allan Hanson (Ed.), *Studies in Symbolism and Cultural Communication* (Vol. 14, pp. 25–41). Lawrence: University of Kansas.

Turner, Victor. (1986). *The Anthropology of Performance*. New York: PAJ.

Turner, Victor, & Turner, Edith. (1978). *Image and Pilgrimage in Christian Culture: Anthropological Perspectives*. New York: Columbia University Press.

van Eenwyk, J.R. (1997). *Archetypes & Strange Attractors*. Toronto, Canada: Inner City Books.

van Gennep, Arthur. (1960). *The Rites of Passage* (Monika B. Vizedom & Gabrielle L. Caffee, Trans.). Chicago: The University of Chicago Press.

Verplanken, B., & Melkevik, O. (2008). Predicting habit: The case of physical exercise. *Psychology of Sport and Habit,* 9(1), 15-26.

Vogel, Martin. 2012. "Story matters: An inquiry into the role of narrative in coaching." *International Journal of Evidence Based Coaching and Mentoring* 10 (1):1-11.

Vogler, Christopher. (1998). *The Writer's Journey: Mythic Structures for Writers* (2nd ed.). Studio City: Michael Wiese Productions.

Vygotsky, Lev S. (1934/1987). Thinking and speech (N. Minick, Trans.). In R.W. Rieber & A.S. Carton (Eds.), *The Collected Works of L.S. Vygotsky* (Vol. 1: Problems of general psychology, pp. 39–285). New York: Plenum Press.

Vygotsky, Lev S. (1934/1998). Infancy (M. Hall, Trans.). In R.W. Rieber (Ed.), *The Collected Works of L.S. Vygotsky* (Vol. 5: Child psychology, pp. 207–241). New York: Plenum Press.

Vygotsky, Lev S. 1962/1986. *Thought and language.* Cambridge MA: MIT Press.

Vygotsky, Lev S. (1978). *Mind in Society: The Development of Higher Psychological Processes* (Michael Cole, Vera John-Steiner, Sylvia Scribner, & Ellen Souberman, Trans.). Cambridge, MA: Harvard University Press.

Wachtel, Paul L. 1991. "The role of accomplices in preventing and facilitating change." In *How people change: Inside and outside of therapy,* edited by R. Curtis and G. Stricker, 21-28. New York, NY: Plenum.

Waitzkin, Josh. 2007. *The art of learning: An inner journey to optimal performance.* New York: Simon & Schuster.

Wallin, David J. 2007. *Attachment in psychotherapy.* New York, NY: The Guilford Press.

Watkins, Mary M. (1976). *Waking Dreams.* New York: Gordon and Breach.

Weick, Karl E. (1984). Small wins: Redefining the scale of social problems. *American Psychologist,* 39(1), 40–49.

Weick, Karl E. 1995. *Sensemaking in organizations.* Thousand Oaks, CA: Sage.

Wheatley, Margaret J. (1994). *Leadership and the New Science*. San Francisco: Berrett-Koehler.

White, Hayden. (1981). The narrativization of real events. *Critical Inquiry*, 793–798.

White, Michael. (1988). The process of questioning: A therapy of literary merit? In Michael White (Ed.), *Collected Papers* (pp. 37–46). Adelaide, South Australia: Dulwich Centre Publications.

White, Michael. (1989). The externalising of the problem and the reauthoring of lives and relationships. In Michael White (Ed.), *Selected Papers* (pp. 5–28). Adelaide: Dulwich Centre Publications.

White, Michael. (2004). Folk psychology and narrative practices. In Lynne E. Angus & John McLeod (Eds.), *Handbook of Narrative and Psychotherapy: Practice, Theory, and Research* (pp. 15–51). Thousand Oaks, CA: Sage.

White, Michael. 2005. "Workshop notes." Dulwich Centre, accessed September 21st. www.dulwichcentre.com.au.

White, Michael. (2007). *Maps of Narrative Practice*. New York: W.W. Norton.

White, Michael, & Epston, David. (1990). *Narrative Means to Therapeutic Ends*. New York: W.W. Norton.

Wiener, Daniel J. (1994). *Rehearsals for Growth: Theater Improvisation for Psychotherapists*. New York: W.W. Norton.

Wilkinson, Margaret. (2010). *Changing Minds in Therapy: Emotion, Attachment, Trauma & Neurobiology*. New York: W.W. Norton.

Winnicott, Donald W. (1965). *The Maturational Processes and the Facilitating Environment*. New York: International Universities Press.

Winnicott, Donald W. (1971). *Playing and Reality*. New York: Basic Books.

Winnicott, Donald W. 1988. *Babies and their mothers*. London, UK: Free Association Books.

Woodman, Marion. (1987). From concrete to consciousness: The emergence of the feminine. In Louise Carus Mahdi, Steven Foster, & Meredith Little (Eds.), *Betwixt & Between: Patterns of Masculine and Feminine Initiation* (pp. 201–222). La Salle, IL: Open Court.

Yalom, Irving D. (2000). *The Theory and Practice of Group Psychotherapy* (4th ed.). New York: Basic Books.

Yanno, Drew. (2006). *The 3rd Act: Writing a Great Ending to Your Screenplay.* New York: Continuum.

Yontef, Gary. (1980). Gestalt therapy: A dialogic method. In K. Schneider (Ed.), *Therapy and Neurose.* Munich: Pfeiffer Verlag.

Zadra, Dario. (1984). Victor Turner's theory of religion: Towards an analysis of symbolic time. In R. L. Moore & Frank E. Reynolds (Eds.), *Anthropology and the Study of Religion.* Chicago: Center for the Scientific Study of Religion.

INDEX

ABOUT THE AUTHOR

David B Drake, PhD, is founder and CEO of the Moment Institute in the San Francisco Bay Area. Its mission is to develop post-professional practitioners who can facilitate real change in real time using accelerated narrative practices.

He pioneered the field of Narrative Coaching, and he has taught coaching skills to over 15,000 leaders, managers, and professionals in twenty countries. He has partnered with WBECS, the world's leading coaching community, to launch his Narrative Coach program on a larger scale.

David has also contributed to narrative-based change and coaching initiatives in over seventy organizations. Clients include: Commonwealth Bank of Australia, Dropbox, Google, Logitech, Nike, PwC, Westpac, and the US and Australian federal governments.

He is the author of over fifty publications on narratives and coaching, including as lead editor of *The Philosophy and Practice of Coaching* (2008) and as co-editor of the reference–level *SAGE Handbook of Coaching* (2016). He is a Thought Leader for the Institute of Coaching at Harvard.

David splits his time between San Francisco and Amsterdam, relishes his life as a father, spends as much time in nature as possible, and is grateful for the opportunity to share this work with people like you.

CONTACT

www.momentinstitute.org
david@momentinstitute.org
1 707.772.9012 (San Francisco)

CONNECTING WITH US

If you are interested in having David (1) speak at your event, (2) contribute to or collaborate on a project, or (3) consult with your organization, please contact us via the form on our website. We would love to hear from you.

TRANSLATIONS

If you or someone you know would be interested in translating this book into another language, please contact admin@cncpress.com. While narrative coaching is based in universal human processes, we welcome opportunities to bring this work to people in their native tongue.

Author photo by Tomo Saito

Made in the USA
Columbia, SC
23 June 2021